# FREE Study Skills DV.

M000280088

Dear Customer,

Thank you for your purchase from Mometrix! We consider it an honor and privilege that you have purchased our product and want to ensure your satisfaction.

As a way of showing our appreciation and to help us better serve you, we have developed a Study Skills DVD that we would like to give you for <u>FREE</u>. **This DVD covers our "best practices" for studying for your exam, from using our study materials to preparing for the day of the test.**

All that we ask is that you email us your feedback that would describe your experience so far with our product. Good, bad or indifferent, we want to know what you think!

To get your **FREE Study Skills DVD**, email <u>freedvd@mometrix.com</u> with "FREE STUDY SKILLS DVD" in the subject line and the following information in the body of the email:

    a.   The name of the product you purchased.

    b.   Your product rating on a scale of 1-5, with 5 being the highest rating.

    c.   Your feedback. It can be long, short, or anything in-between, just your impressions and experience so far with our product. Good feedback might include how our study material met your needs and will highlight features of the product that you found helpful.

    d.   Your full name and shipping address where you would like us to send your free DVD.

If you have any questions or concerns, please don't hesitate to contact me directly.

Thanks again!

Sincerely,

Jay Willis
Vice President
<u>jay.willis@mometrix.com</u>
1-800-673-8175

# NASM
## Personal Trainer Exam
# SECRETS

## Study Guide
### Your Key to Exam Success

NASM Test Review for the National
Academy of Sports Medicine Board of
Certification Examination

**Published by**
## Mometrix Test Preparation
NASM Exam Secrets Test Prep Team

Written and edited by the NASM Exam Secrets Test Prep Staff

Printed in the United States of America

This paper meets the requirements of ANSI/NISO Z39.48-1992 (Permanence of Paper).

Mometrix offers volume discount pricing to institutions. For more information or a price quote, please contact our sales department at sales@mometrix.com or 888-248-1219.

Mometrix Media LLC is not affiliated with or endorsed by any official testing organization. All organizational and test names are trademarks of their respective owners.

ISBN 13: 978-1-61072-190-5
ISBN 10: 1-61072-190-X

Dear Future Exam Success Story:

Congratulations on your purchase of our study guide. Our goal in writing our study guide was to cover the content on the test, as well as provide insight into typical test taking mistakes and how to overcome them.

Standardized tests are a key component of being successful, which only increases the importance of doing well in the high-pressure high-stakes environment of test day. How well you do on this test will have a significant impact on your future- and we have the research and practical advice to help you execute on test day.

The product you're reading now is designed to exploit weaknesses in the test itself, and help you avoid the most common errors test takers frequently make.

## How to use this study guide

We don't want to waste your time. Our study guide is fast-paced and fluff-free. We suggest going through it a number of times, as repetition is an important part of learning new information and concepts.

First, read through the study guide completely to get a feel for the content and organization. Read the general success strategies first, and then proceed to the content sections. Each tip has been carefully selected for its effectiveness.

Second, read through the study guide again, and take notes in the margins and highlight those sections where you may have a particular weakness.

Finally, bring the manual with you on test day and study it before the exam begins.

## Your success is our success

We would be delighted to hear about your success. Send us an email and tell us your story. Thanks for your business and we wish you continued success-

Sincerely,

Mometrix Test Preparation Team

**Need more help? Check out our flashcards at: http://MometrixFlashcards.com/NASM**

# TABLE OF CONTENTS

# Top 20 Test Taking Tips

1. Carefully follow all the test registration procedures
2. Know the test directions, duration, topics, question types, how many questions
3. Setup a flexible study schedule at least 3-4 weeks before test day
4. Study during the time of day you are most alert, relaxed, and stress free
5. Maximize your learning style; visual learner use visual study aids, auditory learner use auditory study aids
6. Focus on your weakest knowledge base
7. Find a study partner to review with and help clarify questions
8. Practice, practice, practice
9. Get a good night's sleep; don't try to cram the night before the test
10. Eat a well balanced meal
11. Know the exact physical location of the testing site; drive the route to the site prior to test day
12. Bring a set of ear plugs; the testing center could be noisy
13. Wear comfortable, loose fitting, layered clothing to the testing center; prepare for it to be either cold or hot during the test
14. Bring at least 2 current forms of ID to the testing center
15. Arrive to the test early; be prepared to wait and be patient
16. Eliminate the obviously wrong answer choices, then guess the first remaining choice
17. Pace yourself; don't rush, but keep working and move on if you get stuck
18. Maintain a positive attitude even if the test is going poorly
19. Keep your first answer unless you are positive it is wrong
20. Check your work, don't make a careless mistake

# Basic and Applied Sciences

## Anatomy and Exercise Physiology

**Nervous system**

The brain and spinal cord make up the central nervous system. The brain controls bodily processes consciously (e.g., higher thinking/mental faculties, voluntary muscle action, memory, etc.) and unconsciously (e.g., heart rate, blood pressure, breathing, digesting food, etc.). The spinal cord has nerves that innervate major organs and muscles and initiate muscle movement or organ function at the command of the brain.

<u>Nervous system functions</u>
The nervous system has three main functions:
1. Sensing—perceive internal and external alterations to the body.
2. Integrating—compute sensory information to communicate to the body the correct action to take.
3. Communicating—transmit information to the muscles of the body when it is time to initiate movement and control this movement.

The human body uses sensory inputs to gather information about itself and the surrounding world. This information travels to the central nervous system where the information will be processed and acted upon through a process called integration. The brain will make decisions based on the information gathered, or reject the information if necessary. If the brain decides to act on the information gathered, it initiates movement through motor pathways. Because the nervous system controls all human movement, it is important to train it to ingrain correct movement and improve reaction time.

<u>Nervous system structure</u>
The nervous system is composed of the central and peripheral nervous systems. The central nervous system includes the main organs of the nervous system: the brain and the spinal column. The peripheral nervous system includes all parts of the nervous system that branch off from the central nervous system, such as cranial and spinal nerves.

The nervous system consists of billions of neurons—special cells made up of a cell body, axon, and dendrite. Function determines neuron nomenclature:
- Afferent neurons—transmit information from muscles and organs to the central nervous system.
- Interneurons—transmit information from neuron to neuron.
- Efferent neurons—transmit information from the central nervous system to muscles or glands.

<u>Mechanoreceptors, muscle spindles, Golgi tendon organs, and joint receptors</u>
Mechanoreceptors reside in the joints and connective tissues of the body (tendons, ligaments, and muscles). They sense changes in the compression or stretching of the muscles or tissues. Muscle spindles, Golgi tendon organs, and joint receptors are types of mechanoreceptors.

Muscles contain muscle spindles. They sense alteration in the length of the muscle and the rate of alteration. Muscle spindles contract when they are stimulated to protect the muscle from overstretching.

Golgi tendon organs sense alteration in muscle tension and the rate of alteration. Golgi tendon organs operate at the junction of a muscle and a tendon. Golgi tendon organs relax when they are stimulated to protect the muscle from overstressing.

Joint receptors sense changes in speed in the joint. Joint receptors sense overextension of the joint and respond to provide protection for it.

Possible nervous system injuries

Cerebrospinal fluid (CSF) surrounds the brain and central nervous system. It helps insulate and protect the brain and central nervous system from hard blows to the head or unanticipated change in speed. The head and neck must be protected during sports play because a hard blow (e.g., tackle in football) could damage the brain and central nervous system by disrupting the CSF.

Afferent neurons pass information to the brain via the spinal cord. Efferent neurons transmit information from the brain to effector cells. Effector cells initiate action in the muscles or organs. Acute or chronic injury, illness, or inflammation can disrupt afferent and efferent pathways. If this occurs, messages will not travel efficiently to the brain or the body. In extreme cases, the message will not travel at all.

**Skeletal System**

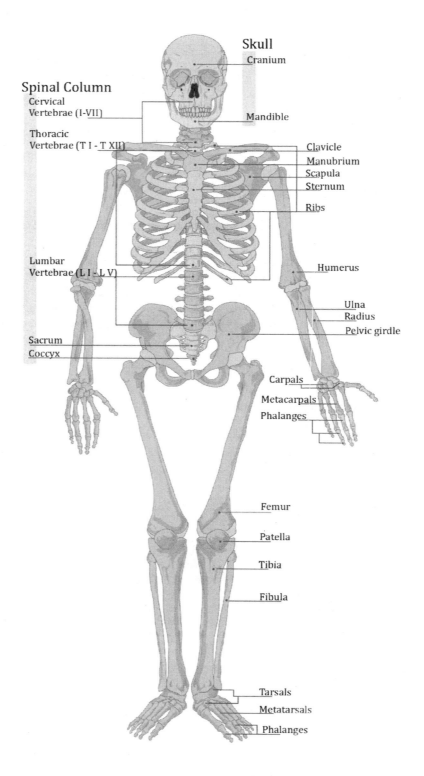

The skeleton provides a support system for the muscles and organs of the body and initiates movement. Additionally, the skeletal system protects major organs (heart, brain, etc.) and creates red blood cells (this takes place in the bone marrow). The skeletal system stores minerals (such as calcium and phosphorus) and releases them into the body, which regulates mineral balance and promotes proper body function.

The skeletal system contains into two major sections: the axial skeletal system and the appendicular skeletal system. The axial skeletal system has nearly 80 bones and is composed of the head, spine, and rib cage. The appendicular system contains the appendages, the shoulders, and the hip complex. It has more than 120 bones.

The two types of tissue that exist within human bones are compact bone and spongy bone. Compact bone resides on the outer layer of bones (the surface). Compact bone is very tough and serves a protective function by allowing the bone to bear the entire weight of the body. Spongy bone contains more spaces than compact bone and houses bone marrow.

The skeleton is composed of long bones, short bones, flat bones, irregular bones, and sesamoid (round) bones. Examples of long bones are the humerus and the femur. The shaft of a long bone, which is called the diaphysis, is made up of compact bone. The ends of a long bone are called the epiphyses, and these are made up of cancellous bone. The epiphyses are the sites of bone growth. Short bones are found in groups, and aid in movement. This type of bone is found in the wrist and ankle. Examples of flat bones are the ribs, scapula, sternum, and cranial bones. The vertebrae, facial bones, and skull bones are irregular bones. Sesamoid bones are located within a tendon. The patella, for example, is a sesamoid bone.

### Bone markings
Every bone has markings on its exterior that serve various functions. One major function is to provide place for muscles or other connective tissue to attach. There are two major categories of bone markings: processes and depressions.

Processes are bulges that protrude from the bone. Some examples include the rounded ends of the femur or humerus. Listed here are examples of bone processes:
- Trochanters—the rounded end of the femur; the hip bone is known as the greater trochanter.
- Tubercles—the top of the humerus; there are tubercles in the shoulder complex also.
- Condyles—the bottom of the femur, where condyles help form the knee joint.
- Epicondyles—the bottom of the humerus, where epicondyles help form the elbow joint.

Depressions are parts of the bone that are smooth or flat. Common depressions are the fossa or sulcus. These are locations where muscle or body tissues can attach or pass between.

## Joints

A pivot joint (C1 and C2 of the neck) provides rotation of one bone around another. A hinge joint (elbow) provides flexion and extension. A saddle joint (between the carpal and metacarpal of the thumb) provides flexion, extension, adduction, abduction, and circumduction. A gliding joint (tarsal bones) provides gliding movements between two bones. A condyloid joint (between the metacarpals and phalanges) can provide flexion, extension, abduction, adduction, and circumduction. A ball and socket joint (e.g., hip) provides flexion, extension, abduction, adduction, internal and external rotation.

| Joint type | Example | Movement provided |
|---|---|---|
| **Pivot** | C1, C2 of neck | Rotation about an axis |
| **Hinge** | Elbow | Flexion and extension |
| **Saddle** | Carpal and metacarpal of the thumb | Flexion, extension, adduction, abduction, and circumduction |
| **Gliding** | Tarsal bones | Back and forth or side to side |
| **Condyloid** | Metacarpals and phalanges | Flexion, extension, abduction, adduction, and circumduction |
| **Ball and socket** | Hip | Flexion, extension, abduction, adduction, internal and external rotation |

There are two major types of joints, designated by physiology: synovial and nonsynovial:
- Synovial joints are those pulled together by a system of ligaments, which give these types of joints greater range of motion. Some specific types of synovial joints include ball-and-socket joints (such as the hip joints), hinge joints, and pivot joints.
- Nonsynovial joints have no system of ligaments and have a limited range of motion. Examples include some of the flat joints of the skull and some of the nonmoving joints in the ankle.
- Ligaments are the main connective tissue between the bones of a joint.

## Hematopoiesis

Hematopoiesis refers to the formation of new red blood cells within the bone marrow. Red blood cells come from hemocytoblasts that quickly replicate themselves. Red blood cells have a lifecycle of three months, platelets of seven days, and granulocytes of seven hours. Healthy red blood cells are necessary for energy maintenance (among other vital processes) since oxygen must bind to each red blood cell as part of the aerobic energy pathway.

## Muscular System

The primary function of muscle is to produce skeletal movement. Muscle fibers contain myofibrils consisting of actin (thin) and mysoin (thick) filaments. A repeating section of actin and myosin is called a sacromere (the functional unit of a muscle). Muscle contraction is controlled by motor neurons. A motor neuron and the fibers it activates are called a motor unit. According to the sliding-filament theory, when a motor neuron inervates a muscle fiber, the thick and thin filaments shorten by sliding past one another, which produces force. If there is enough action potential, the stimulus is strong enough to contract the muscle fiber. If there is insufficient stimulus, the muscle will not contract. This phenomenon is referred to as the "All or Nothing" law.

Two vital protein structures that affect muscle contraction are troponin and tropomyosin. The actin filament houses troponin and tropomyosin. Troponin provides a place for tropomyosin and calcium

- 6 -

(which are essential for muscle contraction) to bind. Tropomyosin blocks myosin from binding to keep the muscle relaxed.

The three different types of muscle tissue are cardiac, smooth, and skeletal. The heart is composed of cardiac muscle. Organs (e.g., the liver or kidneys) contain smooth muscle. Skeletal muscle attaches to the skeletal system. Examples of skeletal muscle include the deltoid and trapezius muscles. The central nervous system (CNS) controls cardiac and smooth muscle with automatic processes. Skeletal muscle appears striated is voluntary control of the CNS.

Type I fibers are considered slow-twitch fibers. They require oxygen and provide power during endurance activities (e.g., running a marathon). Type II fibers are fast-twitch fibers. They rely on anaerobic metabolism (glycolysis, and the ATP-PC systems) as their energy source. These fibers are helpful for power- or speed-related activities that require explosiveness in the individual (e.g., sprinting). Type II fibers are subdivided into type IIa and type IIb fibers. Type IIa are known as intermediate fast-twitch fibers because they can use aerobic (oxygen) and anaerobic energy pathways. They are a combination of type I and II fibers. Type IIb fibers use only the anaerobic energy pathways. The term fast-twitch refers to Type IIb fibers.

The endomysium surrounds the muscle fiber (or cell), which separates it from the other muscle fibers. The fascicle surrounds a bundle of muscle fibers and is itself wrapped within the perimysium. The epimysium (outer covering of the muscle) holds several bundles of muscle fibers. Blood vessels are between each fascicle of muscle fibers. The blood vessels act to supply nutrition and energy to the muscle fiber. Each muscle in the body contains the endomysium, fascicle, perimysium, epimysium, and blood vessels.

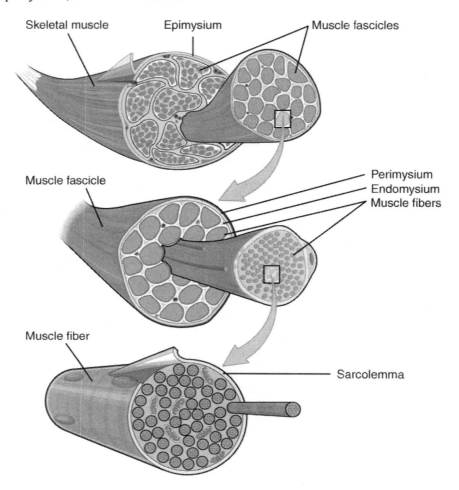

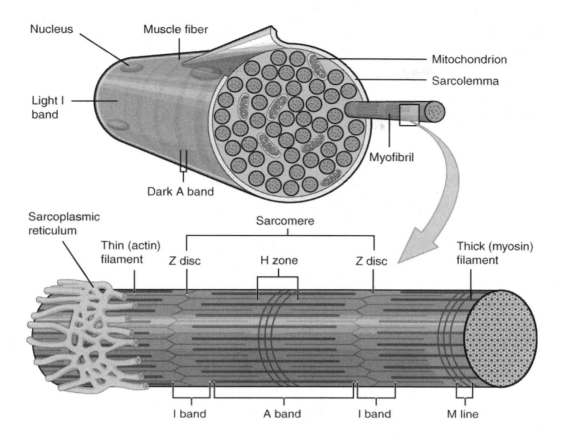

Some common muscular injuries that occur during physical activity include, but are not limited to, sprains, strains, tears, bursitis, and tennis elbow. A sprain occurs when a ligament tears or stretches excessively, whereas a strain is an injury to the tendon or muscle. Tearing of the ligament can lead to a sprain or muscle strain. Bursitis affects the bursa between joints (e.g., shoulder, hip) and causes inflammation of the bursa. Tennis elbow is a condition occurring when the tendons connecting the forearm to the outside of the elbow become inflamed.

Muscle groups
There are four major categories of muscles, differentiated by the primary function of the muscle:
1. Agonists—create primary movement. They are called prime movers. The gluteus maximus is an agonist muscle when performing a squatting movement.
2. Antagonists—counteract the actions of agonist muscles. The psoas muscle performs the opposite action as the gluteus maximus when performing a squatting movement.
3. Synergists—act at the same time as an agonist muscle to assist in the primary movement. The hamstrings are the synergist muscles when performing a squatting movement.
4. Stabilizers—stabilize and support agonist muscles while they perform a primary movement. The transversus abdominis stabilize the body during a squatting movement.

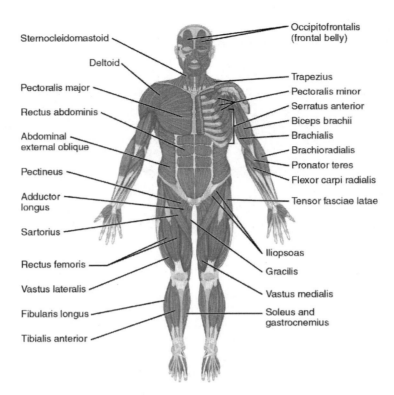

Sternocleidomastoid

Deltoid

Pectoralis major

Rectus abdominis

Abdominal
external oblique

Pectineus

Adductor
longus

Sartorius

Rectus femoris

Vastus lateralis

Fibularis longus

Tibialis anterior

Occipitofrontalis
(frontal belly)

Trapezius

Pectoralis minor

Serratus anterior

Biceps brachii

Brachialis

Brachioradialis

Pronator teres

Flexor carpi radialis

Tensor fasciae latae

Iliopsoas

Gracilis

Vastus medialis

Soleus and
gastrocnemius

Major muscles of the body.
Right side: superficial; left side:
deep (anterior view)

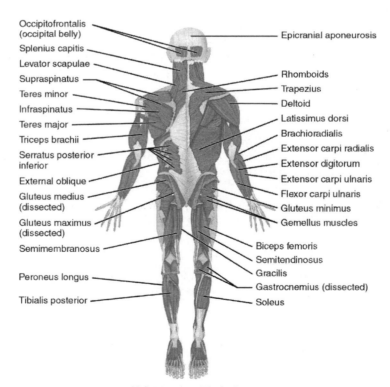

Occipitofrontalis
(occipital belly)

Splenius capitis

Levator scapulae

Supraspinatus

Teres minor

Infraspinatus

Teres major

Triceps brachii

Serratus posterior
inferior

External oblique

Gluteus medius
(dissected)

Gluteus maximus
(dissected)

Semimembranosus

Peroneus longus

Tibialis posterior

Epicranial aponeurosis

Rhomboids

Trapezius

Deltoid

Latissimus dorsi

Brachioradialis

Extensor carpi radialis

Extensor digitorum

Extensor carpi ulnaris

Flexor carpi ulnaris

Gluteus minimus

Gemellus muscles

Biceps femoris

Semitendinosus

Gracilis

Gastrocnemius (dissected)

Soleus

Major muscles of the body.
Right side: superficial; left side:
deep (posterior view)

## Lower leg complex

*Anterior tibialis*—runs along the outside of the tibia from under the knee to the ankle. It helps stabilize the foot.

*Posterior tibialis*—runs along the back of the tibia, under the fibula. It helps control the foot.

*Soleus*—the fleshy part of the back of the lower leg. It also runs down the sides of the Achilles' tendon. It controls walking motion in the leg and ankle and supports the foot.

*Gastrocnemius*—on the back of the leg below the knee. It works with the soleus to control walking and stabilize the foot.

*Peroneus longus*—runs along the tibia on the outer part of the leg. It flexes and everts the foot.

## Hamstring complex

*Biceps femoris* (long head)—emanates from the pelvis and inserts at the top of the fibula. It is essential in knee and hip movement.

*Biceps femoris* (short head)—runs along the lower part of the back of the femur. It is essential to knee and tibia movement.

*Semimembranosus*—runs along the back femur, through the center of the leg. It is essential to hip, knee, and tibia movement.

*Semitendinosus*—runs along the back of the femur toward the inner thigh. It is essential to hip, knee, and tibia movement.

## Quadriceps complex

*Vastus lateralis*—runs along the outside of the front thigh. It stabilizes the knee and controls all movement for that joint.

*Vastus medialis*—runs along the inner thigh close to the knee. It is essential to all movement for the knee joint.

*Vastus intermedius*—runs along the vastus lateralis, the length of the front thigh. It is also essential to all movement for the knee joint.

*Rectus femoris*—runs down the center of the front thigh. It is also essential to knee motion and stability.

## Hip musculature complex

*Adductor longus, adductor magnus* (anterior fibers), *adductor magnus* (posterior fibers), and *adductor brevis*—fall under the pelvis, interwoven at the top of the femur. Together, they control hip adduction, abduction, flexion, and rotation.

*Gracilis*—runs along the interior of the top of the femur. It is also essential to all elements of hip movement.

*Pectineus*—runs along the back edge of the upper part of the femur. It is also essential to all elements of hip movement.

*Gluteus medius* (anterior fibers), gluteus medius (posterior fibers), gluteus minimus—run along the outer edge of the back of the pelvis. Together, they control hip adduction, abduction, flexion, and rotation.

*Tensor fascia lata* (TFL)—runs along the top of the outer part of the hip. It is essential to hip flexion, abduction, adduction, and rotation.

*Gluteus maximus*—the fleshy part of the buttocks. It affects hip rotation and extension as well as stabilizing the lumbo-pelvic-hip (LPH) complex.

*Psoas*—run along the top of the hips to the base of the lowest vertebrae. These muscles are essential to hip movement and the rotation of the lumbar spine.

*Iliacus*—runs along the iliac crest. These muscles are essential to hip movement and lumbo-pelvic stability.

*Sartorius*—runs across the top of the thigh from the outer hip to the inner thigh. This muscle affects hip and knee function.

*Piriformis*—rests along the front of the sacrum. It affects hip movement stabilizes the hip joint.

Abdominal musculature
*Rectus abdominis*—run along the midline of the abdomen. They affect and control all core motion.

*External oblique*—run down the sides of the torso. They affect and control all core motion.

*Internal oblique*—run under the external obliques along the sides of the torso. They affect and control all core motion as well as stabilize the lumbo-pelvic-hip (LPH) complex.

*Transversus abdominis*—run along the side of the torso up and across under the ribs. They help stabilize the internal organs and the LPH complex.

*Diaphragm*—runs underneath the rib cage. It pulls open the thoracic cavity to accommodate oxygen intake.

Muscles of the back
*Superficial erector spinae*—the following muscles run down the length of the spine. Together they control spinal movement and stabilize the spine during activity:
- *Iliocostalis*
- *Longissimus*
- *Spinalis*

*Latissimus dorsi*—runs across the back under the scapula. It is critical to shoulder movement.

*Quadratus lumborum*—runs along the lower back and connects to the top of the pelvis. It affects spinal flexion and also stabilizes the lumbo-pelvic-hip (LPH) complex.

Transversospinalis complex

*Semispinalis* —the following muscles run from the bottom of the back of the skull to the top of the shoulders and spine. Together they control the movement of the upper spine as well as the head:

- *Iliocostalis*
- *Longissmus*
- *Spinalis*

*Multifidus*—run along the spine down into the sacrum. They control spinal flexion and lower-hip rotation.

Muscles in the shoulder

*Serratus anterior*—runs around the rib cage underneath the armpit. They affect the movement of the scapula.

*Rhomboids*—run across the top middle of the back, just under the neck. They also affect the movement of the scapula.

*Lower trapezius, middle trapezius, and upper trapezius*—run along the sides of the spine from the base of the neck down. They are also essential to all aspects of movement of the scapula.

*Pectoralis major*—runs along the front of the chest. It is essential to all movement of the shoulder complex.

*Pectoralis minor*—connects the front of the shoulder to the top ribs. It pulls the scapula forward.

*Deltoid*—the fleshy muscle that runs along the top of the arm. It is essential to all shoulder movement.

*Teres major*—runs along the chest to under the armpit. It is essential to shoulder rotation and movement.

Muscles in the arm

*Biceps brachii*—runs along the top length of the humerus. It is essential to shoulder and elbow movement.

*Triceps*—runs along the bottom of the humerus (the back of the upper arm). It supports shoulder and elbow movement.

*Brachioradialis*—runs along the outside of the humerus (the side of the upper arm). It supports elbow movement.

*Brachialis*—runs along the outside of the humerus (the side of the upper arm). It supports elbow movement.

Muscles in the rotator cuff

*Teres minor*—runs along the lateral edge of the scapula. It accelerates and decelerates shoulder rotation.

*Infraspinatus*—sits under and along the scapula. It accelerates and decelerates shoulder rotation.

*Subscapularis*—covers the back along the scapula. It accelerates and decelerates shoulder rotation.

*Supraspinatus*—runs along the interior of the top of the shoulder. It helps accelerate abduction and decelerate adduction of the arm.

<u>Muscles in the neck</u>
*Sternocleidomastoid*—runs from the side of the back of the head down to the cervical collar. They help control the movement of the head and cervical spine.

*Scalenes*—run down the sides of the neck at the shoulders. They help stabilize and control the movement of the cervical spine.

*Longus coli*—run along the sides of the cervical vertebrae. They help control the movement of the cervical spine.

*Longus capitis*—runs along the side of the neck. It helps stabilize and move the cervical spine.

*Levator scapulae*—runs along the side of the neck down to the top of the shoulder. It affects the up/down motion of the scapula.

## Cardiovascular system

The elements in the body that create and circulate blood (e.g., the heart, the blood, the veins, and the capillaries) comprise the cardiovascular system.

The cardiovascular system has several functions. It removes metabolic waste from and delivers nutrients to the body. White blood cells provide protection from foreign microbes and viruses. Finally, the cardiovascular system helps keep our bodies in a state of homeostasis by controlling body temperature, pH balance, and cellular water retention.

<u>Blood and channels of blood distribution</u>
Blood is the liquid that flows throughout the body, carrying out several functions. The average person has about 1.5 gallons of blood circulating at one time, and blood makes up a little less than 10 percent of a person's overall weight on average. Blood:
- carries oxygen and nutrients to the body systems.
- acts as a conduit to rid the body of waste products.
- regulates the body, helping keep body temperature constant and maintaining acid balance.
- is a defensive mechanism, clotting when necessary to prevent bleeding and creating and circulating defensive cells to help fight infection.

The cardiovascular system circulates five liters of blood through the body. It takes approximately one minute for a red blood cell to make its way through the entire human body.

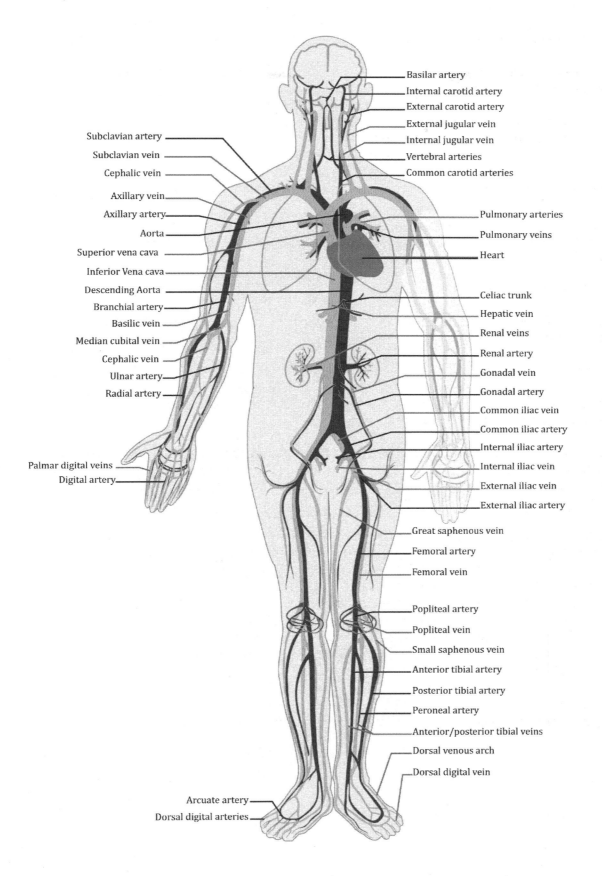

Basilar artery
Internal carotid artery
External carotid artery
External jugular vein
Internal jugular vein
Vertebral arteries
Common carotid arteries

Subclavian artery
Subclavian vein
Cephalic vein
Axillary vein
Axillary artery
Aorta
Superior vena cava
Inferior Vena cava
Descending Aorta
Branchial artery
Basilic vein
Median cubital vein
Cephalic vein
Ulnar artery
Radial artery

Pulmonary arteries
Pulmonary veins
Heart

Celiac trunk
Hepatic vein
Renal veins
Renal artery
Gonadal vein
Gonadal artery
Common iliac vein
Common iliac artery
Internal iliac artery
Internal iliac vein
External iliac vein
External iliac artery

Palmar digital veins
Digital artery

Great saphenous vein
Femoral artery
Femoral vein

Popliteal artery
Popliteal vein
Small saphenous vein
Anterior tibial artery
Posterior tibial artery
Peroneal artery
Anterior/posterior tibial veins
Dorsal venous arch
Dorsal digital vein

Arcuate artery
Dorsal digital arteries

- 15 -

## The Heart

The superior vena cava collects blood from the upper half of the body, while the inferior vena cava collects blood from the lower half of the body. The superior and inferior vena cava take oxygen-deficient blood to the right atrium. The tricuspid valve pushes blood into the right ventricle. From the right ventricle, it moves through the pulmonary valve and travels through the pulmonary artery to the lungs to become oxygen enriched. Once the blood has become oxygen-rich, it returns to the left atrium via the pulmonary vein. The left atrium contracts and pushes the blood through the mitral valve into the left ventricle. Blood is through the aortic valve into the aorta when the ventricle contracts. Blood travels to the rest of the body from the aorta. Blood flows away from the heart in arteries, which branch into arterioles, and then into capillaries. Blood returns to the heart in veins.

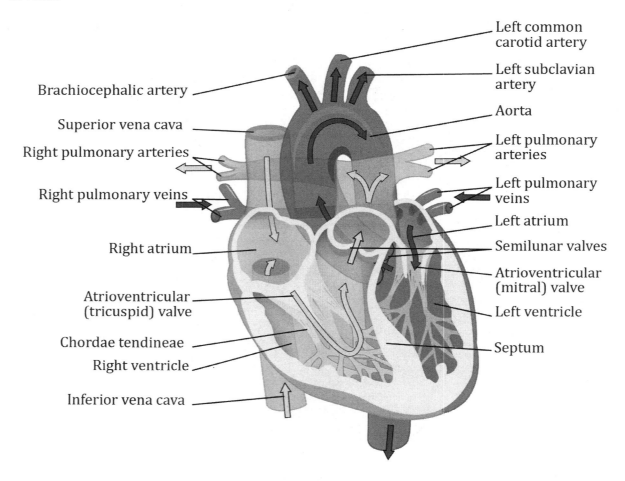

Heart rate is how fast the heart pumps. The resting heart rate is how fast the heart beats when the body is at rest. The average adult has a resting heart rate of between 70 and 80 beats every minute.

Stroke volume refers to much blood the heart pumps out with each beat. The average adult has a stroke volume of between 75 and 80 milliliters per beat. Stroke volume is a more complex measurement than heart rate.

Cardiac output is a measure of the heart's performance. To determine cardiac output, multiply the stroke volume by the heart rate.

## Respiratory system

The respiratory (pulmonary) system brings oxygen to the entire body. Inhalation occurs through the nose and mouth. The warm, moist environment of the nose and mouth warms the air. The air then travels to the lungs through the bronchial tubes; while in the lungs, cilia trap foreign particles and germs and remove them through sneezing or coughing. Carbon dioxide exits the body through exhalation. The body remains in homeostasis throughout the process.

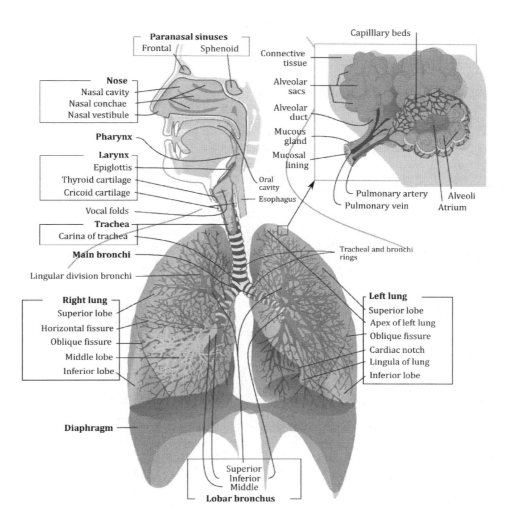

Human respiration is a four-step process involving breathing, external respiration, internal respiration, and cellular respiration. Breathing is the process of bringing oxygen into the lungs. External respiration occurs when oxygen replaces carbon dioxide within the alveoli. Internal respiration removes excess carbon dioxide from the lungs. Cellular respiration, involves oxygen breaking down sugar within the cells to produce water, ATP, energy, and carbon dioxide.

Breathing is the process of inhaling oxygen (inspiration) and exhaling its waste product, carbon dioxide (exhalation). Inspiration requires the muscles to work while exhalation is an involuntary, reflexive action.

The respiratory pump is the entire respiratory physiology, located in the chest and body. It includes hard and soft tissues (bones such as the sternum and ribs) and muscles such as the diaphragm and the sternocleidomastoid.

Respiratory process

The respiratory process operates in the following order:

1. Oxygen is inhaled through the nose and mouth and down the trachea
2. The oxygen passes into the bronchi
3. The oxygen fills the lungs and alveoli
4. The blood is pumped into the heart
5. The blood is pumped into the lungs
6. The blood is infused with oxygen
7. The oxygenated blood is pumped back into the heart
8. The oxygenated blood is pumped throughout the body

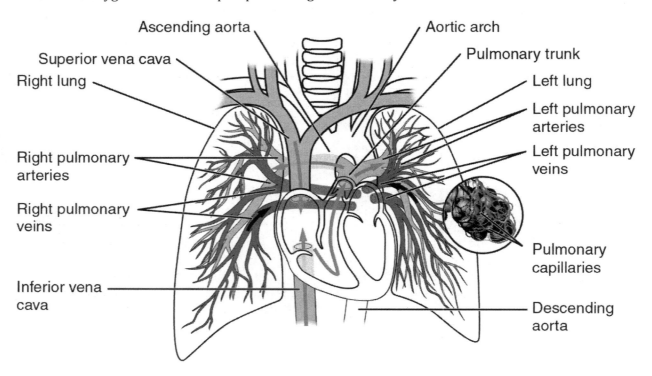

VO$_2$

The efficient delivery of oxygen depends on the respiratory and cardiovascular systems working in synergy. This process is called oxygen consumption, denoted using VO$_2$. The formula for determining oxygen consumption is:

VO$_2$ max = cardiac output (which is heart rate × stroke volume) × ($C_aO_2 - C_vO_2$) (which is the difference between the oxygen content of arterial blood and venous blood)

Oxygen and energy

Oxygen is necessary for activity lasting longer than 30 seconds. Aerobic activities require oxygen. Anaerobic activities are short (less than 30 seconds) and sustainable without oxygen. Although only aerobic activity requires oxygen, all activity requires sufficient energy.

Energy is the fuel that powers the body. Bioenergetics is the study of how the body converts fuel (in the form of food and nutrients) into mechanical energy. Converted fuel must travel to a conductor mechanism to a place where muscles can use it. Adenosine triphosphate (ATP) is the most common conductor mechanism.

ATP is composed of adenine, ribose, and a series of phosphates. The body can make ATP in three ways (referred to as the bioenergetic continuum): without the use of oxygen (anaerobic), with the use of oxygen (aerobic), or through the oxidative pathway.

## Dysfunctional respiration
Breathing is the foundation of movement and cardiovascular function. Disruption in proper breathing or glitches in the physiology of breathing can affect overall health, act as an impediment to proper training, and disrupt the movement continuum.

Stress and anxiety can affect proper breathing. Altered breathing can result in:
- The wrong muscles being used to breathe
- Overuse of the muscles needed to support the spine and skull, resulting in tension and headaches
- Improper oxygen ratio caused by breathing too much (hyperventilation).

These problems can be precursors to sleep disorders, psychiatric problems such as heightened anxiety, and headaches.

## Exercise

## Parasympathetic and sympathetic nervous systems affect on heart rate
In the early stage of exercise, the sympathetic nervous system activates to increase heart rate and blood pressure, which help handle the stress of exercise. The parasympathetic nervous system activates later to help blood pressure and heart rate plateau during the session. During the cool down phase, it allows the heart rate and blood pressure to return to resting levels. Over time, exercise conditions the sympathetic system to become less active during rest, and the parasympathetic system to become more active during rest. Consistent exercise allows blood pressure and heart rate to remain low and keeps them near normal levels during stressful situations.

## Action potential
A neuron is not sending a signal when at rest (resting potential). Potassium ions cross through to the inside of the cell membrane, but chloride and sodium ions do not travel as easily. For every two potassium ions that pass through to the inside of the cell, only three sodium ions pass to the outside. At rest, there will be more potassium inside the cell membrane and more sodium on the outside. An outside stimulus can cause the inside of the cell to move toward positive voltage. Once it moves from -70 mV to -55 mV, an action potential begins. Sodium channels open and sodium rushes inside the cell, causing it to become more positive, and it changes polarity. The potassium channels open more slowly than the sodium channels, and when the potassium comes back in the polarity reverses. The cell becomes negatively charged on the inside.

## Various receptors
Mechanoreceptors respond to mechanical stress, such as lifting a load during resistance training. Mechanoreceptors can be found in the joints and connective tissues of the body (tendons, ligaments, and muscles). They sense changes in the compression or stretching of the muscles or

tissues. Muscle spindles, Golgi tendon organs, and joint receptors are forms of mechanoreceptors. Muscle spindles are found in the muscles. They sense alteration in the length of the muscle and the rapidity of that alteration. When stimulated, they will contract in order to prevent overstretching of the muscle. Golgi tendon organs can be found at the junction of a muscle and a tendon. They sense alteration in muscle tension and the rapidity of that alteration. When stimulated, they will relax in order to prevent overstressing the muscle. Joint receptors are found around the joints. They sense changes in speed in the joint. Joint receptors also have a protective mechanism; they help sense when a joint is in an overextended position and reflexively respond to protect that joint.

Chemoreceptors, which respond to chemical interactions, convert a stimulus into an action potential. When the sympathetic nervous system activates at the beginning of physical activity, chemoreceptors aid in that process. Photoreceptors, which respond to light, include the rods and cones in the eye and provide a picture of the environment around us. Photoreceptors allow someone to see the exercise environment. Nociceptors, which respond to pain, identify stimuli that could be dangerous for the body and send a signal to the brain. Nociceptors activate if a client performs a resistance exercise outside the proper range of motion. Thermoreceptors identify changes in temperature. During activity in a hot, humid environment, thermoreceptors identify a change in core temperature caused by the environment. Osmoreceptors detect a change in osmotic pressure. If one's blood pressure drops drastically during an exercise session, the osmoreceptors identify that issue.

## Muscle action spectrum

The muscle action spectrum includes concentric, eccentric, isometric, isokinetic, and isotonic force. Concentric force is the shortening phase of a movement (e.g., the part of a biceps curl where the biceps is overcoming the load of the weight and gravity to shorten the muscle). Eccentric force is the lengthening phase of a movement (e.g., the part of a biceps curl where the biceps muscle is lengthening by not overcoming the load of the weight and gravity). With isometric movement, force production is equal to the load. (e.g., maintaining a plank position). With isokinetic force, the resistance varies depending on the force exerted (e.g., This movement requires sophisticated machinery that increases the load in proportion to the force exerted on it by the individual.). Isotonic movement produces force and tension through a given range of motion.

| Muscle Action | Example | Purpose |
|---|---|---|
| Concentric | The part of a biceps curl where the biceps is overcoming the load of the weight and gravity to shorten the muscle | The shortening phase of a movement |
| Eccentric | The part of a biceps curl where the biceps muscle is lengthening by not overcoming the load of the weight and gravity | The lengthening phase of a movement |
| Isometric | Maintaining a plank position | Force production equals the load |
| Isokinetic | This movement requires sophisticated machinery that increases the load in proportion to the force exerted on it by the individual. | The resistance varies depending on the force exerted |
| Isotonic | A client performs a squat. | Produces force and tension through a given range of motion |

Lactic acid buildup

When the body breaks down carbohydrates into usable energy, lactic acid is a byproduct. Lactate serves as fuel during endurance activities. Lactic acid is also used by the liver to generate more glycogen and glucose. Lactic acid splits into lactate and hydrogen ions. The buildup of hydrogen causes muscle soreness and fatigue.

## Arthrokinematic movement vs. osteokinematic movement

Arthrokinematic movement refers to movements that occur within joints. Rolling, gliding, or sliding motions are examples of arthrokinematic movements. Osteokinematic movement refers to motor movement. For example, flexion, extension, internal rotation, external rotation, adduction, and abduction are osteokinematic movements. Kicking a soccer ball is an osteokinematic movement. Twisting movements of the spine are arthrokinematic movements.

## Planes of movement

The skeleton can move through the coronal (frontal) plane, transverse (horizontal) plane, sagittal plane, and midsagittal plane. A Warrior II pose in yoga is an example of moving through the coronal plane. Performing twisting or turning movements is an example of moving through the transverse plane. Performing lunges is an example of moving through the sagittal or midsagittal plane.

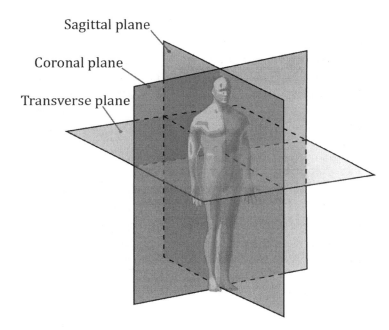

| Plane | Bisector | Movement | Example |
|---|---|---|---|
| **Coronal (frontal)** | Front and back halves | Side to side | Side Lunge |
| **Sagittal** | Left and right sides | Front to back | Lunges |
| **Transverse (horizontal)** | Top and bottom halves | Rotation (twisting) | Golfing |

## Catecholamines

The body releases epinephrine and norepinephrine rapidly at the beginning of aerobic activity. As the body reaches the exercise threshold, the increase becomes more gradual. The body releases epinephrine and norepinephrine more rapidly during anaerobic activity than during aerobic activity. Epinephrine stimulates an increase in heart rate and blood pressure at the onset of exercise, and norepinephrine causes a plateau in heart rate and blood pressure to maintain exercise. The increase in epinephrine and norepinephrine helps stimulate the release of glucagon. The release of glucagon triggers the release of glucose body uses for fuel.

## Cortisol

The body releases cortisol from the adrenal glands in response to stress, and to regulate the body's immune system and sleep cycle. The body releases cortisol during exercise. As someone exercises consistently, the body responds by decreasing cortisol levels post-exercise. The effect of consistent training is better control over cortisol release from the adrenal glands.

## Positive vs. negative feedback mechanisms

A negative feedback mechanism (the most common in the body) is the body's attempt to bring aspects of our system back to their original states. For instance, the release of insulin when sugar level rises in the bloodstream returns the body to normal levels. A positive feedback mechanism increases the stimulus acting within the body. For instance, a clot begins to form to repair a damaged blood vessel, and the creation of more platelets increases the size of the clot.

## Effect of exercise on blood pressure and heart rate

Heart rate and blood pressure increase somewhat rapidly at the onset of exercise. This process increases blood flow to the working muscles while keeping the heart nourished with a steady supply of blood. When an individual reaches an exercise plateau, blood pressure and heart rate level off to maintain the flow of blood to the working muscles and the heart. When a client engages in the Valsalva maneuver while exercising, the resulting spike in blood pressure and heart rate can cause the client to lose consciousness.

## Ventilation

The intake of oxygen and expulsion of carbon dioxide requires proper ventilation. Oxygen makes its way into the bloodstream and helps create ATP. ATP is broken down into usable energy in the muscles so it can continue to fuel exercise. Hyperventilation can prevent the body from replenishing oxygen efficiently, reducing the amount of oxygen that makes it into the bloodstream, which results in less available energy for ATP creation. The client can begin to feel sluggish at this point in the workout.

## Anaerobic vs. aerobic metabolism

The primary fuel source for aerobic metabolism is oxygen. Anaerobic metabolism does not require oxygen. The ATP-PC system and glycolysis create usable energy during anaerobic metabolism. A walk or light jog are examples of light aerobic activity. An example of an anaerobic activity is explosive powerlifting or plyometrics.

## ATP formation

ATP stands for adenosine triphosphate. The energy found in ATP comes from a process called hydrolysis. The enzyme ATP-ase separates a phosphate ion from the ATP, creating usable energy during hydrolysis. ATP becomes ADP (adenosine diphosphate) since it only has two phosphate ions attached. Food is the fuel source consumed during ADP to create more ATP formation.

## Glycolysis

Glycolysis converts glucose into pyruvate, with two net ATP and two NADH as byproducts. The process of glycolysis occurs during aerobic and anaerobic activities. Pyruvate then enters into the Krebs cycle, where it will produce an additional two ATP. The process of glycolysis does not require oxygen (anaerobic) and does not result in substantial energy production.

## Krebs cycle

The Krebs cycle is also called the citric acid cycle or the tricarboxylic acid cycle (TCA). It is a catabolic pathway in which the bonds of glucose and occasionally fats or lipids are broken down and reformed into ATP. It is a respiration process that uses oxygen and produces carbon dioxide, water, and ATP. Cells require energy from ATP to synthesize proteins from amino acids and replicate DNA. One of the products of the Krebs cycle is NADH, which is then used in the electron chain transport system to manufacture ATP. From glycolysis, pyruvate is oxidized in a step linking to the Krebs cycle. After the Krebs cycle, NADH and succinate are oxidized in the electron transport chain.

## Different types of levers

There are three classes of levers. The first class of lever has the fulcrum positioned between the resistance and output force (e.g., performing conventional sit-ups). The second class of levers has the resistance positioned between the fulcrum and the output force (e.g., hitting a baseball with a bat). The third class of levers has the output force positioned between the fulcrum and resistance (e.g., performing tire flips).

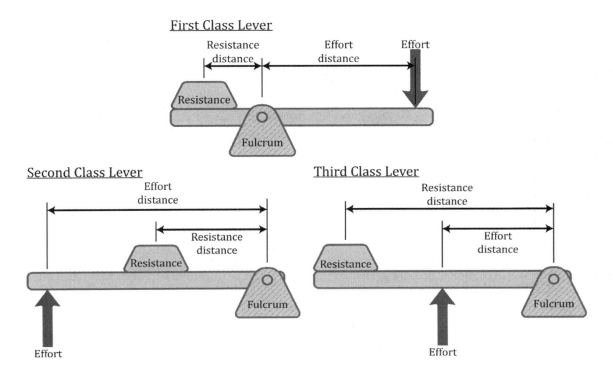

- 23 -

| Lever Type | Description | Example |
|---|---|---|
| First Class | Fulcrum in the middle | Nodding the head |
| Second Class | Resistance in the middle | Push-up |
| Third Class | Effort in the middle | Biceps curl |

## Force and torque

Force occurs when two objects meet resulting in the acceleration or deceleration of the objects. Applied force occurs when a person pushes or pulls on an object. During physical activity, an individual constantly uses applied force. Normal force refers to objects exerting force upon each other by resting in a stable position on top of one another (e.g., a stack of weighted plates). Friction force occurs when the surface of one object slides across the surface of another object (e.g., tennis shoes sliding across the floor in basketball drills). Tension force occurs when a string, wire, or cable exerts a force on an object (e.g., pulley resistance exercises). Spring force occurs when there is a compressed or stretched wire or string with an object at the end of it (e.g., weight machines). Torque refers to a force that rotates around an axis (e.g., oblique crunches).

| Force type | Description | Example |
|---|---|---|
| Applied | Person pushes or pulls on an object | Bench press |
| Normal | Objects resting one on top of the other | Stack of weights |
| Friction | Two surfaces slide against each other | Shoes sliding on the floor |
| Tension | String, wire, or cable exerts force on an object | Pulley resistance exercises |
| Spring | Compressed or stretched wire attached to an object | Weight machines |

A force-couple refers to two forces acting simultaneously on an object with equal force in the opposite direction; for example, pedaling a bike or working an arm ergometer. Force-couples can also exist inside the body when opposing forces act upon bones. One example would be moving the arm backward in the horizontal plane. The agonist and antagonist muscles are exerting force to pull and push the arm backward.

## Muscle length-tension relationship

The length of a muscle at rest, and the amount of tension the muscle can produce at rest is referred to as the length-tension relationship. The optimal muscle length occurs when the actin and myosin have the greatest degree of overlap. Optimal muscle length results in maximal force production. Increasing the length of a muscle reduces force production because actin and myosin overlap is limited. Shortening a muscle causes excessive overlap of actin and myosin which limits force production. When the length-tension relationship is altered, the entire HMS is adversely affected.

## Reciprocal inhibition

Reciprocal inhibition occurs when the muscles on one side of a joint relax while the muscles on the other side of the joint contract. Reciprocal inhibition helps to create coordinated movement during exercise. During a bicep curl, for instance, reciprocal inhibition is the way in which the biceps contract while the triceps lengthen.

## Synergistic dominance

Synergistic dominance occurs when the secondary mover initiates muscle action in place of the prime mover. Synergistic dominance can occur because of an injured prime mover, an underdeveloped prime mover, or an overdeveloped secondary mover (synergist). An injury is likely once the synergist dominates because it was not designed to handle the load appropriately.

## Closed vs. open kinetic chain movements

With closed chain movements, feet or hands are on a surface that is not dynamic. An example of a closed chain movement would be squats. In an open chain movement, the feet or hands are free to move and attached to a movable surface. One example of an open chain movement would be a biceps curl.

## Motor learning

Any movement pattern must be learned and filed in the brain. Motor learning allows this to happen by memorizing and understanding a sequence of steps related to a movement pattern. When teaching movement patterns, less complex patterns should be taught first, with more complex patterns saved for later in the training process. Repetition should be emphasized to increase memory retention of the pattern.

## Motor control

Motor control is the unified activation of the neuromuscular system to initiate and complete a movement. The neuromuscular system can respond to more challenging sequences once movement patterns are established, memorized, and practiced. For example, balance control coupled with open kinetic chain movements challenges the neuromuscular system. As the client masters difficult movements, the foundational movements will become second nature to the individual.

# Considerations in Nutrition

Nutrition refers to everything that is consumed or processed by the human body, which nourishes it and provides essential building blocks for growth, repair, energy, and all other necessary body functions. Nutrition can come in the form of food, beverages, vitamins, and topical exposure to such things as sunlight.

It is important for a trainer to be aware of basic nutrition because working out is not the only aspect of a healthy life. A client's diet and supplementation routine can directly affect his or her ability to train, and a poor diet can sabotage some of the gains made in training. While a trainer is not a nutritionist, and should refer a client to a nutritionist for specific diet planning, client should be steered away from fad diets and toward a healthful, balanced diet that provides adequate energy for the client's training program.

## Body composition

Food consumption contributes to the shape and makeup of the human body. Modern culture promotes thinness over health, causing many people to seek quick weight loss methods, resulting in many fad diets. Unfortunately, these fad diets are ineffective, provide misinformation and spread myths that may be difficult to deprogram from a new client.

A person must burn more calories than they ingest to lose weight (the opposite is true for weight gain). Calories ingested include all food and beverages that are consumed. Calories expended include daily functional activities and fitness activities. In modern society, high-calorie food is readily available, while sedentary work and personal lifestyles are more prevalent than in the past.

Understanding basic nutritional information will greatly enhance a trainer's ability to guide the client.

## Nutrients for specific goals

### Losing weight

If a person is seeking to lose weight, it is likely that he or she is looking to alter body composition by losing fat. To accomplish this, balance micronutrients and include carbohydrates, fat, and protein in each meal. Six smaller meals consumed throughout the day ensure the body is continually processing fuel. Complex carbohydrates and fiber are preferable to simpler sugars. Staying hydrated by drinking up to twelve glasses of water will also help aid digestion and prevent edema, or water retention.

Encourage clients to measure portions to get a realistic sense of portion control. They should also be encouraged to avoid junk food and processed foods to avoid nonnutritive calories.

### Building muscle

Another common fitness goal is to increase muscle mass. Certain dietary suggestions should be adhered to, so the body has sufficient materials with which to build lean muscle tissue.

Include a balance of micronutrients in the diet and consume carbohydrates, fat, and protein at each meal; protein alone will not suffice. To encourage protein synthesis, the client should eat six times daily.

When food is consumed is important. Ingesting protein and carbohydrates within two hours of working out will encourage the body to maximize its muscle-building activities, perhaps due to the increase in blood flow that occurs after a workout. Consider using a liquid supplement product that can be quickly absorbed into the body.

## Protein

Proteins act as a building block for new or damaged body tissues. Proteins are a viable energy source and are required by the body to synthesize other necessary nutrients.

Proteins are composed of amino acids. There are two types of amino acids: essential (meaning the body cannot create them itself) and nonessential (meaning the body can create them from other sources). The eight essential amino acids have to be ingested from a direct source. The ten nonessential amino acids can be pieced together by the body from nitrogen and other source material (lipids and carbohydrates).

<u>Digestion and use of proteins</u>
Proteins are made up of chains of amino acids held together by peptides. For the body to be able to use these amino acids, the entire protein chain has to be broken down into its individual amino acids. This begins when the proteins come into contact with the hydrochloric acid in the stomach, and it continues as the proteins enter the large and small intestines.

Proteins can then be used in different ways, depending on what the body needs at that time. There are three main things a protein can do once released into the blood via the liver: be used immediately as energy, be stored as fat, or be used to build or repair body tissues.

*Amino acids*
There are three different categories of amino acids: essential (meaning the body cannot create them itself), nonessential (meaning the body can create them from other sources), and semi-essential (meaning elements can be made by the body, but other parts need an external source).

| Nonessential amino acids | Essential amino acids | Semi-essential amino acids |
|---|---|---|
| Glutamine | Tryptophan | Histidine |
| Alanine | Isoleucine | Arginine |
| Tyrosine | Valine | |
| Asparagine | Threonine | |
| Serine | Leucine | |
| Cystine | Lysine | |
| Aspartic acid | Phenylalanine | |
| Proline | | |
| Glycine | | |
| Glutamic acid | | |

<u>Foods that contain proteins</u>
A variety of foods contain proteins. Food that comes from animals (e.g., animal meat, eggs, milk, and dairy products) contains substantial amounts of protein. Food that contains all of the essential amino acids is called a complete protein. If it only has some of the essential amino acids, it is called an incomplete protein (such as peanut butter).

The amino acid that is missing or only present in trace amounts is the limiting factor. A complete protein must be synthesized. The missing protein determines (limits) the amount of protein that can be made. Think of a spice recipe that calls for 2 cups of salt, pepper, and garlic. If the chef only has 1 cup of garlic, the spice mix cannot be made, and the garlic is said to be the limiting factor. Vegetarians eat only certain types of protein, which may be incomplete or have a low limiting factor. Vegetarians should work with a nutritionist who specializes in vegan or vegetarian diets to ensure they eat enough complete protein sources.

Complete protein profiles
Protein is evaluated on how well it functions as a complete nutrient, and if it provides all of the essential amino acids in the ratios needed for consumption.

Biologic value (BV) is a popular term used to describe how much a given protein satisfies the needed amino acid values. It is a common catchphrase used in fitness circles and in vitamin supplement advertising. The higher the BV of the protein, the more closely it supplies all the needed amino acids.

Net protein utilization (NPU) and protein efficiency ratio (PER) are two terms that mean the same thing: how well a given protein meets the needs of the human body.

Amounts of proteins
The amount of protein that an individual needs to consume will depend on various factors such as height, weight, activity level, and activity level. For example, if a person does intense aerobic and anaerobic exercises, his or her protein requirements may be higher.

Most of a person's basic energy needs should be met with carbohydrates and lipids, with protein used for tissue repair and as a backup energy source, unless the client is a competitive weight lifter.

If a person consumes high-quality protein sources, less of it will be needed. If the protein sources are less complete, with a lower BV, more protein will be needed to provide all the essential amino acids.

Negative energy balance
A negative energy balance (achieved by burning more calories than are consumed) is required if a client wants to lose weight or reduce body fat percentage. When this state is achieved, amino acids are used by the body to generate energy in a process called gluconeogenesis. Protein is required to fuel this process.

Clients who reduce overall calorie intake and increase activity levels will require an increase in lean protein consumption. Protein will be used for energy, to repair tissues from exercise, and to help prevent the loss of muscle mass that often accompanies a weight-loss regimen.

Protein needs
Because protein acts as a building block for body tissues, persons interested in hypertrophy, particularly weight-lifting clients seeking maximal hypertrophy for competitive bodybuilding purposes, will need to ingest much more protein than the average healthy adult. This will also help taper body fat down to very low ratios, a necessity during the competition season.

However, this should be used as a temporary diet strictly for use during competition times. Because the body's protein needs will be higher because of the specific training, protein will be upped dramatically while overall calories from other sources will be reduced. Consuming a high-protein diet on a long-term basis is not recommended, and keeping body fat to single-digit percentages is not healthy beyond this purpose.

By cycling back to a regular diet when not competing, the bodybuilding client will be able to achieve better muscle mass when competing in the future than he or she would if the high-protein diet was constantly employed.

Satiety
A feeling of fullness (satiety) after eating is important for several reasons. First, it gives a signal to stop ingesting more calories at that sitting. It also signals to the body that calories have been consumed, something that may not be triggered when a person drinks the same number of calories in a beverage or shake form. Protein also takes longer to process, leading to feeling full for a longer period, with steadier energy levels throughout the day.

Protein is more satisfying than other nutrients, specifically lipids (fats) and carbohydrates. Animal studies have shown that when the animals are given protein, they can go longer until the next feeding than when given fat or carbohydrates alone. This indicates that protein satisfies hunger for a longer period and provides more satiety.

RDA of protein
An average healthy person should aim to ingest 0.8 grams of protein for every kilogram of body weight (approximately 30 percent of daily calorie intake).

Those who are engaged in fitness or training activities should ingest more protein to help with tissue repair and muscle building. For a person who works out regularly, this would include a minimum of 1 gram of protein for every kilogram of body weight and somewhere around 1.5 grams of protein for every kilogram of body weight when doing muscle-building activities.

For an endurance athlete, 1.4 grams of protein for every kilogram of body weight is needed during regular training, bumped up to as much as 2 grams per kilogram of body weight during competition training.

Competitive weight lifters would need 1 gram of protein for every kilogram of body weight during noncompetitive periods and jump up to somewhere around 2 grams per kilogram of body weight during competitive training times.

| Normal activity Level | Recommended daily protein intake |
|---|---|
| Sedentary | 0.8 g/kg (0.4 g/lb.) |
| Strength athlete | 1.2–1.7 g/kg (0.5–0.8 g/lb.) |
| Endurance athlete | 1.2–1.4 g/kg (0.5–0.6 g/lb.) |

Protein-based diet drawbacks
High-protein diets have enjoyed popularity in the last decade, touting weight loss benefits. However, research shows that such diets are not best for people in the long run. High-protein diets tend to include higher levels of bad fats and reduce ingestion of dietary fiber, which can lead to a higher risk of serious diseases.

High-protein diets require much more water to digest properly, raising the risk that a person can become dehydrated more easily.

Another serious problem associated with high-protein diets is potential calcium loss. When people eat more protein than they need, their bodies lose calcium.

High-protein diets also force the body into ketosis (a state where the body uses fat as its main source of energy), which many doctors and nutritionists feel is unsafe on a long-term basis.

<u>Extra protein</u>
There is no scientific evidence to prove that consuming extra protein in the form of supplements gives a uniform result to overall fitness gains or muscle hypertrophy. However, when a person is working out, his or her protein needs may go up to supply the body with building blocks to build and repair tissues and as a backup fuel source.

Ingesting protein after a workout has been shown to increase important endocrine activities that may support muscle building, rather than straight repair.

Supplements can also be used when a client is trying to lose body fat by acting as a replacement, giving needed protein while avoiding excess calories. Supplements can be consumed very quickly and easily in the form of portable shakes or bars, ensuring that a client ingests needed fuel before a workout.

<u>Supplemental protein</u>
Many supplement manufacturers attempt to create a perfect protein that can be used by the body better than actual food sources or other supplements. The perfect protein would assimilate quickly and contain the perfect balance of amino acids.

A popular trend in supplemental protein is whey protein, which can be found in a variety of supplements. Whey protein has the best biologic value of all supplemental proteins and has been shown in studies to provide greater benefits than other kinds of protein.

It is debatable if extra protein is necessary, even for active individuals. Whey protein supplements are appropriate for competitive weight lifters in competition mode; these athletes have high protein needs and are seeking to reduce overall calories.

## Carbohydrates

Carbohydrates are made up of three basic elements: oxygen, hydrogen, and carbon. Carbohydrates are macronutrients that fall into three categories:
- Fiber
- Simple carbohydrates (sugar)
- Complex carbohydrates (starch)

Sugars can further be classified as mono- or disaccharides—having one or two sugar units. Fructose (plant sugar) and glucose (blood sugar) are common monosaccharides. Lactose (milk sugar) and sucrose (table sugar) are common disaccharides.

Carbohydrates are the body's main supply of energy and have other wide-ranging functions, including playing a part in the digestion of other micronutrients.

## Digestion and use

Different forms of carbohydrates are digested differently by the body. Simple sugars are easily assimilated with little work by the body. These types of sugars are found in various fruits as well as honey.

Starches take more work to break down because of their double bond. Grains, potatoes, rice, and table sugar fall into this category and require more effort for the body to process.

Fiber in the form of cellulose, the fibrous element of many fruits and vegetables, cannot be completely broken down by the body. Roughage (undigested fiber) is extremely important to healthy intestinal function because it helps clean out the digestive tract and regulate bowel movements.

## Glycemic Index (GI)

The glycemic index (GI) measures how much a given micronutrient affects a person's blood sugar level and the body's insulin response. The test is simple: The measurement is made when a single food is eaten after a fasting period. The blood sugar is measured before and after the food is eaten to gauge the change in blood sugar level.

Eating different foods in combination may change the effect on blood sugar entirely.

Some diets tout the benefits of eating only foods that have a low GI score, claiming that foods with high GI scores will lead to negative effects, such as increased weight and fat gain. These diets tend to clump foods into positive and negative categories, ignoring the basic premise of energy balance (weight gain is the result of more calories taken in than are expended).

The concept of good versus bad foods is a bit misguided, though foods with a low GI score do tend to be very healthy for the diet.

### Foods across the glycemic index

The highest level on the GI chart is pure glucose (commonly known as blood sugar), which is immediately assimilated by the body and causes blood sugar to spike.

The next highest range includes honey, cooked potatoes without skins, and carrots. These are followed (in descending order) by whole wheat bread, cooked potatoes with the skins on, and rice; white bread and bananas; sucrose (table sugar) and corn; pasta, oatmeal, and oranges; dairy products and apples; fruit sugar (fructose) and legumes (such as beans); lowest on the GI scale are soybeans and legumes (such as peanuts).

| GI # | Classification |
|------|----------------|
| > 70 | High |
| 56–69 | Moderate |
| < 55 | Low |

## Fiber

Fiber is an extremely important part of a healthy diet for many reasons. Fiber consists of indigestible cellulose or plant matter that travels through the digestive tract in its original form. Benefits of fiber include:

- Helps keep blood sugar levels even and manageable
- Helps keep a person regular and avoid constipation
- Helps avoid appendicitis
- Helps maintain a healthy bacteria balance
- Helps a person feel more full
- Helps prevent diverticulitis, an infection of the intestines
- Helps lower bad (LDL) cholesterol levels

Diets high in fiber are linked to lower risk factors for diseases such as some cancers and cardiac-related disorders (heart disease).

### Athletic ability

Carbohydrates are essential for fitness and sports performance because they provide the body with the most accessible source of energy, especially for anaerobic exercises or activities. (These would be categorized as quick, high-impact activities, typical of most sporting activities.) During long-term activities, the body relies on stored glycogen first and then on fat.

The phrase "Fat burns in a carbohydrate flame" has a specific meaning in the context of training. There must be sufficient carbohydrates available to keep the body's energy cycle even and continually burning fat, which maximizes fat loss If there are not enough carbohydrates, muscle glycogen will be depleted, and performance will suffer. This can happen even when sufficient oxygen is circulating in the body.

### Recommended grams of carbohydrates

For endurance athletes, carbohydrates are essential. There must be sufficient carbohydrates available to keep the body's energy cycle even without relying on muscle glycogen stores, which are finite. If there are not enough carbohydrates, muscle glycogen will be depleted, and performance will suffer. This can happen even when sufficient oxygen is circulating in the body.

Endurance athletes need high-carbohydrate diets. Carbohydrates should comprise about two-thirds of calories consumed, or somewhere between 5 and 10 grams of carbohydrate per kilogram of body weight. Complex carbohydrates are the best choice because of the variety of other nutrients and vitamins available in these food sources.

Because a person should not exercise on a full stomach, it is a good idea for him or her to eat several hours before a workout. The meal should include an ample supply of carbohydrates sufficient to build up glycogen stores before exercise. Research has shown that people who eat a solid carbohydrate source four hours before exercising get a noticeable improvement in performance for that workout, well over ten percent.

Eating before a morning workout is very important because energy stores will be depleted after a long sleep. If a full meal is not practical, an energy shake or fitness bar will suffice, so the stomach isn't full, and the body can quickly process the fuel.

## Carbohydrate loading

Carbo-loading is a system of ingesting large quantities of carbohydrates before an endurance activity that will last more than an hour and a half. This is common for people who run long distances, such as marathoners. This is done because this activity uses a high percentage of the body's stores of glycogen. If there is insufficient carbohydrate available and the glycogen stores are used up, a bottoming-out effect can occur. By carbo-loading, the body can reinforce its glycogen stores, doubling its available energy stores.

A carbo-loading diet typically occurs over several days. First comes four days of lowering glycogen stores by eating few carbohydrates and engaging in heavy exercise activities. Then, the person recuperates for three days and ingests up to 10 grams of carbohydrates for each kilogram of body weight.

Traditional carbo-loading consisted of four days of exhaustive exercise and limited carbohydrates followed by three days of recuperation and maximal carbohydrate intake. This method can be hard on the body by adding extra stressors right before an endurance event, which can lead to increased injury risk and cause blood sugar levels to slip too low, causing fatigue and crankiness.

An alternate carbo-loading routine, aimed at increasing the body's stores of glycogen, was formulated in the early 1980s. The client ingests four grams of carbohydrate for every kilogram of body weight on the sixth, fifth, and fourth days before an endurance event. High-intensity exercise is also engaged in for a half hour on the sixth day and for three-quarters of an hour for the fifth and fourth days.

On the third and second days prior, high-intensity exercise is engaged in for only 20 minutes. However, 10 grams of carbohydrates for every kilogram of body weight are ingested. The day before the event entails no workout, but it does include the elevated carbohydrate count.

If a client is going to be doing more than an hour of fairly intense exercise, ingesting carbohydrates during the training session may be advisable. This would help keep available energy in a reasonable range, prevent an exhaustion of glycogen stores from muscle tissue, and increase endurance and performance for up to an additional hour.

If the exercise or training requires endurance, hourly intake of carbohydrates is a necessity. The best method would be through sports beverages; these not only replace lost fluids, but they also give a balanced stream of carbohydrates to the body without filling the stomach with the bulk that accompanies solid food consumption. NASM recommends drinking from 20 to 40 fluid ounces of liquid with around a 5-percent carbohydrate solution.

Ingesting carbohydrates after working out can have several benefits: It helps the body replenish glycogen stores that were depleted in training; ingesting carbohydrates after exercise also helps the body repair itself after strenuous workouts.

It is important that carbohydrates be ingested fairly quickly after exercising to maximize benefits. It is advisable to consume between 1 to 2 grams of carbohydrates for every kilogram of body weight within 30 minutes of completing a workout.

Research has shown that waiting two hours to ingest carbohydrates can have a serious negative impact on glycogen replenishment. This could be because the body is more receptive after the rigors of working out, due to its systems working at a higher performance level and the blood rapidly circulating.

<u>Percentage of diet</u>
If a person is looking to lose fat and gain lean muscle, carbohydrates should be the most plentiful aspect of the diet, comprising at least half to three-quarters of all calories consumed. The person can further maximize the benefits of that carbohydrate intake by ingesting a good deal of dietary fiber in that 50 to 75 percent.

This advice is contrary to many popular fad diets, which continue to assert that carbohydrates are a dieter's enemy and contribute significantly to fat gain or the body's inability to lose fat. This is based on junk science. The more reasoned and accepted point of view is that a diet must consist of a higher percentage of carbohydrates to prevent the body from sapping muscle glycogen stores for energy, which then strips lean muscle. Water loss associated with this process can account for apparent weight loss, but it does little in the way of altering body composition.

<u>Weight gain</u>
There is an ongoing claim that carbohydrates contribute to the increase in obesity in the United States. Because the fitness industry and the diet and supplements industry are so powerful, a substantial amount of time and scientific research has been devoted to proving that carbohydrate consumption leads to weight gain.

Research indicates that even though Americans ate a higher percentage of carbohydrates and less fat at the turn of the twentieth century, obesity was far less widespread than it is today. This is due to two simple factors: Modern people are less active and ingest far more overall calories than did their ancestors.

This supports the basic theory that body composition, weight gain, and obesity are not related to high carbohydrate intake as much as to energy imbalance (more calories consumed than burned).

**Lipids**

A lipid is a macronutrient that can be used by the body for various functions and includes oils, fatty substances, sterols, and phospholipids. Lipids in foods are almost always either oil or fat, which are also called triglycerides. This is also the form that lipids are stored in the human body.

Lipids, or fatty acids, are further classified as unsaturated or saturated, sometimes labeled good and bad fats respectively. Unsaturated fats have a double-bond structure and cannot only lower bad cholesterol (LDL) but also can also raise good cholesterol (HDL). These kinds of fats come from plant sources, such as olive oil and avocados.

Saturated fats, on the other hand, do not have this double bond and raise LDL levels, which can lead to atherosclerosis (plaque collecting in the arteries and narrowing them). Saturated fats come from animal sources, such as meat, milk, and eggs and fried foods.

<u>Monounsaturated and polyunsaturated fatty acids</u>
Monounsaturated and polyunsaturated fatty acids are two different categories of unsaturated fats, one of two categories of fatty acids. (The other category is saturated fats.) These terms derive from the way the atoms are formed. If there is one double bond of carbon holding the fatty acid together,

it is monounsaturated. If there are two or more double bonds of carbon holding the fatty acid together, it is polyunsaturated.

Monounsaturated fats are usually liquid when at room temperature. They include a host of natural oils: olive, grapeseed, flaxseed, and peanut, to name just a few. Monounsaturated fats lower so-called bad cholesterol (LDL).

Polyunsaturated fats come from a variety of sources, such as grains and oily fish. They provide benefits against cardiovascular disease and cancer.

Both fats provide needed elements that help the body run properly and are a necessary part of a balanced diet.

Purpose of lipids
Although low-fat diets have been in vogue at various times, based on the misguided belief that fat is harmful, lipids serve a vital role in a healthy diet. Lipids have the most energy per gram when compared to other macronutrients, with nine calories per gram. Lipids are essential for carrying some vitamins, such as vitamin D, and are needed for calcium to be absorbed in the body.

Lipids are important for many other reasons:
- Body fat is used as a thermal layer and as an energy source for a nursing mother
- Fats are needed for proper cell growth and regeneration
- Fats digest more slowly and help a person feel full longer
- Fat plays a role in endocrine function

Digestion and use of lipids
Fat is digested along the entirety of the digestive tract. The process begins when it comes into contact with saliva. Body acids from the stomach and the intestines continue to break the fats down into components that can be used by the body. From the intestines, these components enter the bloodstream. The process goes like this:

- Lipids are broken down through the digestive tract
- Triglycerides are formed in the intestines
- Chylomicrons are formed in the lymphatic system
- Chylomicrons are distributed from the lymphatic system into the bloodstream

Triglycerides are broken down by the lipoprotein lipase (LPL) enzyme and used by body tissues, and the fat content can then be stored in muscle, organs, and fat cells.

Fat can be used as an immediate fuel source if the body has no available carbohydrate energy. However, if a person eats too much fat, it is far easier for the body to convert this into stored fat than it is for the body to alter excess carbohydrates chemically and store them as fat.

Satiety
Lipids have a very distinct effect on satiety, beginning with a hormonal response triggered in the mouth and stomach. Fats begin to trigger hormones that tell the brain the body is full. Fats also take longer to digest, giving the body a steady supply of fuel to process, leading to a full feeling for a longer period.

Many factors contribute to satiety beyond caloric intake (which is why people rarely feel full after drinking a high-calorie protein shake). Food volume and some of the actions of eating (such as crunching, ingesting mass, and getting a full stomach) are also important and cannot be satisfied by lipids alone.

A diet containing 30 percent fat or less will gain the benefits of containing fats while providing enough other foods and nutrients to satisfy a person's sensations of hunger.

Ingesting extra fat

There has been research in recent years regarding different types of lipids and how they might be used to the advantage of athletes and others who are engaged in fitness training. As a general rule, fats take a long time to digest and are not necessarily the ideal supplement for sports or fitness activities.

However, some lipids can be more quickly digested for use in the body, namely medium-chain triglycerides. Unlike long-chain triglycerides, which are the most-common types of lipids people ingest, medium-chain triglycerides do not go through such a long digestive process and can be used by the body more quickly.

While there is a theory that this energy could be a viable backup source for athletes, sparing glycogen sources, there is not enough current research to support this claim. Therefore, supplementation with fat should not be a top priority.

Metabolic syndrome is an umbrella term for a host of problems associated with digestive and endocrine problems such as diabetes, insulin resistance, obesity, and high blood pressure. People who tout protein-rich diets point to high carbohydrate consumption as being the underlying cause of metabolic syndrome, also known as syndrome X.

However, it seems more likely that the common denominator for these conditions is not carbohydrates, but rather an excess of free fatty acids. When free fatty acids are available, the body will use them first instead of more-optimal fuel sources, which in turn leads to problems processing glucose. This will lead to elevated insulin levels, which can then lead to insulin resistance and a host of other problems.

Therefore, it is more likely that higher fat content in the diet is the actual culprit, not high-carbohydrate diets.

**Water**

Water is composed of two hydrogen molecules and one oxygen molecule ($H_2O$). Water is one of the most abundant compounds on the planet and makes up almost two-thirds of the human body. Because it is used for many purposes (e.g., cooling the body off and removing waste from the body) and excreted, it must be regularly replaced to avoid dehydration. While nutritional deficiencies can take a long time to become a problem, humans cannot live for very long without ingesting clean water, or they will suffer serious, and potentially fatal effects. Basic body functions are impacted if a person loses as little as 2 percent of his or her total weight in water.

Benefits of adequate hydration include adequate blood levels, consistent body temperature, optimally functioning hormonal systems, and preventing edema, or water retention.

## Training and sports activities

Water and fluids are essential to fitness training. The body is composed largely of water and needs a continual replenishment to function properly. Exercise and fitness activities hasten the loss of fluids, primarily through perspiration, and require a person to replace lost fluid to maintain performance capabilities.

Dehydration is associated with lower blood volume, lower blood pressure, heightened heart rate, and sodium retention, which in turn lead to fluid retention.

A person's weight can be used as a starting point to determine how much liquid is needed. An individual's weight upon waking in the morning can be considered 0. Before exercising or beginning any strenuous fitness activity; a person should ingest enough liquids to put his or her weight back to the 0 mark.

## Guidelines for hydration

NASM has developed guidelines for how an athlete should rehydrate to make up for fluids lost through sweat and elimination. A few hours before any exercise, the client should drink 16 ounces of fluids and consume up to twice that amount if it is hot out. During exercise, the client should replenish each hour with 20 to 40 ounces of fluids. After exercising, the client should weigh him- or herself and assess how many pounds off the 0 mark he or she is; the client should then drink 20 ounces per pound lost, especially if he or she is in heavy training or is an endurance athlete.

If the client is having a regular training session and the exercising will last approximately an hour, water will be the best choice for rehydration. If the client plans to train for more than an hour, Gatorade or a similar drink will be most beneficial. To stimulate faster stomach emptying, encourage the drinking of cold beverages.

## Vitamins and supplements

### Discovery and initial use

The importance of vitamins was not completely understood until early in the twentieth century. Augmenting diet through the use of supplements then became popular.

Early supplements were a one-size-fits-all variety, a one-a-day pill which included all of the essential vitamins and minerals was the most-common. While this is still popular today, there are thousands of varieties of supplements now, with individual vitamins or minerals in a plethora of dosages and special blends touting specific health benefits.

In 1990, it was estimated that there were over $3 billion in vitamin-supplement sales in the United States. This figure skyrocketed to almost $18 billion by the year 2002.

In 1994, the federal government passed the Dietary Supplement Health and Education Act (DSHEA) to supply guidelines for the manufacture and sale of vitamins and supplements. These are different than the guidelines used by the Food and Drug Administration (FDA).

### Supplements

DSHEA specifically states what can be classified as a supplement. This definition includes:
- The item must be intended to be ingested as a liquid, powder, or pill/caplet/capsule
- It is not marketed as food
- It clearly marked as a dietary supplement

- It is intended to increase the regular intake of a particular vitamin or mineral
- It is a concentrated version of the vitamin or mineral, a metabolized version, a part of a vitamin or mineral, an extract of a vitamin or mineral, or a mixture of these components
- It is a nontobacco product with at least one of the following: a mineral, a vitamin, some plant product, or an amino acid compound

Supplements are used to augment a diet in which some component is missing or lacking.

## Reasons for taking dietary supplements

Supplements can be used for a variety of reasons: to augment a diet that may be missing some nutrients, to prevent particular health problems, or to encourage better fitness performance. Some use supplements for better mental clarity, for help sleeping, and for possible weight-loss benefits.

There are many reasons why a diet may be deficient in some nutrients. This can include not eating a healthy number of calories, not eating healthy foods, eating a restricted diet (such as vegetarian or vegan), overuse of fad diets, and even financial barriers to purchasing nutrient-rich foods.

Seniors can often use supplementation to make sure they are receiving the proper amount of vitamins and minerals needed for healthy body function. Pregnant and nursing women can also greatly benefit from supplementation, but they must do so under a doctor or nutritionist's supervision.

## General parameters

As with any substance that can be introduced to the body, supplements, while usually helpful and beneficial, can be overused or used incorrectly. Therefore, it is necessary to determine appropriate supplemental quantities.

The best reference guides available are the dietary reference intakes (DRIs), a series of reviews performed by the Food and Nutrition Board of the Institute of Medicine. These give not only the recommended healthy dosage but also the dosage considered excessive and potentially harmful. DRIs also account for different gender, age, and special-needs groups (such as pregnant women and nursing mothers).

The goal of DRIs is to give a person an adequate amount of a given vitamin or mineral without overdoing it.

## Supplementation terms

When discussing supplements, there are many terms to describe the ideal dosages and the point at which doses are too high for safe or recommended consumption. These terms include:
- Recommended dietary allowance (RDA)—the total amount that persons of a given age range, gender, and possibly special population group (such as pregnant women) should ingest in one day to get all the needed vitamins and nutrients. From this amount, percentage values can be calculated to show how much of the RDA is met with one serving.
- Estimated average requirement (EAR)—how much of a nutrient will satisfy the dietary needs of half the population.
- Adequate intake (AI)—an estimated figure used when an RDA cannot be calculated; it indicates how much should be enough of a given nutrient to satisfy the body's needs.

- Tolerable upper intake level (UL)—the high end of what should be ingested in a day: the point at which further intake could be harmful.
- Safe upper limit (SUL)—the maximum amount a person should take on a daily basis.

## Toxicity

Vitamins and minerals are necessary for proper body function, but can be toxic or cause adverse health effects when taken in excessive amounts. For example, too much vitamin B6 can affect the nerves, while too much vitamin D can cause kidney damage.

For this reason, tolerable upper intake levels (ULs) are set when possible to give individuals guidance on just how much should be ingested. ULs are set using a normal, healthy individual as the basis for the measurement. This means that these values may not apply to members of special populations, people on special diets, or those who are taking certain medications.

The absence of a UL value does not mean that a possible toxic level does not exist. Rather, this could indicate that there is not enough information to make a determination.

## Recommended values

### Vitamin A

The RDA, or adequate intake (AI) amount, for vitamin A is 700 for women and 900 for men. The DV for vitamin A is 5,000 international units (IU), or 1,500 mg. The UL is 3,000 IU; this value is based on a person who is approximately 130 lbs. The SUL is 5,000 IU or 1,500 mg.

There are potentially serious side effects associated with ingesting too much Vitamin A, including vomiting, headaches, pain in the joints, dry hair and skin, and damage to the liver.

### Beta carotene

The RDA, (AI amount), DV and the UL, values are not defined for beta carotene. Although these values have not yet been defined, there are still potential risks. The values are undefined because there is insufficient information to make a determination. The SUL is 11,655 IU or 7 mg.

There are potentially serious side effects associated with ingesting too much beta carotene, which include a higher risk of developing cancer of the lungs for those who are in high-risk groups (those chronically exposed to asbestos as well as smokers).

### Vitamin D

The RDA, or adequate intake (AI) amount, for vitamin D is 5 mg for women and men. The DV for vitamin D is 400 international units (IUs), or 10 mgs. The UL is 50 mg; this value is based on a person who is approximately 130 lbs. The SUL is 1,000 IU or 25 mg.

There are potentially serious side effects associated with ingesting too much Vitamin D, which include nausea and an increase of calcium in the blood, which can lead to calcification of brain and artery tissue.

### Vitamin E

The RDA, or AI amount, for vitamin E is 15 mg for women and men. The DV for vitamin E is 30 IU or 20 mg. The UL is 1,000 IU; this value is based on a person who is approximately 130 lbs. The SUL is 800 IU or 400 mg.

There are potentially serious side effects associated with ingesting too much Vitamin E, which include a lowered ability for the body to clot blood, leading to bleeding problems.

### Vitamin K

The RDA, or AI amount, for vitamin K is 90 for women and 120 for men. The DV for vitamin K is 80 mg. There is no defined UL, although there is an SUL of 1,000 mg.

There are potentially serious side effects associated with ingesting too much Vitamin K, including damage to the liver, blood problems such as anemia (not enough iron), and red blood cell disorders

### Thiamine (vitamin B1)

The recommended daily allowance (RDA), or adequate intake (AI) amount, for thiamine, or vitamin B1, is 1.1 for women and 1.2 for men. The daily value (DV) for thiamine is 1.5 mg. The tolerable upper level intake (UL) has not been defined, although this does not mean there is not a safe upper level, only that not enough information is available to set a value. The safe upper level (SUL) is 100 mg.

There are potentially serious side effects associated with ingesting too much Vitamin B1, which include nausea, headaches, crankiness, and an inability to sleep properly. An elevated heart rate and dizziness can occur at doses above 7,000 mg.

### Riboflavin (vitamin B2)

The RDA, or AI, for riboflavin (vitamin B2) is 1.1 for women and 1.3 for men. The DV for riboflavin is 1.7 mg. The UL has not been defined, although this does not mean there is not a safe upper level, only that not enough information is available to set a value. The SUL is 40 mg.

Ingesting too much riboflavin is considered fairly harmless, although it may cause a slight discoloration of urine.

### Niacin

The RDA, or AI amount, for niacin is 14 for women and 16 for men. The DV for niacin is 20 mg. The UL is 35 mg; this value is based on a person who is approximately 130 lbs. The SUL is 500 IU.

There are potentially serious side effects associated with ingesting too much niacin, including redness in the face, nausea, damage to the liver and digestive problems.

### Vitamin B6

The RDA, or adequate intake (AI) amount, for vitamin B6 is 1.3 for women and men. The daily value for vitamin B6 is 2 mg. The UL is 100 mg; this value is based on a person who is approximately 130 lbs. The SUL is 10 international units (IU).

There are potentially serious side effects associated with ingesting too much Vitamin B6, which may cause discomfort and a loss of feeling in the limbs.

### Vitamin B12

The RDA, or AI amount, for vitamin B12 is 2.4 mg for women and men. The DV for vitamin B12 is 6 mg. The UL has not been defined, although this value has not yet been defined, there are still potential risks. The value is undefined because there is insufficient information to make a determination. The SUL is 2,000 IU.

There have been no recorded cases of toxic reactions to excessive doses of vitamin B12 when taken orally.

*Folic acid*
The RDA, or AI amount, for folic acid is 400 for women and men. The DV for folic acid is 400 mg. The UL is 1,000 mg; this value is based on a person who is approximately 130 lbs. The SUL is 1,000 mg.

There are potentially serious side effects associated with ingesting too much folic acid, which include hiding a deficiency of the vitamin B12, which in turn can result in nervous-system problems involving brain function.

*Pantothenic acid*
The RDA, or AI amount, for pantothenic acid is 5 mg for women and men. The DV for pantothenic acid is 10 mg. Although the UL has not yet been defined, there are still potential risks. The value is undefined because there is insufficient information to make a determination. The SUL is 200 IU.

Ingesting too much pantothenic acid can cause adverse effects, which include digestive-tract problems, general stomach upset, and diarrhea.

*Biotin*
The recommended daily allowance (RDA), or adequate intake (AI) amount, for biotin is 30 mg for women and men. The daily value (DV) for biotin is 300 mg. The tolerable upper level intake (UL) has not been defined, although this does not mean there is no upper limit, rather there may is insufficient information to determine a value. The safe upper level (SUL) is 900 mg.

There have been no noted cases of toxic reactions to excessive doses of biotin taken orally.

*Vitamin C*
The RDA, or AI amount, for vitamin C is 75 mg for women and 90 for men. The DV for vitamin C is 60 mg. The UL is 2,000 international units (IU); this value is based on a person who is approximately 130 lbs. The SUL is 1,000 mg.

There are potentially serious side effects associated with ingesting too much Vitamin C, including kidney stones, nausea, gastrointestinal upset, and diarrhea.

*Boron*
The RDA, (AI amount), DV and the UL, values are not defined for boron. Although these values have not yet been defined, there are still potential risks. The values are undefined because there is insufficient information to make a determination.

The UL is 20 IU; this value is based on a person who is approximately 130 lbs. The SUL is 9.6 mg.

There are potentially serious side effects associated with ingesting too much boron, which include problems with the reproductive systems of men and women.

*Calcium*
The RDA, or AI amount, for calcium is 1,000 mg for women and men. The DV for calcium is 1,000 mg. The UL is 2,500 mg; this value is based on a person who is approximately 130 lbs. The SUL is 1,500 mg.

There are potentially serious side effects associated with ingesting too much calcium, including kidney stones, nausea, and constipation.

### Chromium

The RDA, or adequate intake (AI) amount, for chromium is 35 international units (IU) for women and men. The DV for chromium is 120 IU. The UL has not been defined, but this does not mean there is no UL value; rather, there may not be enough information to make this determination at present. The SUL is 10,000 IU.

There are potentially serious side effects associated with ingesting too much chromium, including damage or malfunction of the kidneys or liver. It is also possible that chromium picolinate may cause cell mutations.

### Cobalt

The RDA, or AI amount, DV, and UL for cobalt have not been defined for women or men. This is not to suggest there are no upper limits or daily recommendations; rather, there may not be enough information from which to make these determinations. The SUL is 1.4 mg.

There are potentially serious side effects associated with ingesting too much cobalt, which include toxicity in heart function. It is understood that cobalt should not be used as a supplement unless it is in the form of vitamin B12.

### Copper

The RDA, or AI amount, for copper is 900 IU for women and men. The DV for copper is 2,000 IU. The UL is 10,000 IU; this value is based on a person who is approximately 130 lbs. The SUL is 10,000 IU.

There are potentially serious side effects associated with ingesting too much copper, including problems with digestive function, upset stomach, and damage to the liver.

### Fluoride

The recommended daily allowance (RDA), or adequate intake (AI) amount, for fluoride is 3 mg for women and 4 mg for men. The daily value (DV) for fluoride has not been defined, although this should not be taken to mean that a daily value does not exist; rather, there may not be sufficient information to determine this value.

The tolerable upper level intake (UL) is 10 mg; this value is based on a person who is approximately 130 lbs. The safe upper level (SUL) has not been defined yet.

There are potentially serious side effects associated with ingesting too much fluoride, including damage to body tissues, such as bones, muscles, and nerves. Fluoride should only be added to the diet with the advice and supervision of a medical professional.

### Germanium

The RDA, AI amount, DV, and UL values for the micronutrient germanium are undefined. The SUL value has been determined to be none, or zero.

Ingesting too much germanium can cause serious adverse effects, given that this is a known toxic substance for the liver. Because of this, germanium should not be used as a supplement or be included in any other supplemental mixture.

This trace mineral is not considered necessary for proper body function and has been deemed by the Food and Drug Administration (FDA) to be potentially hazardous to human health.

## Iodine

The RDA, or AI amount, for iodine is 150 international units (IU) for women and men. The DV for iodine is 150 IU. The UL is 1,100 IU; this value is based on a person who is approximately 130 lbs. The SUL is 500 IU.

There are potentially serious side effects associated with ingesting too much iodine, which include endocrine irregularities—specifically higher thyroid hormone levels.

## Iron

The RDA, or AI amount, for iron is 8 mg for women and 18 mg for men. The DV for iron is 18 mg. The UL is 45 mg; this value is based on a person who is approximately 130 lb. The SUL is 17 mg.

There are potentially serious side effects associated with ingesting too much iron, which include a higher risk for cardiovascular problems and digestive-system problems including upset stomach.

## Magnesium

The RDA, or adequate intake (AI) amount, for magnesium is 320 for women and 420 for men. The daily value for magnesium is 400 mg. The UL is 350 mg; this value is based on a person who is approximately 130 lbs. The SUL is 400 mg.

There are potentially serious side effects associated with ingesting too much magnesium, which include gastrointestinal distress in the form of stomachache and diarrhea.

## Manganese

The RDA, or AI amount, for manganese is 1.8 mg for women and 2.3 mg for men. The DV for manganese is 2 mg. The UL is 11 mg; this value is based on a person who is approximately 130 lb. The SUL is 4 mg.

There are potentially serious side effects associated with ingesting too much manganese, which include damage to the brain and nervous-system tissue and functioning, with toxicity more common in children than adults. High levels of manganese exposure occur more often as an occupational or environmental hazard, such as with miners or welders. Manganese exposure is regulated by the Occupational Safety and Health Administration (OSHA).

## Molybdenum

The RDA, or AI amount, for molybdenum is 45 mg for women and men. The DV for molybdenum is 75 mg. The UL is 2,000 mg; this value is based on a person who is approximately 130 lbs. The SUL is none, or zero.

Ingesting too much molybdenum can cause serious adverse effects, which include body toxicity, pain in the connective tissue areas, and side effects similar to those associated with the disease gout.

## Nickel

The RDA, or adequate intake (AI) amount, DV, and UL for nickel have not been defined for women or men. This does not mean there are no daily values or upper levels; rather, there may be insufficient information to determine these values at this time. The SUL is 260 international units (IU).

Ingesting too much nickel can cause serious adverse effects, which include the skin becoming more sensitive to surface touch of nickel, leading to dermatitis or contact allergies.

*Phosphorus*
The RDA, or AI amount, for phosphorus is 700 mg for women and men. The DV for phosphorous is 1,000 mg. The UL is 4,000 mg; this value is based on a person who is approximately 130 lbs. The SUL is 250 mg.

Ingesting too much phosphorus can cause serious adverse effects, which include a decline in the density of bone tissue (a precursor to osteopenia and osteoporosis) and changes in endocrine function.

*Potassium*
The RDA, or AI amount, for potassium is 700 mg for women and men. The DV for potassium is 1,000 mg. The UL is 4,000 mg; this value is based on a person who is approximately 130 lbs. The SUL is 250 mg.

Ingesting too much potassium can cause serious adverse effects, which include a decline in the density of bone tissue (a precursor to osteopenia and osteoporosis) and changes in endocrine function.

*Selenium*
The RDA, or AI amount, for selenium is 55 IU for women and men. The DV for selenium is 70 international units (IU), or 1,500 mg. The UL is 400 IU; this value is based on a person who is approximately 130 lbs. The SUL is 450 IU.

Ingesting too much selenium can cause serious adverse effects, which include gastrointestinal upset such as feeling queasy or loose bowel movements, an overall feeling of tiredness, and damage to the nails and hair.

*Silicon*
The RDA, or AI amount, the DV, and the UL for silicon have not yet been established. This does not mean an upper level does not exist; rather, the information is insufficient at this time to make a full determination. The SUL is 700 mg.

Ingesting too much silicon has not been shown to cause too many serious side effects due to its very low level of toxicity, though there is some evidence that high intake can contribute to kidney stones.

*Vanadium*
The RDA, or AI amount, and the DV for vanadium have not yet been established. This does not mean an upper level does not exist; rather, the information is insufficient at this time to make a full determination. The UL is 1.8 mg; this value is based on a person who is approximately 130 lbs. There is no SUL.

Ingesting too much vanadium can cause serious adverse effects, which include stomach irritation and an overall feeling of tiredness.

*Zinc*
The RDA, or AI amount, for zinc is 8 mg for women and 11 mg for men. The DV for zinc is 15 mg. The ULI is 40 mg; this value is based on a person who is approximately 130 lbs. The SUL is 25 mg.

Ingesting too much zinc can cause serious adverse effects, which include a low count of good cholesterol (HDL) and a dampening of the effectiveness of the immune system.

*Percentage needed*
A person should take the 100% recommended daily allowance of a vitamin or mineral by ingesting a one-a-day type multivitamin.

There are some exceptions to this general rule. For example, if one pill held all the calcium a person needed for the day, it would likely be too large to swallow. Calcium should not be taken all at once, but over the course of the day because of its large size.

Vitamin A intake also differs from the one-a-day formula. If a person is taking vitamin A in the form of retinol, less than 100 percent of the daily dose should be taken, because studies have shown an increase in the risk of hip fracture. Vitamin A in carotene form could be used instead.

There are also mixed results with studies of high use of beta carotene, with some showing higher lung cancer rates, but others showing lower prostate cancer rates. Clients should speak with their physicians about beta carotene supplementation.

Supplement facts panels
A supplemental facts panel is the small panel of information that is on all food products, which indicates the nutritional facts about a single serving of that product. This will include what size a serving is, how many calories a single serving contains, and what nutrients are provided by that serving.

Percent daily value (%DV) refers to how much of the recommended daily value of a given micronutrient is satisfied by ingesting one serving. If the %DV indicates 100%, one serving satisfies all of a person's requirements for that micronutrient for one day. This value is based on what was recommended for an adult in 1968, with the higher value for a man or woman taken as the 100% value. While these have been revised from time to time since then, the values are due for revision because they do not necessarily reflect accurate values. For example, the iron value is calculated for a woman who has her menstrual period and is thus too high for most of the population at any given time.

Supplement considerations
First and foremost, a person should discuss his or her nutritional and dietary needs with a licensed dietitian or physician before beginning any course of supplementation. Tests can be performed to check for deficiencies, and patient/physician can engage in a dialogue about what is needed and how to go about obtaining that. Results can vary, and are dependent on the person's physical and mental state and the quality of the supplement. A good multivitamin should be looked into to ensure that all daily nutritional needs are met. A calcium supplement is also a good idea.

A person should research the brand and company that is producing the supplement. Because supplements are not regulated in the same manner as drugs and the FDA does not check the accuracy of the claims made, it is essential that a person uses a trusted brand with safe products.

# Assessment

The fitness assessment is a tool for gathering information that provides insight into a client's past, present, and future. After determining a person's health issues and fitness level, the Certified Personal Trainer (CPT) can set goals for the client and progress through an integrated training program (as well as modify acute variables— which are important aspects of exercise training that ensure progression through adequate challenge).

By design, the fitness assessment does not replace a medical exam or diagnose medical conditions. A health and fitness professional should refer clients to qualified health-care providers whenever necessary. A CPT should not attempt to provide:
- Medical rehabilitation
- Exercises intended to serve as medical treatments
- Specific diets or nutritional supplements
- Treatment for chronic diseases or injuries
- Personal counseling

**PAR-Q**

PAR-Q stands for Physical Activity Readiness Questionnaire.

The PAR-Q is used to gather information about a client's general history. It is a yes-or-no questionnaire designed to determine if a client can safely begin a fitness regimen. The PAR-Q identifies risk factors that may require clearance from a medical professional before beginning an exercise program. It also allows the fitness professional to determine the client's appropriate fitness level using a low-medium-high scale.

Questions on the PAR-Q are intended to determine whether a potential client:
- Feels chest pain (at any time)
- Loses balance or consciousness
- Experiences bone or joint problems
- Takes medication for high blood pressure or a heart condition
- Knows of any other reason that he or she should not perform physical activity

# Subjective Assessment

## Information and conclusions

Understanding the broad details of a client's personal life can provide details about the way they move throughout their daily life. Subjective information about a person's general history may include his or her occupation, recreational activities, and hobbies.

Knowledge of a client's daily patterns provides the CPT with a better understanding of the client's lifestyle and may provide clues to potential imbalances. The CPT can use this information to determine the client's capacity for movement. For instance, those who enjoy relatively sedentary activities are not likely to start training at the same level as those who regularly play recreational sports. A woman who spends most of her day sitting in front of a computer is likely to have tight hip flexors.

## Medical background

Injury or surgery alters the kinetic chain's function. The CPT must discuss a potential client's medical history to determine dysfunctions that contraindicate physical fitness activities.
Ask about:
- Injuries and pain, including:
  o Sprains of the ankle, groin, or hamstrings
  o Tendinitis of the shoulders, knee (patellar), shins (posterior tibialis), or arch of the foot (plantar fasciitis)
  o Chronic headaches
- Surgeries, especially those that:
  o Are performed on the joints (shoulder, back, knee, ankle, or foot)
  o Involve cutting of the abdominal wall (Cesarean section or appendectomy)
- Chronic conditions or diseases, such as:
  o Coronary heart/artery disease or congestive heart failure
  o Cardiovascular disease or hypertension
  o High cholesterol
  o Lung or breathing problems
  o Diabetes mellitus
- Any medications

## Medical risk factors

Evidence supports the hypothesis that muscular and skeletal ailments are more prevalent in modern society than they were a generation ago. Many factors contribute to this decline in the health of the average American. An increase in automation and a decrease in physical activity have altered the overall health and physical fitness level of Americans over the last century. Extensively researched ailments include:
- Low back pain—This problem is estimated to affect four out of five American adults and is common among those who work in offices and remain seated for long periods of time.
- Knee injuries—There are approximately 100,000 injuries to the anterior cruciate ligament (ACL) each year, with the vast majority resulting from non–sport-related incidents. Most of

these injuries occur to young people between the ages of 15 and 25 and may be a result of a less-active population.
- Chronic disease—A decrease in activity can lead to or exacerbate chronic problems such as obesity, diabetes, hypertension, and other heart conditions.
- Kinetic chain injuries—Kinetic chain injuries are a leading cause of doctor visits. Repetitive sitting and sedentary lifestyles weaken muscle support and contribute to kinetic chain injuries.

## Pharmacological information

While it is never appropriate for a CPT to suggest or administer medications to clients, it is important to know what medications a client is taking and the general effects of those medicines. A summary of common medications and the general physiological effects each might have on the body includes:
- Beta blockers—treat high blood pressure (hypertension) or irregular heart rate (arrhythmia).
- Calcium-channel blockers—treat high blood pressure or angina, which is chest pain caused by inadequate blood flow to the heart.
- Nitrates— treat high blood pressure or congestive heart failure, which results from the heart's inability to pump blood to the body's organs adequately.
- Diuretics—help purge excess water from the body and are used to treat edema, congestive heart failure, or high blood pressure.
- Bronchodilators—alleviate constriction in the bronchi and bronchioles of the lungs and are often used to treat pulmonary disorders such as asthma.
- Vasodilators—relax blood vessels and are often used to treat high blood pressure.
- Antidepressants—mood elevators and stabilizers often used to help alleviate symptoms of depression and other psychiatric disorders.

# Special Population Risk Factors

A special population is a group of people that have a common health problem, impairment, or a particular affliction that makes it necessary to alter the general rules of training to accommodate his or her needs.

The basic concepts that NASM teaches apply to adults who are healthy and can cope with the basic rigors of a workout regimen. Some special populations may require a modified program. Examples of special populations requiring additional considerations include:

- Young persons or those who have not finished growing physically
- The elderly or those older than age 65
- Those with osteoporosis or low bone density
- Pregnant women
- Overweight clients whose body mass index (BMI) exceeds the normal healthy range but does not exceed 30
- Obese clients whose BMI is 30 or more
- Diabetic clients
- Arthritic clients
- Persons with hypertension
- Individuals suffering from coronary heart disease (CHD)

For example, children or adolescents have not completed their growing cycles. They often have superior cardiorespiratory capabilities, but should be monitored in their strength-training routines. Likewise, those with osteoporosis, a disease characterized by low bone density, need to engage in weight-bearing exercise to help increase their bone density, but the condition necessitates special consideration. It is important to perform weight-bearing exercises in a manner that keeps physical limitations in mind to promote client safety.

Pregnant women can also work out effectively, but a trainer needs to be aware of several important physiological changes that take place during gestation. These include a much higher volume of blood as well as a general loosening of the body's ligaments, which may affect stability and limit ability to maintain certain positions.

## Young people

Health and fitness professionals often work with younger clients in varying contexts. This population ranges from grade-school age (from 5 or 6 to 12), through adolescence (12 to 18), and up to young adulthood (approximately 21).

Younger clients differ from the adult population, and a well-designed training regimen should accommodate their unique needs. Many training guidelines for young people deal with physical-education–type training or youth sports. Childhood obesity is a much more widespread problem today than it was in previous generations, and the result has been a dramatic increase in the demand for regular training designed for young people. Younger people need at least 20 minutes of activity that increases the heart rate at least three times each week, with an hour being ideal.

## Oxygen consumption

With proper calibration for height and weight, adults and young clients have similar oxygen consumption rates (VO2). Similar VO2 rates suggest that young people and adults have a similar capacity for performing cardiorespiratory training activities that require endurance. Younger children (6 to 12) should be able to tolerate vigorous activity for 30 to 60 minutes daily.

Increases in training volume should not go beyond 10 percent of the previous week's activity. For example, if a young person engages in 30 minutes of exercise three times per week, or 90 minutes total for the week, the following week should only increase by nine additional minutes (three minutes per session), to progress safely.

## Submaximal oxygen

A young person's submaximal oxygen consumption exceeds that of the average adult for activities such as walking, jogging, and sprinting. Reduced VO2 capacity means that younger people have a higher risk of tiring and overheating during vigorous exercises.

Trainers should make sure that youth clients hydrate adequately. Trainers must take care to ensure that clients do not overexert themselves during high-intensity exercise, particularly when the weather is hot and humid. Exercise that increases the heart rate can safely be enjoyed at least three times a week for at least 20 minutes. An anaerobic activity lasting more than ten seconds is not advisable.

## Glycolic enzyme levels

A young person has lower levels of glycolic enzymes than the average adult, which means that he or she would have a lower tolerance for very intense activities that are anaerobic in nature (lasting more than 10 seconds and up to 90 seconds).

A weight-training regimen should include the following:

Choose between 8 and 10 different exercises. Have the client perform one or two sets of each exercise. Each set should consist of 8 to 12 repetitions. Sets of twenty repetitions promote endurance and sets of six repetitions are ideal when strength is the goal. The trainer should make sure that the client is using proper form and is completely controlling the movements when performing these exercises, so as not to put excessive strain on the joints.

## Rate of sweating

A young person cannot handle extreme environments and require extra caution to exercise safely in hot and humid conditions. Schedule a warm-up and cool-down to give the young person's body enough time to adjust to environmental factors.

Increasing the number of repetitions before adding weight builds tolerance. Add weight only after the repetitions have increased.

Be sure the youth client hydrates properly, watch for diminishing performance, and identify visual cues that might signal distress or overheating. Younger clients may lack the ability to identify abnormalities and may not communicate physical distress as well as adults.

## Weight training

There is a common misconception that weight training is not appropriate for youth clients. Research has shown that it is not harmful and can have positive benefits. Research has demonstrated that weight training has a lower risk of causing a serious injury participation in organized youth sports.

There are some risks involved with resistance training, primarily of pulls and tears. Proper training and effective monitoring can mitigate risk. It is also important to perform a movement assessment much like the one given to an adult client to determine a youth client's capabilities before beginning a systematic, progressive weight-training regimen.

<u>Movement assessment</u>
A youth client can perform 10 squats and 10 push-ups for a modified weight-training assessment (these can be modified for a female client or lower-strength client). Gauge all the of the appropriate kinetic-chain checkpoints, as you would with any NASM fitness assessment. The results will help the trainer determine which exercises will be the best for the particular client and also identify specific areas that require careful monitoring during training sessions.

Weight training for youth clients can increase strength, bone density, and general coordination.

<u>Optimum Performance Training (OPT) model</u>
The health and fitness professional should take into account the fitness assessment of the youth client and other general background information when designing an appropriate resistance-training program. Taking a client from the stabilization level into the higher phases will depend on physical ability, the client's overall ability to handle the regimen, and the recommendation of his or her doctor.

Another important factor is that training for the youth client should be engaging and fun. To maintain motivation and interest and encourage a lifelong interest in fitness, keeping the routines fun is vitally important.

<u>Basic guidelines</u>
Youth clients should have a fun training experience with safe activities that are adequately supervised by an adult. Games, sports, walking, running, water sports, and even weight training are good types of exercise for youth clients. Training can be engaged in from three to five times per week for at least 20 minutes, with an hour being ideal. A movement assessment should observe kinetic-chain checkpoints while the youth client performs 10 push-ups and 10 squats. Follow NASM's flexibility continuum and resistance training guidelines as outlined in the OPT model. High-level training requires physical ability and enough maturity to understand and duplicate instructions safely.

## Seniors

A senior citizen is an individual aged 65 years and older. The senior population is growing exponentially now that the baby boomer generation is maturing. There is a need for health and fitness professionals who understand how to work with members of this population safely and effectively.

Keeping fit can dramatically improve a senior client's quality of life. Training can help increase bone density, maintain coordination, and improve overall muscle tone. Many primary functions of the body decline with age, including:
- Elasticity of tissues
- Muscle mass

- Bone density
- Blood volume output
- Neuromuscular coordination
- Maximum heart rate

## Diseases or chronic conditions

Common chronic conditions associated with older age include lower bone density (osteoporosis), arthritis, weight gain or obesity, and back problems. The CPT should treat any problem that fits into a special population according to NASM guidelines for the relevant condition.

However, just because a senior has a different body condition than a younger adult does not mean there is a problem. An older adult may have a higher resting blood pressure measurement, but this may not indicate that something is wrong or require compensation during training. As with all clients, a senior client should have a thorough medical examination before beginning a training regimen.

## Cardiovascular system

A senior's body is different from that of a younger adult. The cardiovascular output, lung capacity, and maximum heart rate that a senior client can achieve during exercise decrease as they age.

Decreased cardiorespiratory capability means that a trainer should ease into exercise routines with an older client, use lower weight, prescribe light workloads, and increase gradually. Training sessions should last from 20 to 45 minutes. Three to five sessions per week is ideal. Training intensity should be in the middle range, from 40 to 80 percent.

## Body composition

A senior's body composition changes with age, with lean muscle mass and bone density decreasing, and fat stores increasing. Weight training counteracts these changes because it builds muscle and decreases fat. Weight-bearing exercise also helps build bone density.

The health and fitness professional should start the client with lower weights and add more weight gradually. Select 8 to 10 exercises. The client can perform three sets of 20 repetitions to achieve this goal. Training lessons should run for about a half an hour.

## Neuromuscular efficiency

An older adult will have differences in his or her neuromuscular system that can significantly alter balance, and a trainer needs to be aware of this possibility to train the senior safely. Coordination and gait can suffer as well. Observe carefully and identify impairments when performing standard assessments.

The health and fitness professional chooses modes of exercise that account for a client's limitations. Walking on a treadmill with two handrails might be a good option. Training on stationary equipment such as an exercise bike, or performing cardiorespiratory training in an aquatic environment may also benefit seniors.

## Cardiac condition

Older clients have an increased risk of suffering from heart problems, and the condition is often undiagnosed. It is important for an older client to have a full medical exam and to be aware of potential heart complications before beginning a workout regimen.

During the health and fitness professional's assessments, it is important to pay attention to the pulse assessments and note anything unusual. It is important to determine a baseline heart rate for each client, which will help the trainer identify issues during training.

## OPT model

The degeneration that occurs with age, and decreased maximum workout capacity, can make working with the elderly challenging for health and fitness professionals. The goal of a training program should be to counteract these processes.

Walking can be challenging for seniors because of changes to bones, muscles, coordination, and, cardiorespiratory capacity. Physiological changes can cause seniors to become more sedentary, which increases the danger of degenerating. Over time, they can lose their ability to live independently.

The OPT model is an excellent way to work with senior clients because it uses thorough assessments to spot potential existing body concerns, and then takes the client through a systematic workout approach.

*Assessment process and intensity level:* To implement the OPT model with a senior client, a health and fitness professional must begin with a series of assessments that will help gauge the client's current exercise capability, physical condition, and overall fitness goals. Begin this process with NASM's Physical Activity Readiness Questionnaire (PAR-Q).

Introduce cardiorespiratory training gradually. Account for prescribed medications and diseases or chronic conditions. Phases 1 and 2 of training are ideal for the senior client. Explore phase 1 thoroughly to build core stability and improve nervous system communication. The result is improved balance and coordination.

## Communication

When a health and fitness professional works with a senior client, he or she must be aware of potential psychological aspects that may impact the working relationship and approach these with sensitivity and tact.

Senior clients may have reservations about engaging in physical activity. Be sure the client has a thorough physical examination before beginning any new workout routine and speaks with his or her doctor about concerns of legitimate physical limitations.

A senior client might be resistant to incorporating weight training into their workout routine because he or she is afraid of injury. Treat this concern with respect, and offer some insight into research showing that resistance training is highly beneficial for seniors.

## Flexibility training

Flexibility training is important to warm up and cool down muscles, improve range of motion, and add elasticity to connective tissue. Flexibility training reduces the risk of injury. Flexibility training is especially important for senior clients who may experience reduced muscle tone, lower body tissue elasticity, and poor coordination as they age. Increased flexibility is a good foundation for better training results and ultimately increases the ability to perform daily activities necessary for independence.

The senior population can benefit from static stretches and self-myofascial release. Dynamic stretching is an excellent tool to prepare the body for a workout and to preserve the body after physical activity.

Training modes
Seniors can engage in cardiorespiratory and weight-training activities, though the trainer should use extra caution for those seniors with balance or coordination problems. For those seniors, equipment with handrails or exercise bikes may be a good choice. Aquatic activities are also effective for seniors. Seniors should work out two to five times each week for up to an hour each day, depending on their ability. The standard set of movement assessments will help the trainer understand these capabilities before beginning a workout regimen. All forms of stretching are appropriate, depending on the client's ability.

Prescribe three sets of 8 to 10 different exercises, beginning with 20 repetitions per set. Explore the first two phases of the OPT model before moving on. Ensure the client demonstrates adequate stabilization of the core muscles, balance, before advancing.

**Obesity**

Obesity is a clinical term defined as the class of people who have a body mass index (BMI) of 30 or greater. BMI is calculated by taking a person's metric weight (in kilograms) and dividing it by their metric height (in meters) squared. Morbid obesity is considered to be a BMI greater than 40.

An individual with a BMI reading less than 18.5 is considered underweight. A BMI reading between 18.5 and 24.9 falls within the healthy range. Clients with BMI readings between 25 and 30 have an overweight designation.

| BMI | Classification |
|---|---|
| <18.5 | Underweight |
| 18.6–21.99 | Acceptable |
| 22.0–24.99 | Acceptable |
| 25.0–29.99 | Overweight |
| 30–34.99 | Obese |
| 35.0–39.99 | Obesity II |
| ≥40 | Obesity III |

Obese usually seek health and fitness training for weight loss and because their overall health status dictates a more healthful lifestyle. Obesity can cause a long list of physical problems that exercise and a healthy diet can address.

Causes of obesity
Individual factors or a combination of two or more compounding factors can lead to obesity. Improper energy balance is a significant problem in the United States. An energy imbalance is a calorie surplus caused by ingesting more calories than the body burns. The body stores excess calories as fat, which results in weight gain.

Inactivity and consumption of excessive amounts of calories contribute to energy imbalance. Given the fast-food culture of the United States and the prevalence of office jobs, in which sitting all day is the norm, it is not surprising that weight gain and obesity have been steadily on the rise over the past few generations. Recreational activity is often sedentary. Watching television and playing video games are more common than is playing outside.

## Aging

Age can contribute to obesity. As a person ages, the body's lean muscle mass (which burns calories) decreases. Body fat may increase at the same time. Additionally, cardiorespiratory capability and bone density may decrease.

A senior may be less likely to work out regularly because of limitations arising from degenerative conditions, which potentially leads to weight gain. While obesity and age do not correlate directly, the physical problems associated with aging can result in a reduction in physical activity, which leads to the overweight condition.

A health and fitness trainer must take age, weight, and chronic diseases associated with old into account when designing a training regimen. Reducing fat and increasing lean muscle mass are important goals for obese clients.

## Client's gait

When working with an obese client, the health and fitness professional should be aware that the person's gait, or how the core musculature coordinates the lower part of the body when walking, can be significantly different than a person in the healthy BMI range. Changes in gait can have a serious impact on balance and coordination.

Research has shown that obese individuals take shorter strides and have lower balance, even when they have superior strength. Shorter strides and poor balance mean that an obese client should improve coordination by fully exploring phase 1 of the OPT model. Stabilization exercises can help maximize core stability and improve communication between the brain and nervous system, improving overall coordination.

## Weight loss

A two-pronged approach is the most effective path to help an obese client lose weight. Modify the client's diet and prescribe a systematic exercise regime to promote weight loss.

The client should discuss his or her diet issues with a licensed dietitian. The dietitian will design a healthy plan for the individual, taking overall activity level and constraints from work or family obligations into account. It is important to support the client's efforts, which will likely include reducing his or her caloric intake by a few hundred calories per day.

Give the client a combination of cardiorespiratory training and weight training to help spur weight loss. Cardiorespiratory training helps improve the body's energy-burning capabilities. Adding lean muscle mass helps burn calories as well.

## OPT model

When working with an obese client, it may be more comfortable for the client, and more effective for the overall workout regimen, for him or her to perform exercises in an upright or recumbent (standing or sitting) position. Machines with cables, as well as isometric exercises that use body weight may be ideal for a beginning client in this population.

Modification of certain fitness assessments may be advisable. Keep all assessments on a manageable gradient to get a good idea of fitness capability, but also keep the client safe. For example, modify a squat to a simple balance exercise, and pay attention to kinetic-chain compensations that occur while the client is standing on one leg.

Upright stretching may be more comfortable for obese clients. Performing a floor stretch from a modified standing or sitting position is beneficial for obese clients.

### Core training and stabilization exercises

Because obese individuals often have issues with gait and coordination, stabilization exercises, particularly those that focus on the core musculature, are an excellent starting point for the health and fitness professional. Given that stabilization exercises tie in directly with Phase 1 of OPT, the trainer has a great jumping-off point to create a systematic, integrated program that follows the OPT model.

When working with an obese client, it may be advisable to avoid positions in which the client is reclining or positioned on his or her back due to the higher risk of hypertension found in this population. It may also be more comfortable for an obese client to begin working from standing or seated positions. For example, abdominal work might be easier to begin on a reclining bench rather than on the floor, or by using cables in an upright position.

### Psychological aspects

When working with someone who is overweight or obese, it is important for the health and fitness professional to be aware of, and sensitive to, the fact that this condition can often cause intense emotional issues for the client. These issues are real and require professionalism and tact to help the client achieve their ultimate goals.

A trainer must do his or her best to motivate all clients and help them feel as though they are in a safe environment. A feeling of safety is important for physical health and emotional well-being. Creating a safe environment is essential to creating a professional relationship founded on trust and cooperation.

When dealing with an obese client, use language that is neutral regarding weight and make thoughtful, encouraging statements. Choose your words carefully to establish rapport, motivate, and keep the client interested in the training routine. Avoid making comments that can make the client feel, self-conscious or distracted.

### Comorbidities

Obese clients are much more likely to have serious health problems that require special considerations when training than individuals within the healthy BMI range. These problems can lead to obesity, or they can result from obesity, but the CPT must consider them when designing a program.

Some common problems obese individuals may experience include:
- Diabetes
- Arthritis
- Hypertension
- Asthma

Having the client get a full physical examination before beginning a new training routine is essential. A medical examination will help identify physical problems and allow the client to begin necessary medical treatment for those problems. Fitness assessments allow the CPT to tailor the program to the client's capabilities by providing insight into kinetic-chain problems, gait problems, and musculature compensations.

## Cardiovascular abilities
An obese client may have different cardiovascular and cardiorespiratory capabilities than a person in the healthy BMI range. The maximum amount of oxygen that can be taken in during exercise may not be adequate to support his or her body for vigorous activities, and the ability to perform extended, anaerobic workout activities may be limited.

When beginning a workout regimen, include modalities that account for these factors. Beginning in an aquatic environment is very helpful. Submersion in water has many benefits. Water immersion can improve overall conditioning while reducing stress on the body and joints. As the client's capabilities improve, they can progress to walking on flat terrain or on a treadmill to improve cardiovascular endurance and lung capacity.

## Diet program
Obese clients are likely to have spent a good deal of their adult lives dieting. A lifetime of unsuccessful dieting can lead to many hang-ups or misconceptions about diet and exercise that the health and fitness professional must navigate to help the client achieve his or her goals.

Be sure the obese client meets with a registered dietitian or nutritionist to create a healthy eating plan that reduces daily caloric intake. Low-impact exercise should be the starting point, with a goal of increasing the client's daily activity level. Lengthen each training session to an hour before increasing the impact level. Initially, the client should burn approximately 1,200 calories per week. Progress the client until they are consistently burning 2000 calories a week through exercise.

## Body composition
When working with an obese client, it is best to use BMI as the method of measuring body fat composition. Circumference measurements may also work well. Other methods of body composition measurement may not be accurate for a person who is clinically obese, and taking measurements with skinfold calipers may not appeal to an obese client who is already self-conscious about his or her weight.

The exact measurement of body fat is not important when working with an obese client. BMI measurement is not 100 percent accurate. However, it gives an excellent starting point for the client to use. It is valuable for setting goals for the client because it is a concrete number that serves as a baseline for future comparison.

## Modes of training
Low-intensity activities are ideal when beginning a training program with an obese client. Low-intensity activities include walking, using a stationary bike, or training in an aquatic environment. Frequency and duration of exercise are more important when beginning than is intensity level. The client should train as many as five times a week. Initially, workouts should be 20 minutes, and should last increasingly longer as the client's fitness level improves. Increase intensity after the client can perform exercises at low-intensity for an hour. It is important to note that uninterrupted workouts are unnecessary. Two 20-minute walks are as productive as one 40-minute walk if the client reaches the proper heart rate for both sessions.

Movement assessments designed to determine client capability are important, but simple balance exercises can replace squatting exercises if necessary. Observe the kinetic-chain checkpoints for postural distortions.

Select up to ten exercises for the client and have them perform three sets of 15 repetitions.

Other issues

Obesity is a significant problem in modern American society, with record numbers of obese children and adults in the United States. At present, 66% of Americans over 20 are classified as overweight. Approximately 34% (72 million) of those individuals are considered obese. Further, 9 million children between the ages of 2 and 19 are overweight or obese. Many obese people want to begin a training regimen to lose weight and to alleviate other physical problems that obesity exacerbates. Many obese individuals start an exercise program with a goal of improving their overall health and quality of life.

By understanding the common problems associated with this special population, a health and fitness professional can offer superior services to its members. It is important for a trainer to understand not only the additional physical considerations but also the emotional concerns an obese person may have in dealing with a training regimen so the trainer can help guide the client with professionalism and sensitivity.

Reducing calorie intake, increasing activity, and building muscle are the cornerstones of working with an obese client.

## Diabetic individuals

Diabetes describes two related endocrine, or hormonal, disorders. One stems from the inability of the pancreas to produce insulin, a necessary hormone, while the other makes it difficult for the body to convert simple carbohydrates.

More than five percent of the American population has diabetes, with hundreds of thousands of new diagnoses every year. Diabetes affects the young and the elderly, and it is a leading cause of death.

A trainer must be aware that a client with diabetes has limitations on his or her body's ability to process, convert, and utilize glucose (blood sugar). While exercise can be very beneficial for a diabetic client, careful monitoring is required to ensure that exercise regimens are safe. The CPT must protect a diabetic's feet, which are easily injured and slow to heal.

Type 1 diabetes

The pancreas of a Type 1 diabetic does not produce the hormone insulin. Because insulin is not circulating in the bloodstream, the cells of the body are not able to convert blood sugar into energy. An insulin deficiency creates too much blood sugar (hyperglycemia) and not enough available energy. Type 1 diabetics need to introduce insulin manually into their bodies, usually by injecting synthetic insulin.

Synthetic insulin is important because exercise can use blood sugar, so if a diabetic is not mindful of his or her blood sugar levels when engaging in exercise, he or she can use up too much blood sugar, resulting in levels that are too low (hypoglycemia).

Low blood sugar can cause a person to faint or feel lightheaded. Discuss this potential problem with your client, and ascertain what recommendations his or her doctor has made for managing blood sugar during exercise. A common solution is for the client to keep a high-sugar snack or drink on hand for low-blood-sugar incidents.

## Type 2 diabetes

Type 2 diabetes is referred to as adult-onset diabetes. People who are overweight and eat a diet high in refined foods (especially sugars), can be at a higher risk of developing Type 2 diabetes. Young people are at risk of developing Type 2 diabetes because of poor diet and a higher incidence of obesity.

Type 2 diabetics do not usually have trouble making insulin, which is the primary problem of type I diabetics. Rather, the body cannot properly recognize the insulin and allow it to perform its function of converting blood sugar into a form of energy that cells can readily use.

The body's inability to recognize insulin means that the blood sugar levels remain high (hyperglycemia). If the blood sugar remains high over a long period, damage to other parts of the body can occur.

Exercise can help use blood sugar and alleviate some of the stress placed on the body by extra weight.

## Exercise selection

When working with someone with diabetes, it is important for the health and fitness professional to be aware of the method the client uses to control glucose levels. Exercise is a very effective method of controlling blood sugar because it reduces the level of glucose in the bloodstream.

The trainer must have an action plan to manage the client's blood sugar levels. It is important for the trainer to monitor the client, recognize the signs of hyperglycemia and hypoglycemia, and to take appropriate actions based on these observations. In extreme cases, skipping a workout may be necessary to protect the client's health. The action plan should consider all recommendations from the client's physician.

It is also important to help the client avoid damage to the feet (e.g., blisters, infections, cuts), as the feet are a sensitive area of the body for diabetics.

## Comorbidities

People with diabetes are highly likely to have other conditions that place them in other special populations. Diabetics may be overweight or obese, have hypertension (high blood pressure), or a host of other medical issues. It is very important to make sure the diabetic client has a full physical examination before beginning training, so the client's physician can properly diagnose and treat any problems.

Because obesity can be a cause of diabetes, or can be an effect of diabetes, it is advisable to put a diabetic client on a training regimen that encourages weight loss and the building of lean muscle tissue. Set the routine to burn at least 1,000 calories each week, and build to 2,000 calories.

## Glucose control mechanisms

A person with diabetes does not have the same glucose control mechanisms that a nondiabetic has. Introducing exercise, which uses blood sugar, into a diabetic's routine requires caution. Though exercise is very beneficial to a diabetic in the larger scheme, each training session runs the risk of causing hypoglycemia, or low blood sugar.

Because of this, it is important for the trainer to notice when a client's blood sugar drops. Symptoms of low blood sugar include fatigue, dizziness, and disorientation. Set up an action plan with the client in case this happens.

A client should be aware that their blood sugar may drop many hours after a training session. A person who has had diabetes for some time will likely know how to regulate his or her blood sugar, but a person with a recent diagnosis may want to take more frequent blood sugar readings when starting a training regimen.

### Beta blocker medication use

Clients in the diabetic population often have comorbidities. A common comorbidity is high blood pressure (hypertension). Beta blockers are commonly used to treat this hypertension.

Beta blockers can mask the symptoms of low blood sugar that may occur during a workout. If the client is not aware of a dip in blood sugar, hypoglycemia (low blood sugar) may occur during the training session.

It is advisable for the client to take less insulin before working out to compensate for the effects of exercise. The client should have simple carbohydrates (e.g., juice, snack bar) on hand that can be ingested before or during the workout, to assist in regulating blood sugar levels. If a diabetic client also takes beta blockers, encourage them to have a discussion with a physician.

### Tolerance to heat

It is more difficult to recognize the symptoms of low blood sugar (hypoglycemia) when diabetic individuals exercise in hot environments, or when they become overheated. These symptoms include fatigue, dizziness, and disorientation.

Training should begin with low-impact activities and progress to longer training sessions (up to an hour at a time). It is helpful to conduct frequent training sessions (as often as daily). Frequent exercise will help control glucose levels. Initially, intensity should be moderate, giving the client time to acclimate to the workouts and learn to recognize symptoms of hypoglycemia that may occur during training sessions.

### Training modes

The guidelines for working with a diabetic client are similar to those for working with an obese individual. The primary difference is the recommended modality of exercise. While obese clients can greatly benefit from walking as the primary starting point for workouts, this may not be advisable for diabetic clients, whose feet can be susceptible to injuries that do not heal properly. Thus, other exercises, such as aquatic workouts, might be a good starting point.

Use the basic flexibility continuum with modifications for self-myofascial release if the client has nervous-system concerns with their feet. Check with the client's physician before recommending self-myofascial release.

The first two phases of the OPT model are ideal for diabetic clients.

<u>Training length and intensity</u>
Diabetic clients often have the goals of controlling glucose levels and losing weight. Employ low-intensity activities (such as riding a stationary bike or performing aquatic exercises) gradually to accomplish these goals safely. Start with short sessions, work up to hour-long sessions, exercise frequently (as often as seven days a week).

Use the standard assessments unless there is comorbidity that limits the client's ability to perform the test. The flexibility continuum as outlined by NASM is appropriate.

The first two phases of the OPT model are ideal, and two or three resistance-training sessions per week are beneficial. High-level power training is usually not advisable.

Keep all physician recommendations in mind when working with a diabetic client, know the symptoms of hypoglycemia, have a simple carbohydrate source on hand and be sure the client wears appropriate protective footwear.

## Hypertensive individuals

A client has hypertension (high blood pressure) if the systolic (top number) is greater than 140, and the diastolic (bottom number) is more than 90. To be diagnosed hypertensive, a client's systolic and diastolic readings must exceed the normal range. The reading taken when the individual is not taking any medication is the relevant reading.

People who smoke, are overweight, or eat an unhealthy diet are at a higher risk for hypertension. Many individuals diagnosed as hypertensive will be on medication to help control the problem, and they may seek exercise as another way to control hypertension and alleviate some of the underlying causes.

It is important for the health and fitness professional to encourage hypertensive individuals to take the medication prescribed by their doctors. Often, people in this population avoid consistently taking their medications because they do not feel sick.

<u>Body positioning</u>
Proper body positioning is important when working with hypertensive clients because improper body positioning can affect blood pressure. Positions that place the head below the heart can cause the blood pressure to rise. Lying on the back or the stomach are examples of positions that can cause the blood pressure to rise.

Try to keep the hypertensive client in seated or upright positions for all exercises. To perform abdominal work, the health and fitness professional should consider using cable machines or putting the client on an inclined weight bench.

The trainer should advise the client not to overstrain or grip equipment too tightly, as this can increase blood pressure.

It is acceptable to prescribe the first two phases of the Optimum Performance Training (OPT) model for this population. Monitor high-intensity power training carefully.

## Blood pressure change during exercise

Clients without hypertension tend to have predictable blood pressure responses. A client with high blood pressure may not have a predictable blood pressure response. It may spike, rise slightly, or vary from session to session. It is important to create a low-impact training routine that gradually increases in frequency, intensity, and duration to avoid aggravating this condition.

Begin with three twenty minute sessions per week, and build to five to seven one-hour sessions per week, which will help stabilize the body's blood pressure response. Add more exercise to facilitate additional weight loss goals.

## Blood pressure medication considerations

Even with medication, a client with high blood pressure may not have his or her condition completely under control before arriving for an exercise session. To compensate, the health and fitness professional can use program design to support the client's specific needs. Some types of medication to be aware of are:

- Beta-blockers – Used for high blood pressure or arrhythmia.
- Calcium-channel blockers – Used for hypertension and angina.
- Nitrates – Used for hypertension and congestive heart failure
- Diuretics – Used for hypertension, congestive heart failure, and peripheral edema
- Bronchodilators – Used for asthma and other pulmonary diseases
- Vasodilators – Used for hypertension and congestive heart failure
- Antidepressants – Used for psychiatric and emotional disorders

For example, circuit training two or three times a week can be a very effective tool for hypertensive clients. The trainer should select eight to ten exercises and have the client perform up to three sets of twelve to twenty repetitions.

The client should not over-grip equipment and should avoid performing the Valsalva maneuver (forcing expiration when the airway is closed). It is also important for the client to breathe evenly throughout the training session.

## Comorbidities

Hypertension frequently occurs in conjunction with other health problems, such as diabetes and obesity. It is important for the client to have a thorough physical examination before beginning any training regimen and to discuss potential limitations with the physician.

When creating a training regimen for anyone who belongs to more than one special population, the health and fitness professional should take into account all of the special guidelines for each of the special populations.

A hypertensive routine should aim to burn 1,500 calories each week and build to burning 2,000 calories weekly. Burning calories in this range will facilitate weight loss and keep cardiovascular gains on target for supporting the hypertensive condition.

## Beta blocker use

When a hypertensive client utilizes beta blocker medication, this can alter the way the heart responds to training. NASM's formula to determine maximum heart was not designed for clients on beta blockers so the health and fitness professional should use the talk test (which tests the client's ability to maintain a conversation while exercising) as an alternative.

If the client's blood pressure exceeds 200 over 115, he or she should not engage in exercise. A trainer should be aware of the policies at their fitness training facility.

Training length and intensity
Use training modalities that keep the client upright (walking and the stationary bicycle are excellent) to avoid body positions in which the head is even with or lower than the heart. Start with three training sessions per week, and progress to daily workouts. Initially, workouts can last for half an hour, and can increase to an hour in duration. Administer the standard assessments and prescribe stretching according to the flexibility continuum, using upright or seated positioning.

The first two phases of the Optimum Performance Training (OPT) model and circuit training are ideal for this special population.

## Coronary artery disease (CAD)

Heart disease is one of the leading causes of death in the United States. Up to 18 million Americans have received a diagnosis for CAD or another heart issue. CAD is a condition characterized by a narrowing of the arteries caused by a build-up of plaque, resulting in less oxygenated blood traveling to the heart. Eventually, CAD can lead to damage of the heart muscle and, ultimately, heart attack.

Stress, use of tobacco products, and diets high in LDL (bad) cholesterol contribute to plaque accumulation. It is important to determine if the client has heart-related health concerns and to understand the treatment the client's physician has recommended.

Response to exercise
Because the client with CAD has special heart-related limitations, it is important to keep an accurate measure of the upper levels of capability, to ensure client safety. The health and fitness professional should not use the traditional methods of estimating heart rate maximum. The client's physician should determine the maximum heart rate.

Determining the proper heart rate maximum is important because a client with CAD may not have the usual symptoms of impending heart trouble, such as sharp chest pains If the client experiences chest pain frequently, they misinterpret serious chest pains and ignore them. Medication that reduces chest pains may mask these symptoms during exercise. Therefore, self-monitoring of heart rate is vital.

Comorbidities
Clients with CAD often have other related health problems. These can include being overweight or obese, being diabetic, and having high blood pressure. It is important for the client to undergo a thorough physical examination and to discuss potential limitations with a physician before beginning any training regimen. CAD is related to a diet high in saturated fats and cholesterol. Refer the client to a dietitian or licensed nutritionist who can create a healthful and realistic diet plan to help support the training benefits he or she will derive from fitness training.

When creating a training regimen for anyone who belongs to more than one special population, the health and fitness professional should take into account all of the special guidelines for each of the special populations.

## Peak oxygen capacity

When an individual suffers from CAD, the heart muscle is not functioning at capacity, which limits the maximum amount of available oxygen. The health and fitness professional should begin with low-impact workloads under the guidance of the client's physician or heart specialist. Cardiovascular work should stay below the maximum guidelines suggested by the physician.

Opt for short (approximately 20 minutes) workouts three times a week initially, and gradually work up to sixty-minute workouts five times a week. Closely observe how the client is tolerating the workload, and follow the client's capabilities. The goal is to build the client's heart muscle and overall cardiorespiratory conditioning while proceeding with care due to the client's condition and any medications he or she may be using.

## Changes with improvement

A client with CAD should set a goal of burning 1500 calories from exercise per week initially and work toward burning 2000 calories weekly. Given the client's condition and potential limitations, progress gradually and under the advisement of the client's physician to reach these levels.

After the client has trained steadily and tolerated the regimen without cardiac symptoms for three months, it is safe to introduce weight training to the workout routine. Select up to ten exercises based on the client's goals and capabilities, and have the client perform up to three sets of each exercise. NASM recommends prescribing between 10 and 20 repetitions. Circuit training is advisable to maximize the cardiovascular benefits of the routine.

## Perceived exertion scale

Clients with CAD will not be able to use age-related guidelines to determine maximum heart rate because their heart capacity and heart function are lower than the average client's, which means that their heart rate reading will likely also be lower in a given situation. Since this is an unpredictable measure, use other methods.

One way to make sure the client does not exceed the heart rate maximum recommended by his or her physician is by using the perceived exertion scale, a subjective test that allows the client to gauge his or her exertion level based on physical cues. The original scale ranged from 6 to 20. A 6 signified light exertion and a 20 indicated strenuous exertion. The old version was modified, and the new one runs from 0 (no exertion at all) through 11 (absolute top-level exertion).

| Old version | | New version | |
|---|---|---|---|
| 6 | | 0.0 | No intensity |
| 7 | Very, very light | 0.3 | |
| 8 | | 0.5 | Just noticeable |
| 9 | Very light | 0.7 | |
| 10 | | 1.0 | |
| 11 | Fairly light | 1.5 | |
| 12 | | 2.0 | Light |
| 13 | Somewhat hard | 2.5 | |
| 14 | | 3.0 | |
| 15 | Hard | 4.0 | |
| 16 | | 5.0 | Heavy |
| 17 | Very hard | 6.0 | |
| 18 | | 7.0 | |
| 19 | Very, very hard | 8.0 | |
| 20 | | 9.0 | |
| | | 10.0 | Strongest intensity |
| | | 11.0 | |
| | | | Highest possible |

<u>Training length and intensity</u>
NASM recommends beginning work on large muscle areas when commencing training with a person with CAD, including exercises that work the legs and the gluteals, such as walking, rowing, or riding a stationary bike.

Start slowly, and progress to longer and more frequent workouts. Three 20-minute workouts are ideal as a starting point. Gradually increase to hour-long workouts five times weekly, to accomplish the client's overall goals. NASM recommends the talk test and the perceived exertion scale for measuring intensity; use a doctor's guidelines to dictate maximum heart rate.

Include warm-up and cool-down periods for these clients to help the heart prepare for exercise and to relax afterward. Flexibility exercises can follow NASM's flexibility continuum.

**Osteoporosis**

Osteoporosis is the name of a disease typified by a lower level of bone density, leading to brittle bones that are susceptible to breaking. Osteoporosis is an ailment more common in postmenopausal women. When the body of a postmenopausal woman reabsorbs bone cells instead of creating new bone cells, bone density decreases. Decreased bone density leaves extra space between bone cells, making the bones themselves more porous.

There is a precursor to osteoporosis called osteopenia, marked by a decrease in overall bone density that can ultimately develop into osteoporosis.

- 65 -

Osteoporosis can be very dangerous for older women who can suffer irreversible injury if a bone breaks in a fall. Commonly broken bones include the hip and the collarbone; many persons never fully recover from such an injury.

## Preventing osteoporosis

Many factors increase the risk of developing osteoporosis. Although men can develop osteoporosis, postmenopausal females are at greatest risk of developing the disease.

Increased bone density is a benefit of exercise (especially weight-bearing exercise). Weight-bearing exercise places stress on the body, causing the bones to remodel (add more cells) to compensate, resulting in denser bone tissue. Osteoporosis is associated with lower levels of activity because the bones of inactive individuals do not reap the benefits associated with weight-bearing exercise. Other lifestyle choices that can increase the risk of developing osteoporosis include smoking, drinking alcohol, and poor diet.

A health and fitness regimen can address risk factors by increasing physical activity and promote healthier lifestyle choices.

## Osteoporosis vs. osteopenia

It is important for the health and fitness professional to know whether the client has osteopenia or osteoporosis to determine how intense his or her weight training can and should be.

A client with osteopenia can train at a higher intensity level than a client with osteoporosis can. Increased bone density is a benefit of high-intensity weight training, which can reverse the effects of osteopenia. The risk is that high-intensity exercise places strain on already weakened bones, which can lead to injury. The certified personal trainer must weigh the risks versus the rewards when prescribing high-intensity weight training to a client with osteopenia.

When working with older clients, training novices, or individuals who have had low levels of activity throughout life, it may be preferable to develop balance and coordination to avoid falls altogether, rather than focusing on increasing bone density through high-intensity weight training.

## Training length and intensity

Since falls are a very dangerous possibility for people with osteoporosis, cardiorespiratory training that prevents falls is vital. Aquatic activities and supported cardiorespiratory training (recumbent bike or a treadmill with railing) are ideal.

Begin slowly, and gradually increase frequency and duration. Twice-weekly workouts of 20 minutes are a good starting point. Progress the client to complete 60-minute workouts five times weekly. More than one daily session may be useful, so consider breaking the session into shorter chunks of time.

For people with osteoporosis, weakened bones affect core musculature. The first two phases of the OPT model are very important to build muscle strength, coordination, and balance—all of which will help the client to avoid falling and suffering from injuries. Focus on hinging areas, such as the hips and thighs, and monitor for proper alignment and posture.

# Arthritic individuals

Arthritis is a condition that causes chronic pain and inflammation of the joints. There are many different types of arthritis; each causes pain in various joints that can seriously affect a person's ability to function on a daily basis, exercise, and engage in physical activity.

Osteoarthritis is a condition characterized by worn down cartilage, which causes the bones to wear on each other. Rheumatoid arthritis is a condition in which the body attacks its soft tissues, causing pain and stiffness in the joints, especially in the hands and feet. Rheumatoid arthritis is a chronic degenerative disease of the immune system.

It is important for the trainer to monitor how the training regimen affects the client's arthritic condition. The trainer should adjust intensity and frequency to avoid aggravating the condition.

## Oxygen capacity

The chronic pain and loss of mobility associated with arthritic conditions can lead to decreased physical activity levels, which can lower the client's oxygen capacity.

Workouts can be broken into shorter segments performed throughout the day to avoid aggravating the condition. Separate sessions on different equipment can help provide adequate daily cardiorespiratory training while avoiding overstressing any one joint area. Separate sessions are preferable to single high-impact sessions.

Ideally, the client will train for a total of thirty minutes a day, five times each week.

## Ability to exercise

Acute episodes may prevent clients with arthritic conditions from exercising as long or as frequently as desired. The trainer should not force the issue—if a client is having excessive pain and does not feel up to exercising, his or her condition should take precedence. Over time, the client may build up stamina and endurance and be able to exercise more frequently for longer stretches of time.

Consider avoiding morning workouts with clients that suffer from rheumatoid arthritis, because these individuals often have early morning pain and stiff joints. Clients may take medication to manage their arthritis pain; be sure that the client follows doctor recommendations for medication use, especially before training.

## Comorbidities

An individual with arthritis often suffers from other health problems, such as having osteopenia or osteoporosis. It is extremely important for the client to have a thorough physical examination before beginning a training regimen and for him or her to discuss potential limitations with the physician.

When creating a training regimen for anyone who belongs to more than one special population, the health and fitness professional should take into account the special guidelines for each of the special populations.

Weight training is beneficial for clients with arthritis. The client should progress as much as their condition allows. Select as many as 10 exercises, and work through them up to three times a week.

With arthritic clients, the health and fitness professional will want to use a minimal number of repetitions and work up to 12 or repetitions.

Training length and intensity
Select exercise low impact exercise modalities for arthritic clients. These might include aquatic exercise activities or walking on a treadmill with handrails. The health and fitness professional should progress as the client's condition allows, working from three sessions a week up to five. Sessions should be shorter in length, up to a half an hour, and can be broken up into shorter sessions throughout the day. When beginning, five-minute sessions may be required; use the client's pain threshold as a guide.

Administer NASM's regular assessments, and use the flexibility continuum if the client can tolerate it.

During resistance training, prescribe six to twelve repetitions. Avoid having the client lift heavy weights, and make sure the client does not grip equipment too tightly.

## Cancer

Cancer is the umbrella term for a variety of disorders characterized by mutated body cells that attack and damage the body. Even with aggressive treatment, cancer can be fatal. It is one of the top causes of death in the United States.

Improved treatments have dramatically improved the long-term prognosis of cancer patients. Research has shown that exercise can help maximize the benefits of treatment and keep a person healthy after treatment is over.

It is important for the health and fitness professional to understand that many of the medications used to treat cancer can have side effects that may affect the ability of the client to train. Clients may feel ill, be anemic, and have cardiac problems caused by cancer medicines. Cancer treatments fall along a wide spectrum and can have a broad range of effects.

Fatigue
Cancer wreaks havoc on the body by attacking vital cells, organs, and body systems. The medications designed to treat it are also harsh. The cycle of medication exhausts patients physically and emotionally. It can be difficult to rally for a training session even when the session is part of the treatment routine.

Cardiovascular training should be low impact and at 76%-85% of the client's maximal heart rate, in Zone 2, 14-16 on the perceived exertion scale, three to five times a week. Breaking up the training cycle throughout the day, with a target of 30 minutes of exercise in aggregate might be the best option for a client with cancer. Walking, rowing, and using a stationary bicycle are all good options for clients in this population.

Immune function and muscle tissue
Cancer and its various treatments can affect the body in a multitude of ways. Immune system function will be lower due to the onslaught of medications used to kill cancer cells. Exercise can help increase immune function and improve the client's overall condition, adding an emotional boost.

Weight training is especially effective. Select up to 10 appropriate exercises for the client, and have them perform just one set (of around twelve repetitions) a few times per week, as their body allows. Weight training will help combat the atrophy of lean muscle that can result from cancer and its various treatments. Pay special attention to coordination and balance deficiencies that may occur because of the loss of muscle mass.

<u>Training length and intensity</u>
Clients with cancer face physical challenges unique to their special population, including physical weakness and acute fatigue that may vary depending on the day or the stage of their treatment. It is best for the client to do several short cardiorespiratory sessions for a total of 30 minutes to avoid overtaxing the body. As the client's fitness level improves, build to training three to five times per week.

Walking and pedaling on a stationary bicycle are good exercise modalities. Administer the standard NASM assessments, and use the flexibility continuum if the client can tolerate it.

To introduce weight training, select 10 exercise and have the client can perform a low repetition set for each exercise.

## Pregnancy

A pregnant woman is carrying a fetus through a 40-week gestational period. The body of a pregnant woman is undergoing dramatic changes to support the growing baby and prepare for birth. Pregnancy causes physiological changes including hormonal shifts, loosening of ligaments and connective tissue, increased blood volume, and changes in gait and balance.

Exercise is beneficial to pregnant women. Exercise helps prepare a woman's body for the rigors of childbirth, and it promotes recovery once the baby is born. It is very important that the health and fitness professional understand the physical changes that women go through to keep mother and child safe.

<u>Exercise limitations</u>
Although exercise is beneficial for a pregnant woman, there are risk factors for the trainer to consider. There are instances that necessitate restricting or suspending a pregnant woman's exercise program. Constant diligence is required to avoid potentially dangerous situations.

A physician should examine a pregnant woman if she experiences bleeding in the second or third trimesters. She should not resume exercising without clearance from a physician. Heavy vaginal bleeding during pregnancy is a serious warning sign.

A physician must address cervical issues such as early dilation (incompetent cervix) or improper placenta placement, and clear the client before she can continue a training program.

High blood pressure during pregnancy and gestational diabetes (pregnancy hormones interfere with the body's ability to process and use glucose properly) are serious issues that require caution. While exercise can help with these conditions, it is essential that the pregnant woman consults with her physician first.

Blood volume

When a woman is pregnant, her body produces up to a third more blood than it normally does. This is a protective mechanism that helps support the demands of the growing fetus while ensuring the woman has an extra blood supply should she bleed during delivery.

Despite having more blood volume, a pregnant woman may have a lower oxygen capacity for training sessions. She may also experience shortness of breath if the fetus presses upward on her lungs.

NASM advises prescribing low-impact exercises to compensate for these factors. Aquatic exercises or machine-based cardiorespiratory training work well. Avoid having the client lift heavy weights. The trainer should begin with three sessions per week and work up to five.

Nutritional needs

A pregnant woman has increased nutritional demands because she is supporting another life. A pregnant woman needs an extra 300 calories each day to support the fetus and to build fat stores required for breast feeding once the child is born.

When a woman adds exercise to her activities, she must compensate for this added caloric expenditure. It is not advisable for pregnant women to engage in a calorie restricted diet in an attempt to lose weight during pregnancy. A pregnant woman should consume the proper amount of calories and focus on nutritionally sound food sources rich in calcium and other vitamins and minerals to support fetal growth.

The client should discuss her training routine with her physician and a dietitian to determine a positive nutritional balance that is appropriate for her particular gestational stage and fitness activity level.

Risk categories

Some women have a higher risk of developing serious complications during pregnancy. Major risk factors include:

- Age (women older than 35 are at higher risk for complications and for having a baby with certain birth defects)
- History of pregnancy-related problems, such as miscarrying
- Endocrine problems (thyroid or insulin-related)
- Being obese or overweight

These risk factors potentially add more stress onto the already hardworking pregnant body. If the client has risk factors, be sure that she has discussed her training routine with a physician. It is not advisable to engage in weight training without a doctor's endorsement. Closely observe how the client tolerates training and track notable changes.

Loosening of the ligaments

During pregnancy, a woman's body releases hormones to help prepare for childbirth. These include hormones that loosen ligaments. Although the hormones help the pelvis accommodate the baby's head during birth, the hormones do not discriminate among ligaments, and there can be a loosening of all connective tissues throughout the body.

A pregnant woman with loosened ligaments may have impaired balance and less control of her core musculature. She may have dull or sharp pain in the groin and pelvic area from the loosened ligaments. Consider using supported cardiorespiratory training, such as aquatic activities and walking on a treadmill with handrails. Use extra caution with weight-bearing exercises.

Training length and intensity
There are several important things to keep in mind when working with a pregnant client. Due to the added pressure that the fetus places on the circulatory system, avoid exercises that require the client to lie on her back. Core body temperature tends to run higher for pregnant women, so they are at increased risk of overheating, especially if the overexert.

Lower-intensity activities are ideal for pregnant women. The trainer should avoid supine exercises because the weight of the baby can tax the circulatory system by pressing on the vena cava, which can result in dizziness or fainting. Sessions should range from three to five per week, with weight training incorporated once or twice per week. As the pregnancy progresses, use only phase one of the Optimum Performance Training (OPT) model.

Postpartum considerations
Exercise and fitness training are excellent ways for a postpartum mother to combat fatigue and help her body return to its pre-pregnancy shape. However, the health and fitness trainer must be aware of certain aspects of postpartum training before commencing with someone who has recently given birth.

Physicians discourage women from entering into exercise routines for the first six weeks after childbirth. Giving birth is a strenuous task that requires downtime for the body to heal. The period immediately following birth is one of great transition as a woman adapts to caring for a baby, while her hormone levels shift dramatically, and she begins breastfeeding (if she chooses to). Complications during the birth, or a surgical delivery, can lengthen recovery time.

Many women are so keen on returning to their pre-pregnancy weight that they rush to work out before it is advisable. When beginning a training routine with a woman who has just had a baby, be sure her doctor has sanctioned the activity.

**Lung disorders**

Lung disease is an umbrella term for any chronic disorder of the pulmonary system. In many instances, it is caused by smoking cigarettes or having been exposed to second-hand smoke.

There are two types of lung disorders: obstructive disorders and restrictive disorders. Obstructive lung disease is characterized by lower lung function caused by an obstruction (often the body's fluids) of the free flow of gasses. Obstructive lung diseases include emphysema and asthma. In restrictive lung disease (e.g., pulmonary fibrosis), the lung tissue is damaged and does not function properly. Restrictive and obstructive disorders impair oxygen levels, reducing stamina and increasing feelings of fatigue and dizziness at low-impact levels.

Physical characteristic
People who have chronic lung disorders may show the physical signs of the wear the disease places on the body. Those with obstructive lung disease may be underweight and have lower muscle tone. Those with restrictive lung disease may be overweight and have oversized rib cages, which are side effects of constantly working against their bodies to breathe.

Working with a person who has lung disease is similar to working with a regular adult. The health and fitness professional should anticipate lower energy levels and adjust accordingly. Additionally, the trainer should focus on lower-body activities to avoid stressing upper-body muscles that may be compensating for pulmonary issues. Incorporate adequate rest times into the workout to help the person recover from heightened activity.

## Comorbidities

Individuals with lung disease often have comorbidities that can affect a health and fitness training regimen. People with lung disease are often long-term smokers and may have heart issues as a result (over time, lack of oxygen to the heart muscle can enlarge the heart and cause vascular problems).

It is extremely important for a client with a history of lung disease to undergo a thorough examination with a physician before commencing physical training, which will help establish parameters for safely working around the lung disease issues. The physician may diagnose and treat concurrent health problems at this time.

## Oxygen conversion

Lung disease lowers the level of oxygen converted for the body's use at any given time. Reduced oxygen stresses the cardiovascular system. Exercise, even low-impact activities, further taxes the pulmonary system.

The lower oxygen levels can cause shortness of breath even when the client is engaged in low-impact activities. A health and fitness professional should be aware of how to use a pulse oximeter to obtain oxygen levels during exercise to ensure they do not dip below acceptable levels. Record results to use as a point of comparison for future readings, to ascertain whether the client is tolerating certain activities, and to determine if there have been improvements in oxygen levels

## Physical shape

A person with lung disease is likely to be out of shape. Lung disease may limit activities and necessitate a sedentary lifestyle, lowering the client's cardiovascular health level lower and promoting muscle atrophy.

Regular exercise helps to reverse these limitations. Under the guidance and supervision of the client's physician, begin working out five times a week for twenty minutes, and build to 45-minute workouts five times a week. Observe how well the client tolerates the routine, and progress based on the client's comfort level. Consider breaking up training sessions throughout the day, to avoid overtaxing the pulmonary system with one long session. Schedule more rest time to allow recuperation between exercises or sets.

## Upper body training regimen

Training a client with pulmonary considerations impacts exercise selection. A health and fitness professional should choose exercises that target lower-body muscle groups or lower-body activity, such as using a stationary bike, and avoid exercises that tax the upper-body muscles.

Because clients with lung disorders struggle to receive adequate supplies of oxygen, there is a tendency to overuse secondary respiratory muscles to compensate. These secondary breathing muscles stabilize the upper body during certain movements. Stressing the secondary muscles can lead to shortness of breath and fatigue.

## Muscle mass

When a person has a serious pulmonary disorder, it can result in muscle loss from lack of exercise. In extreme cases, severe atrophy occurs, resulting in the client dipping below the healthy BMI range (less than 18).

If the client is dangerously underweight, refer them to a nutritionist or dietitian. The dietitian should place the client on a healthy eating plan designed to return them to a healthy weight. Incorporate weight training into the routine to build muscle mass and to help the client put on weight.

## Oxygen tank consideration

Clients with lung disorders may need an oxygen tank to maintain their oxygen levels during exercise (and possibly in daily life). The use of an oxygen tank can present a unique challenge in health and fitness training activities.

It is vitally important for health and fitness professionals to understand that they may not interfere with or adjust the levels of oxygen that a client is taking. The use of an oxygen tank is a medical treatment that only a physician can administer and control. Use a pulse oximeter to keep track of oxygen saturation levels during exercise and record results for all of the client's sessions to track of notable patterns. Consult the physician if there is an issue with the client's oxygen levels.

## Training length and intensity

Low-impact activities are the best for those with impaired lung function, especially those that work the lower extremities and avoid taxing the upper body. Training sessions should be short, starting with 20 minutes and working up to 45 minutes, depending on the client's tolerance. Several shorter sessions in a day may be more attainable than one long session.

Only employ phase 1 of the Optimum Performance Training (OPT) model. Limit weight training intensity: two or three sessions of one set of repetitions per exercise a couple of times per week.

Have the client perform all of the NASM assessments, and employ the full spectrum of stretching activities.

Give the client adequate rest time between sets or exercises; they might require longer rest than the average client.

## Peripheral artery disease (PAD)/intermittent claudication

Peripheral artery disease (PAD) is a disorder in which a person's arteries do not function properly due to a narrowing of the arteries or a failure of the artery closure flaps. PAD results in poor lower-body circulation that can affect training. Intermittent claudication is the umbrella term for the effects of PAD.

One of the main symptoms of PAD is leg pain, which can limit a client's ability to train. The health and fitness professional will have to proceed cautiously to determine if the pain is due to PAD or if it is associated with beginning a training regimen. It is important for the client to have a full physical examination before beginning the training regimen. The client should follow the doctor's recommendations as prescribed.

Training sessions should proceed according to the client's tolerance for pain or discomfort. If pain continues during training sessions, have the client discuss the problem with a physician before continuing.

## Comorbidities

Clients with PAD are often prone to having other health problems, or comorbidities. Coronary artery disease and insulin-related disorders (e.g., type 1 and type 2 diabetes) are common comorbidities.

If a client has coronary artery disease in addition to PAD, the health and fitness professional should make sure the client stays within a set heart rate maximum. (This upper limit can be determined using a test in which the client walks to the extent his or her pain will permit.)

Acknowledge the client's pain and stop if necessary. Avoid encouraging the client to continue or ignore the pain. Leg pain acts as a good barometer, and it can help prevent overworking the heart.

Walking is ideal for those with PAD, and the client should walk for at least 10-minute sessions.

## Smoking

If a client with PAD smokes, they should be encouraged to quit. Encourage the client to discuss methods of quitting with his or her physician. Advise the client that smoking affects circulation and is very dangerous when combined with PAD. Smoking also lessens the client's ability to perform the exercise routine.

There are many options for quitting smoking to explore, including medications. Tread lightly when discussing this topic because many smokers have indulged for years and may be resistant to any perceived negative judgments of this habit.

If the client cannot or will not quit, try to get him or her to agree not to smoke for a period preceding health and fitness workouts. Ideally, the client will not smoke for 60 minutes before a session.

## Stamina

Clients with PAD are more likely to be significantly out of shape when compared to the average healthy adult due to leg pain, which limits their fitness activities. PAD itself can affect a person's ability to circulate oxygenated blood, leading to fatigue more quickly than with the average healthy adult.

NASM recommends walking for people with peripheral artery disease. Walking is tolerable for clients with PAD. If the client can handle increased intensity, increase the speed or change the incline of the treadmill.

If the client is having difficulty with pain, consider breaking up the workout into shorter chunks of time, aiming to have at least 10-minute segments at a time.

## Weight training

Although weight training has many benefits, it does not specifically improve the issues associated with PAD. The focus of the training program should be on cardiorespiratory exercises. Add a few supplementary weight-training sessions if the client is capable. Incorporate up to 10 exercises and include as many as three moderate repetition sets (around 10). Working in a circuit method maximizes the cardiorespiratory training.

Allow adequate rest time and to progress to the extent that the client's pain will allow.

<u>Training length and intensity</u>
Prescribe aerobic exercises, such as walking and using a stationary bicycle, for clients who have pulmonary issues. Start with three sessions per week and progress to five, as the client can tolerate. Sessions should be relatively short, beginning with 20 minutes and not exceeding 60 minutes. Consider breaking the session up over the day, aiming for shorter sessions of more than 10 minutes each.

NASM's normal range of assessments and the flexibility continuum are acceptable for use with this special population. Avoid SMR with this population.

Weight training is acceptable but focus primarily on aerobic exercise. These sessions should incorporate up to 10 exercises and can include up to three sets of a moderate number of repetitions (around 10). Working in a circuit method maximizes the cardiorespiratory training.

## Abnormal curvatures of the spine

Lordosis is the excessive curvature of the lumbar spine, kyphosis is the excessive curvature of the thoracic spine (i.e., hunchback appearance), and scoliosis is a lateral S-shaped curve of the spine. If a client displays an abnormal curvature, they should avoid performing movements that put excessive stress on the spine. For example, stable, closed kinetic chain movements are more helpful than open kinetic chain movements.

# Objective Assessment

## Five types of objective information

There are five types of objective information a CPT should gather about a client's general history during the fitness assessment:

1. Heart/lung (cardiorespiratory) efficiency
2. Dynamic movement (posture)
3. Physiology, including heart rate and blood pressure
4. Fat and muscle composition, which may include body mass index (BMI) and waist-to-hip ratios
5. Athletic ability or performance, which may include a bench press assessment and a squat assessment

Objective information is essential to a trainer because it establishes a client's fitness capabilities and a starting point. Objective information also provides a baseline to serve as a comparison for future results which can be used to determine client progress and program efficacy.

## Heart rate

To find the radial pulse, place two fingers on the inside of the wrist in line with (and just above) the thumb and count the number of beats. Place two fingers on the neck, just to the side of the larynx, right underneath the jawline to find the carotid pulse. When measuring the carotid pulse, apply minimal pressure to decrease the risk of reduced blood flow to the brain.

Although resting heart rates vary, men average 70 beats per minute, and women average about 75.

To find an estimated maximum heart rate, subtract the client's age from the number 220.

## Blood pressure

Blood pressure is a measurement of the force exerted by the blood on the interior walls of the arteries. Blood pressure emanates from the heart, which pumps the blood throughout the body.

A stethoscope (to listen to the pulse at the brachial artery) and a sphygmomanometer (cuffed around the arm, above the elbow) measure blood pressure).

To take a blood pressure reading, rapidly inflate the cuff to 20–30 mm Hg above the point at which the pulse at the wrist is undetectable. Release the pressure at 2 mm Hg per second.

The systolic reading is the top number of a blood pressure measurement. The systolic reading registers when the pressure releases and the sound of the pulse is audible. It reflects the maximum force produced by the cardiac cycle. The diastolic reading records when the sound of the pulse fades away. It appears on the bottom of the reading and reflects the lowest amount of pressure produced during the cardiac cycle.

A normal reading for an adult is between 120 to 130 mm Hg for the systolic number and from 80 to 85 mm Hg for the diastolic number.

## Body fat percentage

Use of skin calipers

The Durnin-Womersly formula requires caliper measurements (in millimeters) at four sites on the body. To promote consistency when measuring skin folds, take all measurements on the right side of the body. The four measurement locations are:

1. A vertical fold of skin on the anterior side of the biceps, halfway between the elbow and shoulder
2. A vertical fold of skin on the posterior side of the triceps, halfway between the elbow and shoulder
3. An angled fold of skin (about 45 degrees) at the subscapula, about two centimeters below the inner angle of the scapula
4. An angled fold of skin (of about 45 degrees) just above the iliac crest and in line with the apex of the armpit

The Durnin-Womersly chart or formula provides the client's body fat percentage based on the sum of the four caliper measurements, the client's age, and the client's gender.

## BMI and waist-to-hip ratio

To find a person's waist-to-hip ratio, measure the smallest part of his or her waist and largest part of his or her hips. Divide the waist measurement by the hip measurement. Women whose ratio exceeds 0.80 are at risk of having obesity-related health problems. The same is true for men with ratios greater than 0.95.

To reveal whether a person's weight is appropriate for his/her height, simply divide weight (in kilograms) by height (in meters squared). The likelihood of obesity-related health problems increases when BMI exceeds 25.

BMI is an acronym that stands for body mass index. BMI is inexact. It is a simple method to determine if a client's weight is proportional to their height. BMI indicates general health risks but is not a reliable indicator of fitness level. A muscular individual will have a high BMI without the health risks associated with a high BMI. A lean marathon runner may have a low BMI but is still fit. The Quetelet index is another name for BMI.

BMI does not measure body fat, but it is a useful assessment tool to determine whether a person's weight correlates in a healthy manner to his or her height. Use the following formula to determine BMI:

$$\text{BMI} = \frac{\text{weight (in kilograms)}}{\text{height (in meters)}^2}$$

A person is considered overweight when they have a BMI that exceeds 25. A range of 25 to 30 is considered mildly overweight, while 30 to 35 is moderately overweight. Measurements greater than 35 are considered obese, or severely overweight.

| BMI | Classification |
|---|---|
| <18.5 | Underweight |
| 18.6–21.99 | Acceptable |
| 22.0–24.99 | Acceptable |
| 25.0–29.99 | Overweight |
| 30–34.99 | Obese |
| 35.0–39.99 | Obesity II |
| ≥40 | Obesity III |

## Cardiorespiratory assessments

The three-minute step test and Rockport walk test are cardiorespiratory assessments that estimate a cardiovascular starting point (the trainer should modify the assessments according to the person's ability level).

The three-minute step test requires a client to step onto a 12-inch step 24 times per minute, for a total of three minutes (72 steps total). After a one-minute rest, measure the client's recovery pulse for 30 seconds. To determine the client's cardiovascular (CV) efficiency level, locate the client's heart rate in the table below.

### Three-Minute Step Test Chart

| | Age | Very Poor | Poor | Below Average | Average | Above Average | Good | Excellent |
|---|---|---|---|---|---|---|---|---|
| **Male** | 18-25 | 124-157 | 111-119 | 102-107 | 95-100 | 88-93 | 79-84 | 50-76 |
| | 26-36 | 126-161 | 114-121 | 104-110 | 96-102 | 88-94 | 79-85 | 51-76 |
| | 36-45 | 130-163 | 116-124 | 108-113 | 100-105 | 92-98 | 80-88 | 49-76 |
| | 46-55 | 131-159 | 121-126 | 113-119 | 103-111 | 95-101 | 87-93 | 56-82 |
| | 56-65 | 131-154 | 119-128 | 111-117 | 103-109 | 97-100 | 86-94 | 60-77 |
| | 65+ | 130-151 | 121-126 | 114-118 | 104-110 | 94-102 | 97-92 | 59-81 |
| **Female** | 18-25 | 135-169 | 122-131 | 113-120 | 104-110 | 96-102 | 85-93 | 52-81 |
| | 26-36 | 134-171 | 122-129 | 113-119 | 104-110 | 95-101 | 85-92 | 58-80 |
| | 36-45 | 137-169 | 124-132 | 115-120 | 107-112 | 100-104 | 89-96 | 51-84 |
| | 46-55 | 137-171 | 126-132 | 120-124 | 113-118 | 104-110 | 95-101 | 63-91 |
| | 56-65 | 141-174 | 129-135 | 119-127 | 113-118 | 106-111 | 97-103 | 60-92 |
| | 65+ | 135-155 | 128-133 | 123-126 | 116-121 | 104-111 | 96-101 | 70-92 |

To perform the Rockport walk test, have a client walk for one mile on a treadmill as fast as possible without losing control. At the one-mile mark, quickly record the time and the client's heart rate. Determine the client's VO2 (maximal oxygen uptake) score, and locate it in the Rockport Chart.

Male: $$VO_2max \left[\frac{ml}{kg \times min}\right] = 11.33 - (0.42 \times heart\ rate\ in\ beats\ per\ minute)$$

Female: $$VO_2max \left[\frac{ml}{kg \times min}\right] = 65.81 - (0.1847 \times heart\ rate\ in\ beats\ per\ minute)$$

### Rockport Walk Test Chart

|  | Age | Very Poor | Poor | Fair | Average | Good | Very Good | Excellent |
|---|---|---|---|---|---|---|---|---|
| Male | 18-20 | <33 | 38-33 | 45-39 | 50-46 | 56-51 | 62-57 | >63 |
| | 21-25 | <32 | 37-32 | 44-38 | 50-45 | 55-51 | 62-56 | >62 |
| | 26-30 | <30 | 35-30 | 41-36 | 47-42 | 54-48 | 59-55 | >59 |
| Female | 18-20 | <28 | 32-28 | 37-33 | 42-38 | 47-43 | 53-48 | >53 |
| | 21-25 | <27 | 31-27 | 35-32 | 41-36 | 45-42 | 50-46 | >50 |
| | 26-30 | <26 | 30-26 | 34-31 | 39-35 | 43-40 | 48-44 | >48 |

## Functional Biomechanics

Biomechanics is the study of the kinetic chain, including the movements it makes and the forces that act internally and externally upon it. Important elements of biomechanics include joint motion, muscle movement, force, and leverage.

Human movement is an interrelated cycle that encompasses the nervous system, the skeletal system, and the muscular system:
- The central nervous system (CNS) collects information from the internal and external environments
- The CNS processes this information
- Nerve impulses are passed to the muscles
- The muscles move the skeletal system

## Kinetic chain

The kinetic chain refers to the system of bones, joints, and muscles connected through the nervous system that allows the human body to move. The health and stability of the kinetic chain directly correlate to how well a person can move and how comfortable (or uncomfortable) the movement is.

Because the kinetic chain integrates several different body systems, each must be fully functional for optimal movement. If any component of the kinetic chain is impaired, the entire chain will function at a suboptimal level. The CPT should understand each aspect of the kinetic chain and address each particular client's needs in his or her training.

## Planes of motion

Optimal training techniques use exercises that span all three planes of motion. While many movements occur on a primary plane of motion, the movement does not occur solely in one plane.

The best way to visualize these planes is by picturing a pane of clear glass passing through the body:

- Frontal plane—The pane of glass passes through the body from the head to the toes, bisecting the body into front and back halves.
- Transverse plane—The pane of glass passes through the center of the body at the abdomen, bisecting the body into top and bottom halves.
- Sagittal plane—The pane of glass passes through the body from the head to the toes, bisecting the body into right and left halves.

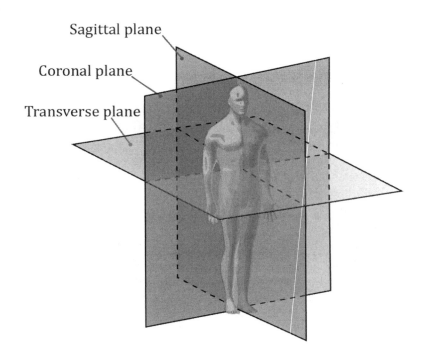

| Plane | Bisector | Movement | Example |
|---|---|---|---|
| **Coronal (frontal)** | Front and back halves | Side to side | Side Lunge |
| **Sagittal** | Left and right sides | Front to back | Lunges |
| **Transverse (horizontal)** | Top and bottom halves | Rotation (twisting) | Golfing |

**Types of motion**

The body can make many different types of motion. Knowing the terminology can help define these movements quickly and efficiently.

- Adduction—movement in toward the center of the body.
- Abduction—movement away from the center of the body.
- External rotation—movement of a joint away from the center of the body.
- Internal rotation—movement of a joint in toward the center of the body.
- Pronation—rotation out of either the radioulnar joint or subtalar joint.
- Supination—rotation in of either the radioulnar joint or subtalar joint.
- Extension—the straightening out of a joint to increase its angle.
- Flexion—the bending of a joint to decrease its angle.

## Muscle actions

There are three main muscle actions:
1. Concentric muscle action—A concentric contraction results in the shortening of the muscle—when the muscle exerts sufficient force to overcome the force acting on it.
2. Eccentric muscle action—An eccentric contraction results in the lengthening of the muscle—when the force acting on the muscle exceeds the force the muscle is exerting. Eccentric contractions are negative forces because the weight exerts a force on the muscle. The negative occurs when a muscle is returning to its original position or decelerating.
3. Isometric muscle action—The muscle is exerting a force equal to the force acting on it—when the muscle is stabilizing and balancing.

## Muscular force

These terms help define the interrelation of the kinetic chain and musculoskeletal system and how force and energy come into play regarding human movement. Understanding these terms improves the health and fitness professional's ability to recognize and describe movement and impairments and improve the client's training regimen.

- Muscular force—describes the interplay between two objects that creates an acceleration or deceleration of one or both objects. Force has magnitude and direction.
- Length-tension relationships—the optimum length for a muscle at which it can achieve its top force. Hyperextension and underextension do not allow the muscle fibers to work at their peak capacity.
- Force-velocity curve—the ability of muscles to produce more force at a higher rate of speed.
- Force-couple relationships—the synergistic relationship between certain muscles and muscle groups that result in the movement of an entire joint. Force-couple relationships often involve a pushing and pulling action on the joint.

## Motor control

Motor control is the body's ability to control the elements of the kinetic chain based on the information it collects from internal and external sources. It is important to train each element individually and in an integrated manner to manipulate motor behavior. Increased motor behavior improves motor control (the body's response to internal and external stimuli).

Muscle synergies (the way muscles interact and work together), proprioception (how the body interprets incoming sense information), and sensorimotor integration (the ability of the nervous system to process sense information and translate it into motion) affect motor control. Each of these components features the interaction of more than one body system. Increased efficiency of individual components positively affects overall motor control.

## Integrating motor behavior and control

Motor learning hones motor behavior and motor control. Motor learning refers to the body's ability to hardwire movement into the body's neuromuscular pathways through repetition and practice.

The body receives sensory feedback from internal and external sources. Internal feedback facilitates motor learning and refers to information that comes from the body via internal sensors.

External feedback is information that comes from an outside source, such as watching oneself in the mirror or working with a trainer. Incorporating external feedback benefits motor learning.

Results and performance are components of external feedback. Knowledge of results focuses on the outcome of a given movement (e.g., a trainer indicating that the client completed the target number of repetitions). Knowledge of performance sheds light on the quality of the movement (e.g., a trainer observing that the client broke form during the set).

## Flexibility concerns

Postural distortions caused by muscle imbalances can lead to poor movement coordination and ultimately to injury. The human movement system responds to poor flexibility by seeking the path of least resistance, a process called relative flexibility. Relative flexibility causes the body to learn to improper movement patterns, and the inefficient movement becomes ingrained (think a shortcut cutting the corner of a ninety-degree angle).

A client's toes pointing out during a squat are an excellent illustration of relative flexibility. When an individual performs a squat correctly, the back is straight, the knees are in line with the toes, and the toes point straight ahead (or point out slightly). If a person has overactive calf muscles, he or she must compensate for a lack of flexion in the ankles by spacing the feet further apart and rotating them out. Poor flexibility (tight calves and poor dorsiflexion of the ankle) causes the body to move in an inefficient manner (toes turn out during a squat), over time the pattern becomes ingrained, and injury can occur.

## Biomechanical assessments

Movement assessments provide information on postural distortions caused by overactive or underactive muscles. The following contains descriptions of assessments, including which muscles are causing the problems:

Overhead squat assessment
The overhead squat assessment is an excellent tool to determine a client's balance, flexibility, core strength, and proprioceptive ability. It will provide evidence of postural distortions or abnormal movement patterns. To administer the test, have the client stand with feet shoulder width apart. With arms raised overhead and elbows fully extended, the client will perform a squat movement. The client will repeat this movement 5 times in a slow, controlled manner. Observe and record any postural distortions.

| | Overactive muscles | Underactive muscles |
|---|---|---|
| **Knees that buckle inward are evidence of:** | Adductor complex<br>Biceps femoris<br>Tensor fascia lata (TFL)<br>Vastus lateralis | Gluteus medius<br>Gluteus maximus<br>Vastus medialis oblique |
| **An arch in the lower back at the lumbo-pelvic hip (LPH) complex is evidence of:** | Hip flexor complex<br>Erector spinae | Gluteus maximus<br>Hamstrings<br>All intrinsic core stabilizers (such as the transverse abdominus, multifidus, transversospinalis, internal obliques, and pelvic-floor |

| | | muscles) |
|---|---|---|

The overhead squat assessment is used by CPTs to determine a client's total body strength and dynamic flexibility.

Single-leg squat assessment

The single-leg squat assessment is an excellent tool to determine a client's balance, flexibility, core strength, and proprioceptive ability. It will provide evidence of postural distortions or abnormal movement patterns. To administer the test, have the client stand on one leg with hands on hips. Have the client perform a squat, but do not require them to go lower than their comfort level allows. For each leg, the client will repeat this movement 5 times in a slow, controlled manner. Observe and record any postural distortions.

| | Overactive muscles | Underactive muscles |
|---|---|---|
| **Knee moving inward is evidence of:** | Adductor complex<br>Biceps femoris<br>Tensor fascia lata (TFL)<br>Vastus lateralis | Gluteus medius<br>Gluteus maximus<br>Vastus medialis oblique |

The single-leg squat assessment is used by CPTs to determine the stability of a person's hip joint, ankle flexibility, and center strength. It may not be appropriate for elderly or obese individuals, who may find it too difficult to perform.

Pulling assessment

The pulling assessment is an excellent tool to determine how efficiently a client moves while pulling. The assessment will reveal postural distortions that affect pushing performance. Administer the test on a cable press machine. The client will stand in a split stance with the abdomen drawn in. Have the client perform 20 pulls (rows) in slow, controlled manner. Observe and record any postural distortions

| | Overactive muscles | Underactive muscles |
|---|---|---|
| **An arch in the lower back at the lumbo-pelvic-hip (LPH) complex is evidence of:** | Hip flexor complex<br>Erector spinae | All intrinsic core stabilizers (such as the transverse abdominus, multifidus, transversospinalis, internal obliques, and pelvic-floor muscles) |
| **Pulling up of the shoulders is evidence of:** | Levator scapulae<br>Sternocleidomastoid<br>Upper trapezius | Mid trapezius<br>Lower trapezius |
| **A head that juts forward is evidence of:** | Levator scapulae<br>Sternocleidomastoid<br>Upper trapezius | Deep cervical flexors |

Pushing assessment

The pushing assessment is an excellent tool to determine how efficiently a client moves while pushing. The assessment will reveal postural distortions that affect pushing performance. Administer the test on a cable press machine. The client will stand in a split stance with the abdomen drawn in. Have the client perform 20 presses in slow, controlled manner. Observe and record any postural distortions.

| | Overactive muscles | Underactive muscles |
|---|---|---|
| **An arch in the lower back at the lumbo-pelvic-hip (LPH) complex is evidence of:** | Hip flexor complex Erector spinae | All intrinsic core stabilizers (such as the transverse abdominus, multifidus, transversospinalis, internal obliques, and pelvic-floor muscles) |
| **Shoulder elevation is evidence of:** | Levator scapulae Sternocleidomastoid Upper trapezius | Mid trapezius Lower trapezius |
| **A head that juts forward is evidence of:** | Levator scapulae Sternocleidomastoid Upper trapezius | Deep cervical flexors |

**Strength assessments**

Davies and shark skill tests
To administer the Davies test, have the client begin in a push-up position with the hands positioned one yard (3 feet) apart. Instruct the client to move one hand rapidly to touch the other in an alternating fashion while maintaining a push-up position. Record the number of completed in a 15-second period. Repeat three times.

The Davies test evaluates upper-body strength, agility, and stability; it may not be appropriate for people with shoulder problems or injuries.

To give a shark skill test, create a 3X3 square grid on the floor numbered one through nine (masking tape works well). Start the client in the center box. Have the client stand on one leg with hands on hips. Have the client hop from the center box to square one, then to the center, then to square two, then to the center, and so on, until the client has hopped into each square. Switch legs and repeat the exercise. Do this four times, twice for each leg, recording the time for performance. Add one-tenth of a second for mistakes, such as the raised foot falling to the ground, stepping into an incorrect square, or the hands dropping.

The shark skill test evaluates lower-body strength and agility as well as a person's muscle coordination; it may not be appropriate for people with lower-extremity problems or injuries.

Upper- and lower-extremity strength assessments
The bench press is the standard upper-extremity strength test. The client should warm up with a comfortable weight and then rest for 60 seconds. Add 10 to 20 pounds, have the client do three to five repetitions and then rest for two minutes. Add another 10 to 20 pounds, and have the client do another three to five repetitions. Repeat this progression until the client cannot complete the repetitions. Use the NASM chart to establish the maximum level of intensity for one repetition.

The upper-extremity strength assessment evaluates the maximum level of intensity for one repetition; it is an advanced assessment and is not appropriate for novice clients.

The squat is the standard lower-extremity strength test. Have the client warm up with a comfortable weight, and then rest for 60 seconds. Put on an additional 30 to 40 pounds, have the client do three to five repetitions, and then rest for two minutes. Add another 30 to 40 pounds, and have the client do another three to five repetitions. Repeat this progression until the client cannot complete the repetitions. Use the NASM chart to establish the maximum level of intensity for one repetition.

The lower-extremity strength assessment evaluates the maximum level of intensity for one squat repetition; it is an advanced assessment and is not appropriate for novice clients.

## Postural and movement dysfunctions

### Deconditioned states

A deconditioned state is a decline or lack of physical fitness characterized by low stamina, decreased strength, muscle distortions, lack of flexibility, and lack of overall muscle stability and agility. A deconditioned state is not merely being overweight; it describes a decline in physical ability, reduced musculoskeletal strength and capability, and limited cardiorespiratory capacity.

When sedentary individuals begin a typical training program, they substantially increase their risk for injury and overwork muscles. It is important to modify typical training programs to ensure that the client increases fitness in a safe and steady manner.

Proprioception is the information transmitted through the body via the senses. A training program that incorporates movements throughout the different planes of motion and through all muscle actions and contractions increases the level of neuromuscular communication throughout the body results in a proprioceptively enriched environment that forces the body to increase its ability to stabilize and balance. The use of a stability ball when doing any number of training exercises creates a proprioceptively challenging environment.

### Postural distortion

Muscle imbalances cause postural distortions. Imbalanced muscles alter joint mechanics, decrease functionality, and lead to injury. There are three common postural distortions. Pronated feet and knees that rotate inward characterize pronation distortion syndrome. An arch in the lower back characterizes lower crossed syndrome. Rounded shoulders and a protruding head characterize upper crossed syndrome. Each distortion has a number of shortened and lengthened muscles, increased and decreased joint function, and possible injuries.

|  | Pronation Distortion | Lower Crossed | Upper Crossed |
|---|---|---|---|
| **Shortened Muscle** | Gastrocnemius, Soleus, Peroneals, Adductors, Iliotibial head, Hip flexor complex, and Biceps femoris (short head) | Gastrocnemius, Soleus, Hip flexor complex, Adductors, Latissimus dorsi, and Erector spinae | Upper trapezius, Levator scapulae, Sternocleidomastoid, Scalenes, Latissimus dorsi, Teres major, and Pectoralis major/minor |
| **Lengthened Muscle** | Anterior tibialis, Posterior tibialis, Vastus medialis, Gluteus medius, Gluteus maximus, and Hip external rotators | Anterior tibialis, Posterior tibialis, Gluteus maximus, Gluteus medius, Transversus abdominis, and Internal Oblique | Deep cervical flexors, Serratus anterior, Rhomboids, Mid-trapezius, Lower trapezius, Teres minor, and Infraspinatus |
| **Increased** | Knee adduction, Knee internal rotation, Foot pronation, and Foot external rotation | Lumbar extension | Cervical extension and Scapular protraction/elevation |
| **Decreased** | Ankle dorsiflexion and Ankle inversion | Hip extension | Shoulder extension and Shoulder external rotation |
| **Possible Injuries** | Plantar fasciitis, Posterior tibialis tendonitis (shin splints), Patellar tendonitis, and Low-back pain | Hamstring complex strain, Anterior knee pain, and Low-back pain | Headaches, Biceps tendonitis, Rotator cuff impingement, and Thoracic outlet syndrome |

Cumulative injury cycle

Postural distortions coupled with repetitive motions (even those associated with daily living), result in the kinetic chain not working properly. Poor kinetic chain function affects muscles and connective tissue and confuses the body, which reacts as though these distortions are injuries that require repair. The body will try to fix the problem, resulting in the cumulative injury cycle.

This cycle includes the following:
- Muscle imbalance
- Injury to connective tissue
- Inflammation of the injured tissues
- Increased muscle tension and spasms
- Knots in the soft tissue (also called adhesions)
- Altered reciprocal inhibition
- Increased synergistic dominance (when synergist muscles overcompensate for a weak prime mover muscle)
- Altered joint motion

Failure to identify and correct this cycle can lead to permanent changes in the body. Davis's law states that soft tissue will form or rebuild itself along the lines of any stress, which may run contrary to the natural lines of the muscle, which will inhibit optimal muscle function.

## General adaptation syndrome

Hans Selye identified general adaptation syndrome, which states that the body, specifically the kinetic chain, attempts to stay in equilibrium at all times by counteracting any stresses placed on it. There are three types of responses to various stresses:

1. Alarm reaction— The body's initial when it is stressed. In this stage, the body responds to unfamiliar stressors with a variety of physiological changes.
2. Resistance development—The body has become familiar with the stress mechanism and has begun to develop specific responses to handle and adapt to the stress.
3. Exhaustion—Exhaustion occurs when the body has been overwhelmed by a stress mechanism and can no longer cope. Exhaustion can result in damage to the body ranging from emotional wear to physical damage such as stress fractures or muscle tears.

## Muscle imbalance

Muscle imbalance is sub-optimal lengthening or shortening of the muscle around a joint, which causes improper movement. Distortion of the kinetic chain (e.g., an improper length-tension relationship or force-couple relationship) can lead to a muscle imbalance. When there is a muscle imbalance, instead of muscles working together synergistically as they are designed to, one muscle or muscle group works harder than it should, resulting in tightness (overactive muscle), while another muscle or muscle group works less than it should, resulting in weakness (underactive muscle). This cycle can lead to postural distortion and injury.

Muscle distortions are caused by:
- Repetitive motions
- Emotional stress/heightened emotional states
- Stress on the body that affects the kinetic chain
- Cumulative trauma
- Poor nervous system and muscle communication/coordination
- Lack of strength
- Improper physical training

## Altered reciprocal inhibition

Altered reciprocal inhibition refers to an overactive or tight agonist muscle that stifles the proper function of its partner antagonist muscle—as with a tight hip flexor reciprocally inhibiting its antagonist muscle, the hip extensor.

Synergistic dominance occurs when synergist muscles overcompensate for a weak prime mover muscle. This process is the body's backup system, allowing the muscles adjacent to the prime mover to pick up the slack when it is not functioning optimally. Synergistic dominance and altered reciprocal inhibition result in muscle imbalances that affect the kinetic chain.

Arthrokinetic dysfunction refers to alterations to the kinetic chain that change the way joints work. It can also lead to muscle imbalances and other postural distortions.

## Neuromuscular efficiency

Neuromuscular efficiency refers to the body's ability to communicate correct movements properly in response to various stimuli to the nervous system and the muscular system. The result of neuromuscular efficiency is a full, stable kinetic chain

Muscle spindles and Golgi tendon organs, key sensory organs that affect neuromuscular control and efficiency, react to changes in the muscles and have protective mechanisms that react to extreme movement. Muscle spindles detect changes in the length of a muscle and also how quickly the muscle stretches. Golgi tendon organs can sense tension alterations in a muscle and how quickly this tension changes.

Flexibility training challenges these organs in a positive way, increasing neuromuscular efficiency. Autogenic inhibition is an automatic response from the receptors that tells the body to relax the muscle and allow it to stretch. It occurs after a body part receives sufficient stimulation (e.g., a 30-second stretch).

# Program Design and Implementation

In the past, health and fitness professionals worked in a less-systematic manner with clients, merely giving clients exercises and tasks that had worked in the past for the trainer or the trainer's other clients. The program was developed by NASM to tailor fitness regimens for specific clients, factoring in special considerations (such as medical concerns and specific postural distortions or compensations) that might affect the training.

By including these considerations in the program design, following the OPT model, and prescribing the correct exercises (stabilization, strength, or power), the health and fitness professional can work with the client to develop the most efficient regimen, maximize gains, and minimize potential injury. NASM trainers use program design to monitor and tweak acute variables in the regimen, giving it a scientific basis.

## Elements of program design

According to NASM, program design refers to a systematic process for achieving clients' fitness goals. NASM refers to it as a purposeful system, which includes the following:
- OPT model—the foundation of all NASM training. OPT stands for Optimum Performance Training, consisting of a three-pronged approach. These three steps are 1) stability, 2) strength, and 3) power, and they must be applied in that order.
- Phases of training—within the OPT model there are further levels of training. A health and fitness professional must know the five phases for proper program design:
    o Phase 1—stabilization endurance training
    o Phase 2—strength endurance training
    o Phase 3—hypertrophy training
    o Phase 4—maximum strength training
    o Phase 5—power training
- Acute variables— essential program elements that determine how the body is stressed and influence how the body adapts.
- Application—how the acute variables are prescribed, including what exercises will be chosen, how they are to be performed, and how often they are performed.

## OPT method

The OPT method of program design gives a certified health and fitness professional a proven method of designing and tracking the activities and improvements of an individual client. Because specific templates clearly outline the program, trainers can follow parameters systematically instead of guessing what might work for a particular client.

Having this knowledge gives a CPT a distinct edge over other trainers because a CPT using the OPT method can design a program for nearly any client with any of a wide range of fitness goals, from losing weight to increasing athletic ability.

The OPT program design facilitates troubleshooting a fitness regimen by clearly defining the acute variables in the program, making it easy to alter the program for better results.

## Acute variables

An acute variable is an important aspect of exercise training that can be changed to fit a particular client's needs.

NASM details several acute variables:
- Number of repetitions—a single complete movement
- Number of sets—a single round of exercises
- Intensity of training—how hard a person exerts him- or herself during the performance of an exercise compared to their maximum effort level
- Tempo of training—how quickly repetitions are performed
- Length of rest time—downtime between sets of exercise
- Volume of training—the amount of work (training) performed over an extended time
- Frequency of training—how often a client is training
- Duration of training—how long a given training session lasts, and also how long a client stays in one phase of training
- Types of exercises—the specific exercises being chosen for the client

## NASM program design continuum

NASM's program design continuum gives some general guidelines on how to set some of the acute variables involved with fitness training.

For the muscular endurance/stabilization level, the continuum recommends that the client perform one to three sets of each exercise for 12 to 25 repetitions. The intensity level is from 50 to 70 percent of the client's one-repetition maximum percent, and rest should not exceed 90 seconds between sets.

For the hypertrophy level, the continuum recommends that the client perform three to five sets of each exercise for 6 to 12 repetitions. The intensity level is from 75 to 85 percent of the client's one-repetition maximum percent, and rest should not exceed 60 seconds between sets.

For the maximal strength level, the continuum recommends that the client perform four to six sets of each exercise for 1 to 5 repetitions. The intensity level is from 85 to 100 percent of the client's one-repetition maximum percent, and the client rest 3-5 minutes between sets.

For the power level, the continuum recommends that the client perform three to six sets of each exercise for 1 to 10 repetitions. The intensity level is from 30 to 45 percent of the client's one-repetition maximum percent, and the client rest 3-5 minutes between sets.

| Phase | Repetitions | Sets | Intensity Level | Rest |
|---|---|---|---|---|
| **Muscular endurance/stabilization** | 12–20 | 1–3 | 50–70% of 1RM | 0–90 s |
| **Hypertrophy** | 6–12 | 3–5 | 75–85% of 1RM | 0–60 s |
| **Maximal strength** | 1–5 | 4–6 | 85–100% of 1RM | 3–5 min |
| **Power** | 1–10 | 3–6 | 30–45% of 1RM | 3–5 min |

## Acute variable: Repetitions

A repetition is the completion of one motion of a given exercise. It is called a repetition because it is repeated several times in a row to perform a complete set in an exercise routine. This usually entails using a muscle or group of muscles to contract and retract.

The number of repetitions is an important acute variable because it can be tailored to a client's ability level and his or her ultimate fitness goals. More repetitions at a lower weight result in increased muscle endurance, while fewer repetitions at a higher weight can lead to increased muscle mass (hypertrophy) and the ability to move faster with more-explosive power.

Trainers can use the repetition continuum guidelines to determine the appropriate number of repetitions to prescribe. While it is best for a client to start with more repetitions at a lower weight and increase to power-building (fewer repetitions at a high weight), it is important to alternate high repetitions and low repetitions once the power level has been achieved to avoid injury.

### Ideal number of repetitions

NASM's repetition continuum gives general guidelines for the appropriate number of repetitions for each of the three main OPT levels: stabilization, strength, and power.

For stability exercises, a larger number of repetitions with a lighter weight load are recommended. Somewhere between twelve and 25 repetitions per set is the standard. The higher end of the spectrum leads to gains in muscle endurance.

For strength exercises, a moderate number of repetitions with a moderate weight load are recommended. Somewhere between one and twelve repetitions per set is the standard. The higher end of the spectrum leads to maximum muscle growth.

For power exercises, a lower number of repetitions with a higher weight load are recommended. Somewhere between one and ten repetitions per set is standard.

## Acute variable: number of sets

A set is a completion of one group of repetitions of a given exercise performed consecutively. Many other acute variables come into play when determining how many sets of one exercise a client should perform. These include the number of repetitions for the client's level of training and the total number of exercises the client will perform in a given workout.

There is a direct relationship between how many individual repetitions and how many sets should go together. As the number repetitions increase, the number of sets decrease, and vice versa. Exercise intensity is also a factor. For example, if a client is working with heavier weights, fewer repetitions with more sets will be used.

The number of sets also correlates to the client's particular fitness goals. When a client is working toward muscle endurance and increased muscle mass, fewer sets consisting of higher repetitions at a lower weight load are best. When a client is working toward strength and power gains, more sets consisting of fewer repetitions at a higher weight load are best.

## Recommended number of sets

The number of sets directly correlates with the number of repetitions and the intensity of the exercise, which often translates into how much weight, is used. The number of sets corresponds with the specific fitness gains a client is working toward.

To increase stability and muscle endurance, NASM recommends up to three high repetition sets (12 to 25) with light weights.

To increase muscle mass, NASM recommends three or four medium repetition sets (8 to 12) with moderately heavy weight

To increase strength, NASM recommends four to six low repetition (up to five) with maximum weight.

To increase power, NASM recommends three to six low repetition sets (up to 10) with weights that weigh 10% of the client's weight.

## Acute variable: training intensity

One way to alter a fitness regimen is by changing the level of intensity at which a workout, or its individual component exercises, is performed. Intensity is a scale that reflects how hard an individual is working compared to how hard that particular client can work. Intensity can be subjective (e.g., talk test, perceived exertion), or objective (e.g., % of 1 rep max, oxygen consumption). Intensity can be measured by the amount of weight lifted and also by how much oxygen the individual is consuming (cardiorespiratory intensity).

The intensity of the work must be balanced with other acute variables, namely the number of repetitions and the number of sets of an exercise. These two variables will be programmed according to the client's capabilities and goals, and then intensity will be factored in according to the intensity continuum.

Other acute variables can affect the level of intensity. For example, taking little rest between exercises makes the subsequent exercises more intense.

## Recommended intensity

The intensity of the exercise, number of repetitions, and number of sets are directly related, and correlate with the specific fitness gains a client is working toward. The following describes NASM's intensity continuum:

- To increase stability and muscle endurance, NASM recommends working at from 40 to 70 percent of the client's maximum weight capability, or one-repetition maximum.
- To increase muscle mass, NASM recommends working at from 71 to 85 percent of the client's maximum weight capability.
- To increase strength, NASM recommends working at from 86 to 100 percent of the client's maximum weight capability.
- To increase power, NASM recommends working at less than 50 percent of the client's maximum weight capability or just one-tenth of total body weight if using medicine balls.

## Acute variable: repetition tempo

Tempo refers to how fast one exercise is performed in a set, which can be changed to meet the capabilities and goals of a particular client. NASM uses its repetition tempo spectrum as a general guideline for how fast exercises should be performed for the three levels of the OPT model.

For stabilization-level exercises, the tempo should remain slow and controlled. This increases stability and endurance while allowing the trainer to observe for postural distortions or compensations. The slower tempo also gives added stimuli to the nervous system and the connective tissue to prepare for more-advanced motion later.

For strength-level exercises, the tempo should be somewhere in the middle.

For power-level exercises, the tempo should be as quick as can be managed while keeping all muscles under control.

## Acute variable: rest time

Rest time refers to the amount of downtime taken between sets of exercise during a training session. Rest time can affect the energy the body uses during the workout and can be calibrated to meet the capability and goals of a particular client.

To achieve maximum power, for example, it may be necessary to take an extended rest time between sets or exercises to give the body a chance to recover. For muscle building, however, shorter rest times (no more than a minute and a half) are advisable.

Stability-level exercises use oxygen and glucose energy stores.

Strength-level exercises use adenosine triphosphate/creatine phosphate (ATP/CP) and glucose energy stores.

Power-level exercises use ATP/CP energy stores.

### Recommended rest period

NASM has a rest interval continuum that details general guidelines for each main level of the OPT model. Rest time gives the body a chance to recover and restore the energy source needed to continue.

Stability-level exercises should be performed with a relatively short rest period between exercises and sets, which may be anywhere from no time to a minute and a half.

Strength-level exercises can be performed in relatively quick succession (less than a minute of rest) or with a longer rest (up to five minutes).

Power-level exercises should have a lengthier rest period—anywhere from three to five minutes.

Keep in mind that within 30 seconds after a set, adenosine triphosphate/creatine phosphate (ATP/CP) levels will be back up to about half capacity; at a minute, there is almost 90-percent recovery. It can take up to three minutes for these levels to be back at full capacity.

**Acute variable: training volume**

Training volume refers the amount of physical activity performed within a defined time frame. It is important for a health and fitness professional to plot this component out in advance when designing a program to ensure accurate monitoring and to avoid overtraining the client.

The amount a client can train depends on many factors, some unrelated to fitness goals or limitations. Lifestyle considerations such as work, family obligations, age, and overall current fitness level will in part dictate how much the client can train. The phase of training will also play a role in determining training volume.

Training volume and the acute variable of intensity are closely related; when there is a higher level of one variable, there must be a lower level of the other and vice versa. A person cannot train hard continually because of the risk of overtraining.

Recommended training volume
NASM has a volume continuum that details general guidelines for each main level of the OPT model. The training volume used will give the desired cellular changes and nervous system changes sought for on each level. Volume is determined by multiplying the number of sets by the number of repetitions.

Stability-level exercises should be performed with a large number of sets and a high number of repetitions. The total number of exercises, determined by multiplying the number of sets with the number of repetitions, should be between 36 and 75.

Strength-level exercises should be more moderate, with the total number of exercises to be determined by multiplying the number of sets by the number of repetitions—between 8 and 36.

Power-level exercises should be at a lower volume, with between 6 and 30 total exercises.

**Acute variable: training frequency**

Training frequency refers to how much training is done within a given period.

The amount a client can train depends on many factors, some unrelated to fitness goals or limitations. Lifestyle considerations such as work, family obligations, age, and overall current fitness level will in part dictate how much the client can train. The phase of training will also play a role in determining training volume.

The underlying goals of the client will be the primary factor in determining training frequency. For general fitness goals, a total-body workout two to three times a week may be adequate. If the client is a competitive athlete, however, body-part-specific workouts may occur up to six times a week.

Training volume adaptations
The manner in which training volume and intensity levels are paired can have a great effect on the end results of training.

Benefits of a high-volume, low-intensity workout schedule can include:
- An increase in the amount of muscle cross-section
- An increase in base metabolism

- An increase in lean muscle tissue
- Better blood results
- Lower overall body fat

Benefits of a low-volume, high-intensity workout schedule can include:
- An increase in how much force a person can deliver
- An increase in nervous-system communication
- An increase in muscle response time

## Acute variable: training duration

Training duration can refer to two separate things when it comes to fitness training:
1. Specific to the NASM system of training, training duration can refer to how long a client stays in one of the OPT phases. Depending on factors such as beginning fitness level, whether injuries occurred, client motivation, and ultimate goals, a client will usually work in a given phase for a month to two months.
2. Training duration can also refer to the actual amount of time from the beginning to the end of a workout session. This is important because training sessions that are too long (exceeding an hour or hour and a half) can result in fatigue and body changes that will negatively impact training.

## Acute variable: choosing exercises

Choosing exercises in a training routine may seem simple, but it can have a profound effect on the outcome of the program. For example, the choice of exercises will be drastically different for a client who wants to exercise to improve his or her overall health versus those chosen for a person who is a competitive bodybuilder or Olympic athlete.

There are three basic categories of exercises (single-joint, multijoint, and total-body), which NASM sorts based on how much of the body is used to perform the exercise. A fitness assessment must be completed, the client's physical history taken, and goals identified to configure this part of the program design for the client. Then the trainer can determine where on the OPT chart to begin the client and which exercises to select from that phase/level of training.

## Typical program design

In a typical program design, in which the goal is overall fitness, the following will give a good idea of how to balance several acute variables:
The overall routine should last from about forty-five minutes to an hour, including a warm-up and a cool-down of ten minutes each. Up to seven exercises should be chosen for the client. Three sets of each of the exercises are done, with a dozen repetitions performed for each set. The tempo is moderate, with up to four seconds to perform the main motion, two beats to release, and only one beat before starting the next repetition.

## Principle of specificity

The principle of specificity states that the body will specifically adapt to particular stresses it is exposed to. This means that the exercises selected should be picked with an eye toward the client's specific goals. For example, if the client is an Olympic bodybuilder, upper-body and arm strength will be the focus for that client.

NASM's exercise selection continuum gives some general guidelines as to what types of exercises work best for different training levels. For the stability level, any of the three main types of exercise (single-joint, multijoint, and total-body) should be performed in a slow, deliberate manner in an unstable environment. For the strength level of the OPT model, the same three exercises can be used. For the power level of the OPT model, total-body exercises are ideal, performed in a fast, forceful motion.

## Examples of exercises

For stability and strength, any of the three general types of exercises are effective. For power, total-body exercises work best.

Exercises appropriate for the stability level include stability-ball exercises such as the crunch, chest press, or hamstring roll as well as one-leg balance exercises, such as any of NASM's step-up exercises.

Exercises appropriate for the strength level include squats, presses, and cable rowing. Exercises appropriate for the power level include medicine-ball exercises, such as overhead throws or presses. Jumps are also effective; tuck jumps and box jumps are ideal.

Keep the progression continuum in mind as a client progresses: the floor, then a sports beam, and then a foam roll or balance disc is an ideal progression of instability to help develop neuromuscular coordination.

## Training plans

Periodization is the basic concept behind NASM's approach to program design. It is a systematic way of changing up a client's training routine, so his or her body does not plateau but continues to make progress toward fitness goals while avoiding overtraining and overuse injuries.

A training plan is a comprehensive written plan that considers all acute variables, the client's assessments, and the client's goals. It views the overall approach to training from long- and short-term perspectives.

An annual plan, as the name implies, details the training plan for an entire year, giving the trainer a good overview while giving the client a visual tool to help him or her see exactly how the OPT plan will be implemented.

## Periodization

Periodization of a training regimen is highly effective because it prevents the negative impact of general adaptation syndrome. Specifically, it assures that the same routine is not employed to the point that the body learns to cope, thus reducing ongoing training gains.

Periodization can improve fitness gains while reducing injuries from repetitive actions. It also gives variations training type, volume, and frequency, opening the door for more interesting and thoughtful programs that keep the client motivated and involved.

Even though periodization has been shown to work well, many health and fitness professionals do not use it in their training programs. This means that the training programs they use are repetitive, which can result in overuse injuries and a plateau effect in training. These results, in turn, can lead to low client motivation and cessation of regular training.

Scientific research

Many scientific studies support the idea that an integrated training program, such as the one adopted by NASM, is the ideal way to train clients to maximize gains while minimizing injuries and other barriers.

B. Tan found that changing the variables in a men's resistance-training program encouraged ongoing adaptations while minimizing injury.

W.J. Kraemer and N.A. Ratamess determined that well-thought-out strength-training programs using periodized training methods not only increased physiological benefits but also showed better performance improvements when compared to nonperiodized regimens.

M.R. Rhea discovered that daily tweaking of a training program's variables resulted in better improvements than changing them monthly. This researcher also found that ongoing increases in training volume, coinciding with decreases in intensity, were the best method for increasing the endurance of muscles.

Periodization approach and OPT system

For each period of training, which can also be referred to as a phase, there is a corresponding OPT level. The period model includes a preliminary phase (or anatomic adaptation), a muscle-building phase (or hypertrophy adaptation), a power-building phase (or a maximum-strength adaptation), and an explosive-power phase.

The levels of OPT are stabilization, strength, and power.
NASM likens the OPT model to a staircase. Each of the OPT levels is a series of steps, with each step representing a specific phase of that level. Periodization consists of taking the client not just straight up the staircase, but up and down in a particular design according to his or her specific goals and capabilities. This is done to avoid general adaptation syndrome, in which not varying from the same routine leads to a plateau effect.

## Phases of training

The stabilization level of the OPT model has one phase of training: stabilization endurance, which focuses on stabilizing the kinetic chain, core musculature, and connective tissue and increasing cardiorespiratory and muscular endurance.

The strength level of the OPT model has three phases: strength endurance, hypertrophy, and maximal strength. During the strength-endurance phase, the client's strength and stabilization endurance will improve, and they may experience hypertrophy. The hypertrophy phase focuses on building muscle mass. The maximal-strength phase focuses on increasing the load placed on the body's tissues. Per NASM, the strength period has several goals. The first goal of the strength period is to improve the core's ability to stabilize the pelvis and spine when they are exposed to heavy weight. To promote weight loss or hypertrophy, the strength phase aims to increase the load-bearing capabilities of muscles, tendons, ligaments, and joints by increasing the training volume and increasing metabolic demand. To promote maximal strength, the body increases motor unit recruitment, frequency of motor unit recruitment, and motor unit synchronization. .

The power level of the OPT model has one phase: the power phase, in which the main goal is to increase the speed at which maximum force can be produced.

### Stabilization level

Stabilization training is the cornerstone of the OPT model; without stabilizing the kinetic chain and working through body compensations and postural distortions, more-advanced training will be reduced in effectiveness and may result in injury.

Stabilization specifically seeks to correct muscle imbalances, repair kinetic-chain distortions, increase cardiorespiratory and muscular endurance, and ease connective tissues (such as ligaments and tendons) into increased activity.

Stabilization training focuses on increasing proprioceptive demand. Performing low-intensity exercises for high repetitions in a controlled, unstable environment increases proprioceptive demand. This is particularly useful for out-of-shape, overweight, or older clients. The level of instability is increased to progress the client.

The stabilization level has one phase: stabilization endurance.

### Strength level

Strength training is an important part of the OPT model, helping clients progress and achieve a variety of different fitness goals. It follows stabilization training, which helps prepare the body for more-advanced strength training.

The main goal of the strength level is to accomplish several adaptations in strength, including increased endurance, building muscle mass, and increasing how much weight or stress the body can handle. This is accomplished through increasing the number of exercises, performing more repetitions, adding sets, and increasing intensity.

The strength level is essential for anyone who wants to increase metabolism, promote higher bone density, and build muscle mass.

The strength level has three different phases of training. These are called strength endurance, hypertrophy, and maximal strength.

### Power level

Power or reactive training is not a necessary component of NASM's OPT model and is reserved for athletes or clients with advanced fitness goals. Power training focuses on increasing a client's ability to produce explosive but controlled movement at a high rate of speed (velocity).

The CPT increases the amount of weight client must move, the speed at which this load is moved, or both to progress a client through the power phase of training. Light and heavy loads must be used at high rates of speed to maximize power training. This helps the body increase its level of neuromuscular efficiency, or the method in which the brain communicates with the nervous system and muscles.

The power level has one phase of training: the power phase.

## Phases

### Phase 1: Stabilization endurance phase

The first phase of training in the OPT model is stabilization endurance training. This is the ideal phase for clients who are new to training, overweight, or elderly. While beneficial for all clients, those who wish to increase their base fitness level and lose body fat will gain the most benefit from this phase.

The primary goals of this phase are increasing stability, muscular endurance, neuromuscular efficiency of the core musculature and improving intermuscular and intramuscular coordination. It is important that training occur in a slow, systematic manner to prepare connective tissue, which has fewer blood vessels and less vascular support than muscle tissue and thus adapts more slowly to increased activity.

Accomplishing these goals reduces injury risk, maintains client interest, and sustains motivation.

### Phase 2: Strength endurance phase

The second phase of training is strength endurance training. This phase eases the client into strength training from the stabilization phase of training, continuing to work on core stabilization while increasing endurance and beginning to build muscle mass. This is accomplished by performing a superset consisting of a stable exercise with a similar one that maximizes proprioceptive instability (controlled instability). This results in a high volume of work, which helps the client progress through the phase.

For a client who is seeking to improve base-level fitness or reduce body fat, acute variables can be tweaked when phase 1 has been completed. If the client seeks to improve lean muscle mass and overall athletic ability, repetitions should be reduced, and intensity should be increased, over a four-week period.

### Phase 3: Hypertrophy phase

The third phase of training is the hypertrophy phase. This phase focuses on increasing muscle mass, accomplished by performing a high volume of work with short rest intervals. This encourages the body to compensate through the growth of additional muscle tissue.

The hypertrophy phase is initiated after the client has successfully progressed through phases 1 and 2. To increase lean muscle mass and overall athletic ability, increase intensity and training volume while reducing repetitions over a period of four weeks. Upon completion of phase 3, the client should be progressed (to phases 4 and 5) or cycled backward through phases 1 and 2. This creates the periodization scheme that helps reduce injury and maximize gains.

### Phase 4: Maximal strength training phase

The fourth phase of training is the maximal strength phase, which increases the ability of the body to cope with a higher weight or workload. This is done by focusing on the neuromuscular system—improving communication between the brain, nervous system, and muscles—and how fast the muscles can respond to stimulus. This phase can also act as an excellent foundation for power training.

The focus of the phase should be on placing an increased load on the body to achieve these goals. The client should remain in this phase of training for approximately four weeks before progressing to phase 5 or cycling back to stabilization exercises (phases 1 and 2).

Phase 5: Power training phase
The fifth phase of training is the power training phase. The main focus of power training is to increase the rate of force production by pairing a strength exercise with a power exercise. Basic strength exercises are performed at the upper range of intensity (from 80 to 100 percent), while speed drills are performed as quickly as can be managed while maintaining proper form, but at a lower intensity level (from 30 to 50 percent). This creates two combinations that increase power: 1) high weight with intense, powerful movement, and 2) low weight with rapid movement.

Progression by tweaking acute variables should only be performed if the client has successfully progressed through the other levels of OPT.

A client should remain in this phase for approximately four weeks and then return to stabilization exercises (phases 1 and 2).

Time frame
The stabilization level of the OPT model consists of one phase: strength endurance. This phase of training should be performed for approximately four weeks to allow for an increase in stabilization of the core musculature as well as muscular endurance.

The strength level of the OPT model consists of three phases: strength endurance, hypertrophy, and maximal strength. Each of these phases should be performed for four weeks.

The power level of the OPT model consists of one phase: power. This phase is optional, as only a client attempting to increase explosive power would benefit from power level training. For clients who are bodybuilders, athletes, or have specific power goals, this phase should be progressed through for approximately four weeks before returning to earlier phases of training.

**Fitness goals**

Reducing overall percentage of body fat
To reduce the overall percentage of body fat, a client must use more energy than he or she consumes. The best way to accomplish this is through a two-pronged approach: increasing calorie-burning muscle while increasing calorie expenditure through cardiorespiratory exercise.

Because the client does not wish to maximize muscle mass or build explosive power, he or she will only need to be progressed through the first two phases of training: stabilization and strength endurance. The client should spend approximately four weeks in each phase, and then go back and forth between the two phases.

A sample plan could include working out three days a week for a month in phase one, and then three days a week for a month in the second phase. These workouts include cardiorespiratory exercises and weight training, with simple flexibility exercises done daily, if desired.

Increasing the amount of lean muscle mass
To increase lean muscle mass, a client must take in more energy than he or she burns to gain weight in the form of muscle. The best way to accomplish this is by ingesting more high-quality proteins

while increasing the overall volume of training, which will help the body create additional muscle fibers.

Because hypertrophy is the main goal, the client will need to be progressed through three, and possibly four phases of the OPT model: stabilization endurance, strength endurance, hypertrophy, and maximal strength.

The client begins by spending approximately four weeks in phase 1 to prepare for the more-advanced training. After four weeks in phase 2, the client can progress to a month in phase 3. Depending on the client's goals, he or she can revert to phase 2 and cycle through phases 2 and 3 or work up to phase 4 and then cycle between phases 2, 3, and 4.

Improving overall base level of fitness

Improving base level fitness requires making strides in several different areas, including endurance, strength, and power. This will require the client to be systematically taken through four phases of the OPT model, including stabilization endurance, strength endurance, maximal strength, and power: The first two phases and the final phase are the most vital for this particular goal. Because the client is not seeking to build maximum muscle mass, phase 4 (hypertrophy) can be bypassed.

The client should be taken through each of these phases (1, 2, 3, and 5) for approximately four weeks each, after which phases 1, 2, and 5 should be systematically alternated in a manner known as undulating periodization. In undulating periodization, the three phases are alternated weekly instead of monthly.

# OPT Model

To address the wide spectrum of fitness needs the modern training client demands, NASM uses an integrated, progressive system that incorporates many different training techniques, such as:

- Cardiovascular training
- Stretching
- Coordination
- Strength or resistance training
- Balance

These methods are introduced in a progressive manner, using the OPT method, which takes a client through levels of training commensurate with ability and improved performance.

By using a wide variety of training techniques introduced on a gradient, a client will experience physiological benefits (e.g., higher bone density and enhanced lung function), physical benefits (e.g., weight loss), and increased ability to perform (e.g., enhanced flexibility and increased strength).

The OPT model consists of three distinct levels: stabilization, strength, and power. The client should complete a phase before progressing to the next phase.

1. The stabilization phase assesses and addresses specific weaknesses in a client and improves those areas first. This stage improves neuromuscular communication and lays a foundation for more-intense training. It includes phase 1: stabilization endurance training.
2. The Strength phase strengthens prime movers and sustains the stabilization endurance that the first phase developed. It includes three phases: strength endurance training (Phase 2), hypertrophy training (Phase 3), and maximal strength training (Phase 4). Strength endurance training increases strength and endurance. Hypertrophy training increases the size of muscle fibers. Maximum strength training increases the body's ability to handle heavy loads.
3. The Power phase increases the body's ability to create maximum force as rapidly as possible. It includes phase 5: power training.

## Stabilization level

The stabilization level is the first phase of the OPT model. The primary goals of this phase are:

- Enhanced muscle suppleness and flexibility
- Increased joint balance
- Increased muscle endurance
- Improved posture
- Improved neurological/muscular coordination

The training strategies employed for this phase of stabilization training include:

- Using light weights at a high number of repetitions
- Using increased proprioception (such as with a balance ball) to challenge the nervous system and increase balance and neuromuscular efficiency
- Using flexibility training to address problem areas

Because each level of NASM's Optimum Performance Training (OPT) model has different overall goals, the trainer should select exercises that promote the goals of the phase.
Some ideal exercises for the stabilization level include:

- Floor prone cobra—performed by lying on the flat on the floor on the stomach with the arms down by the sides. Keeping the core muscles firm, lift the torso off the ground for two seconds.
- Quadruped arm/opposite leg raise—performed by lying on the stomach flat on the floor with the arms over the head. Keeping the core muscles firm, raise the opposite leg and arm off the ground, hold for 2 to 4 seconds, and then switch sides.
- Prone iso-abs (also known as a plank)—performed by resting on the forearms (with the elbows at ninety degrees) while holding the body in a rigid position using the core muscles.

## Strength level

The strength level includes phases 2, 3, and 4 of the OPT model. The primary goals of *phase 2* (strength endurance training) include:

- Increased lean muscle
- Increased joint balance
- Increased endurance
- Enhanced strength in prime mover muscles

The training strategies employed for this phase of strength training include:

- Using midrange weights and a comparable number of repetitions
- Using flexibility training for activity
- Using superset training (a dual combination of exercises with no rest time in between)

The primary goal of *phase 3* (hypertrophy) is:

- Increasing muscle size

The training strategies employed for this phase of strength training include:

- Using flexibility training for activity
- Many sets of heavy weights for a midlevel number of repetitions (fewer than 10)

Phase 4 is an optional phase of the OPT model. The primary goals of *phase 4* (maximum strength training) are as follows:

- Increase top level of force
- Enhance neuromuscular efficiency

The training strategies employed for this phase of strength training include:

- Using flexibility training for activity
- Heavy weights at a low number of repetitions (fewer than 5)

## Power level

The power level is the fifth phase of the OPT model. This level is optional and requires successful completion of the stabilization and strength levels.

The primary goals of *phase 5* (power training) are as follows:
- Increased strength of prime mover muscles
- Increased strength at higher speeds
- Increased ability to produce higher levels of force
- Enhanced neuromuscular efficiency

The training strategies employed for this phase of strength training include:
- Using flexibility training for high levels of activity and movement
- Performing repetitions as quickly as safely viable
- Using superset training (a dual combination of exercises with no down time in between)

## Implementation

After conducting a full range of fitness assessments, the trainer will design an effective fitness program using the OPT program template. The NASM Program Template is a special form that helps the trainer design an integrated program that improves all functional abilities (e.g., flexibility, stability, strength, balance, speed, agility, and quickness). The template contains sections to prescribe exercises in the primary training modalities (e.g., warm-up, core/balance/plyometric training, speed, agility and quickness (SAQ) drills, resistance training, and cool-down). The template also has sections for sets, repetitions, tempo, and rest. Each training session should follow the OPT template to ensure adequate progression.

# Flexibility Training

Flexibility training prevents various neuromuscular injuries and corrects movement inefficiencies by including exercises and activities that improve a person's ability to move efficiently. Efficient movement is especially important in a training program to increase joint and muscle mobility for physical activity and to counteract postural imbalances caused by over- and underactive muscles that have lost their flexibility, which inhibits the proper movement of surrounding muscles and muscle groups.

### Flexibility Training Benefits

| Increase | Decrease | Maintain |
|---|---|---|
| Joint range of motion<br>Neuromuscular efficiency<br>Muscle function<br>Flexibility of musculotendinous junction | Excessive tension<br>Joint stress | Normal muscle length |

## Important terms

**Flexibility** refers to the level to which a person can extend the muscles and soft tissues, allowing the joint a full range of motion.

**Dynamic functional flexibility** refers to the cycle of flexibility that comes from extensibility, which allows for a wide range of motion of a joint, coupled with optimal communication between the nervous system and the muscles.

**Extensibility** refers to the general ability of muscles and soft body tissues to stretch or be elastic.

**Dynamic range of motion** refers to the body's ability to move freely in all planes of movement coupled with the ability of the nervous system to handle and control these movements in a safe manner.

Flexibility training seeks to improve all of these different areas to increase flexibility and extensibility to accommodate a better range of motion. This improves posture and blood flow and can decrease the incidence of injury.

## Multiplanar flexibility

Multiplanar flexibility refers to the flexibility that allows the joints, muscles, and soft tissue to extend into all planes of motion.

For the biceps femoris, multiplanar flexibility refers to:
- Frontal plane—flexibility needed for optimal adduction of the hip
- Transverse plane—flexibility needed for optimal rotation of the knee and hip
- Sagittal plane—flexibility needed for optimal hip flexion and extension of the knee

For the gastrocnemius, multiplanar flexibility refers to:
- Frontal plane—flexibility needed for optimal calcaneus inversion
- Transverse plane—flexibility needed for optimal rotation of the femur
- Sagittal plane—flexibility needed for optimal ankle dorsiflexion

For the latissimus dorsi, multiplanar flexibility refers to:
- Frontal plane—flexibility needed for optimal shoulder abduction
- Transverse plane—flexibility needed for optimal rotation of the humerus
- Sagittal plane—flexibility needed for optimal shoulder flexion

## Scientific approach

Flexibility training, one important component of a balanced, integrated training program, has many benefits:
- Improving extensibility of muscles and soft tissue
- Alleviating stress on joints
- Improving overall range of motion
- Lowering muscle tension
- Correcting or maintaining proper muscle lengths

Pattern overload is damage resulting from repeatedly doing the same activity, repeatedly stressing the muscles and joints. The activities associated with daily living and repeatedly using the same physical training routine cause pattern overload. Incorporating flexibility training into an integrated training program can help introduce varied forms of movement into a person's routine and combat muscle imbalances that may result from pattern overload.

## Flexibility continuum

Much like the different stages in the OPT model; flexibility training should likewise take a progressive approach. By introducing different types of flexibility training over time, a CPT can help a client maximize results, minimize injuries, and avoid potential pitfalls of repetitive training routines.

The following are the three stages of flexibility training:
1. Corrective flexibility addresses basic problems such as joint range of motion, muscle imbalance, joint mobility issues, using self-myofascial release, and static stretching techniques.
2. Active flexibility improves extensibility of soft tissues and neuromuscular system communication through reciprocal inhibition, using stretches that work the muscles and joints through a range of motion. It employs self-myofascial release and active-isolated stretching.
3. Functional flexibility takes active flexibility to the next level, using stretching techniques that move through all planes of motion to simulate correct muscle use and stretching. It employs self-myofascial release and dynamic stretching.

## Self-myofascial release

Self-myofascial release refers to a system of stretching that targets the communication system between the nervous system and the body's fascia, or connective tissue. A foam roller applies light pressure to the muscle where there is an adhesion. The goal is to stimulate the Golgi tendon organs, induce autogenic inhibition, and allow the body to release the knot.

Self-myofascial release requires an application of pressure to the knot for at least 30 seconds, giving the Golgi tendon organs time to react to the pressure. Self-myofascial release is an element of all stages of flexibility training to help reprogram the soft tissue of the body.

### Latissimus dorsi and piriformis muscles
To perform self-myofascial release on the latissimus dorsi, the client lies on his or her side on the floor. The foam roll rests along the upper torso close to the armpit, with the lower arm raised parallel to the ground. The client should gently roll on the foam roll to find a knot on the muscle, holding the position for at least 30 seconds until there is some sensation of release or relief.

To perform self-myofascial release on the piriformis, the client sits on the floor with knees bent. The client should cross one leg over the other, with the ankle resting on the top of the knee, and use one arm for balance. The client should place the foam roll under his rear end and lean toward the side with the leg that is up, finding a tender spot on the posterior hip area. The client gently rolls on the foam roll, holding the position for at least 30 seconds until there is some sensation of release or relief.

### Adductors, gastrocnemius, and soleus
The client should lie in a prone position, with the arms bent in front for support to perform self-myofascial release on the adductors. Have the client position one leg toward the side, with the foot parallel to the floor. Have the client place the foam roll under his or her extended leg near the groin area. The client should gently roll on the foam roll, find a tender spot, and hold the position for at least 30 seconds until there is some sensation of release or relief.

To perform self-myofascial release on the gastrocnemius and soleus, the client should begin by sitting down on the floor with the legs extended in front. The calves rest on the foam roll, with one leg on top of the other. The client should gently roll on the foam roll, find a tender spot, and hold the position for at least 30 seconds until there is some sensation of release or relief.

### Tensor fascia lata/iliotibial (TFL/IT) band
To perform self-myofascial release on the TFL/IT band, have the client lie on his or her side on the floor. The client can bend the lower arm underneath for support, with the torso elevated off the ground. Have the client place the foam roll underneath the lower leg above the knee but below the hip, and then cross the top leg over and in front of the other leg, so it is on the floor just in front of the knee. The client should gently roll on the foam roll, find a tender spot, and hold the position for at least 30 seconds until there is some sensation of release or relief.

## Static stretching

Static stretching is familiar to most people. A static stretch involves placing the muscle under steady tension for 20 to 30 seconds to encourage a release or stretch.

Static stretching works through autogenic inhibition, which automatically occurs when the Golgi tendon receptors and muscle spindles activate and trigger a relaxation reflex in the muscles. Performing one or two sets of a stretch lasting at least 20 seconds gives the body's receptors time to react to the stress of the stretch.

Static stretching decreases muscle-spindle reactions and lessens the chance of injury caused by a muscle-spindle protective reaction on chronically tight muscles before activity.

### Psoas and the gastrocnemius

To perform a static stretch for the psoas, the client stands in a forward lunge. The back leg should then rotate inward. Have the client raise the arm on the same side as the back leg and rotate the hip in the direction of that arm, pressing forward to give the hips a stretch. The client holds the stretch for at least 20 seconds; repeat on the other side.

To perform a static stretch for the gastrocnemius, the client lunges with both hands on a wall and arms slightly bent for support. Have the client lean forward to stretch the back leg, making sure to keep the feet pointing forward and not allowing them to roll in on the arches. Hold this stretch for at least 20 seconds, and repeat on the other side.

### Hip flexors

The client performs a kneeling hip-flexor stretch on a small floor mat. Have the client kneel on the mat with one knee with the other knee bent in front of the body. The kneeling position is optimal for stretching the rectus femoris muscle because it crosses both target areas (the knee and the hip). The client raises the arm on the side of the bent knee straight into the air and then presses the hip forward toward the side of the raised arm. The client should feel the stretch on the front of the hip. Instruct the client to hold the stretch for at least 20 seconds; repeat on the other side.

### Latissimus dorsi

To perform the latissimus dorsi ball stretch, you will need a large stability ball. Place the ball on the floor, and have the client get on the floor next to it on his or her hands and knees. Have the client place one arm on the ball with the arm bent at a 90-degree angle. The thumb should be facing up. Pulling the core muscles in and bending the hips to rotate up, the client slowly rolls the ball away from the body by extending the arm straight. Instruct the client to hold the stretch for at least 20 seconds; repeat on the opposite side.

Should this stretch result in uncomfortable sensations in the shoulder, decrease the intensity by having the client place his or her palm down on the ball instead of having the thumb up in the air.

### Adductors

To perform a standing adductor stretch, have the client stand straight up with hands on hips and feet in a wide stance, well beyond shoulder-width distance apart (this is very important to get the best stretch). Have the client bend one knee and move the other leg back so it is approximately six inches behind the front foot. Be sure both feet are on the ground, pointing straight forward (the back leg will be bent at the ankle). Have the client slide sideways toward the bent leg to give the straight leg a flex in the upper interior groin area. Have the client hold this position for at least 20 seconds; repeat on the opposite side.

### Pectorals

To perform a static pectoral-wall stretch, find a stationary object for the client to lean against (a doorway works well). Have the client stand in a lunge position with arms placed at right angles out from the body and lean against the object. Be sure the shoulder-to-elbow area stays flat, and the shoulders stay pressed down during the stretch to maximize its effect. Have the client lean forward into the doorway until a stretch can be felt in the front shoulder muscles. Have the client hold the stretch for at least 20 seconds; repeat for a second set.

### Upper trapezius/scalene muscles

To perform the static upper trapezius/scalene stretch, the client begins in an upright, standing position with feet shoulder-width apart. Check the client's posture, and make sure the body is in optimal alignment. The client extends one arm out slightly away from the body and slightly behind the torso. Have the client gently tilt the head away from the extended arm, pressing the scapula on the side the arm is extended. Be sure the client keeps the shoulders pressed down to increase the effectiveness of the stretch, which will be felt behind the shoulder blade. Hold the stretch for at least 20 seconds, and repeat on the other side.

## Active-isolated stretching

Active-isolated stretching is designed to trigger reciprocal inhibition by actively moving a joint through its full range of motion. Agonist and synergist muscles are activated in these stretches.

These types of stretches are very effective as a warm-up for other training or sports activity. A set of five to ten, held for a minimal period (one or two seconds), helps warm up the body and prepare the muscles for activity.

Some examples of active-isolated stretching include:
- Active pectoral wall stretch
- Active upright adductor stretch
- Active kneeling quad stretch
- Active supine biceps femoris stretch

### Upper gastrocnemius
To perform the active upper-gastrocnemius stretch with pronation and supination, have the client stand facing a wall or other sturdy, flat surface. The client leans forward against the wall and raises one leg. The standing leg is stretched out straight behind. The raised leg should be bent at the knee. Keeping the back foot flat on the ground, rotate the bent leg open to the side, then closed across the other knee like a gate swinging open and closed. Have the client act in a fully controlled, quick manner (one to two seconds). The hip should be the source of the motion, not the leg or knee. Perform a set of ten to fifteen on each side.

### Biceps femoris
To perform the active supine biceps femoris stretch, have the client lie flat supine on the floor. One knee is raised so the thigh is perpendicular to the floor, and the leg is bent at a right angle. Have the client hold the back of the raised leg with the corresponding arm, and then quickly stretch the leg up, holding for one to two seconds. Make sure this is done in a completely controlled manner. To maximize the stretch, shift the hip on the stretching side inward a bit before extending the leg. Do a set of ten to fifteen on each side.

### Psoas
To perform the active standing psoas stretch, have the client stand in a forward lunge. The back leg should then be rotated inward. The client raises the arm on the same side as the back leg and rotates the hip in the direction of that arm, pressing forward to give the hips a stretch as he or she steps forward quickly, but in a controlled manner. Make sure the buttocks are tight when moving into the stretch to maximize effectiveness. Have the client hold the stretch in the hip for one to two seconds, and repeat on the other side. Do a set of ten to fifteen on each side.

### Hip flexors
To perform the active kneeling hip-flexor stretch, have the client kneel on the ground on a small mat. One knee should be down and the other steadying the body at a 90-degree angle in front of the torso. Raise the arm on the same side as the lower knee straight into the air and rotate the hip

inward. Have the client contract the gluteals on the side being stretched while rotating the hips backward. The client slowly leans forward until a stretch can be felt in the front hip, and then bends to the side and rotates the hip back. Have the client hold the stretch in the hip for one to two seconds, and repeat on the other side. Do a set of ten to fifteen on each side.

## Adductors and the latissimus dorsi

To perform an active standing adductor stretch, have the client stand straight up with hands on hips and feet in a wide stance; well beyond shoulder-width distance apart (this is very important to get the best stretch). Have the client bend one knee and move the other leg back so it is approximately six inches behind the front foot. Keep both feet on the ground and pointed straight forward (the back leg will be bent at the ankle). Have the client quickly (but in a controlled manner) slide sideways toward the bent leg to give the straight leg a flex in the upper interior groin area, holding the stretch for one to two seconds. Do a set of ten to fifteen on both sides.

## Latissimus dorsi

To perform the active latissimus-dorsi ball stretch, you will need a large stability ball. Place the ball on the floor, and have the client get on the floor next to it, on his or her hands and knees. The client places one arm on the ball, with the arm bent at an approximately 90-degree angle. The thumb should be facing up. Pulling the core muscles in and bending the hips to rotate up, the client quickly (but in a controlled manner) rolls the ball away from the body by extending the arm straight, holding the stretch for one to two seconds. A set of five to ten repetitions should be performed on each side.

The movement should emanate from the hips moving into an upward (posterior) tilt, not from the arms or hands.

## Pectorals

It is best to perform an active pectoral-wall stretch in an open doorway (although any stationary place a client can lean against as instructed will work just as well). Have the client stand in a lunge with both arms placed at right angles out from the body and lean into the door frame. Be sure the shoulder-to-elbow area stays flat, and the shoulders stay pressed down to maximize the effects of the stretch. The client leans forward in a quick but controlled manner into the doorway until a stretch can be felt in the front shoulder muscles. Have the client hold the stretch for one to two seconds. Have the client perform a set of five to ten repetitions of this stretch.

Make sure the client pulls back the shoulder blades when performing the stretch to maximize its effectiveness.

## Upper trapezius/scalene muscles

To perform the static upper-trapezius/scalene stretch, the client begins in an upright standing position with feet shoulder-width apart. Check the client's posture, and make sure the body is in optimal alignment. Have the client extend one arm out slightly away from the body and slightly behind the torso. The client gently tilts their head away from the extended arm, quickly but in a controlled manner, pressing the scapula on the side the arm is extended. Be sure the client keeps the shoulders pressed down to increase the effectiveness of the stretch. The stretch will be felt behind the shoulder blade. Hold the stretch for one to two seconds. A set of five to ten repetitions is performed on each side.

If the client's hand is numb or tingles, the tilt of the head should be decreased.

## Dynamic stretching

Dynamic stretching is a form of highly active stretching that maximizes the body's production of force and movement through the various planes of motion to increase the extensibility of a joint and its surrounding muscles through reciprocal inhibition. For a client in good physical condition (with good flexibility, strength, and balance) dynamic stretching can be a beneficial warm-up regimen. It is best used on clients that have progressed well through lower levels and phases of training and have no postural distortions.

Dynamic stretching can be performed in a rotation of anywhere from three to ten different stretches, with ten repetitions of each stretch. Some examples of dynamic stretching include tube walking and prisoner squats.

### Prisoner squat
To perform a prisoner squat, the client stands straight up with both arms bent outward at the shoulders, touching the ears. Feet should be shoulder-width apart, and toes should face straight forward. Have the client bend into a squat, careful to keep perfect form without postural distortions or compensations; make sure the toes stay forward and the knees stay in line with the toes. The client straightens the knees and hips, so he or she is standing straight up, rising all the way up onto the toes. Have the client return to the original position and repeat the action 10 times.

### Multiplanar lunge
To perform a multiplanar lunge, the client begins by standing straight up, hands on hips, with feet shoulder-width apart. Make sure the client has proper alignment and maintains it throughout the stretch, keeping toes straight forward through the lunges and keeping knees in line with the toes. The client steps forward into a deep lunge, bending the knees and hips to the floor. Repeat this action ten times on each side. The client switches to side lunges, doing ten repetitions on each side. Finally, the client performs turning lunges, stepping forward and twisting at the hips—ten repetitions on each side.

### Single-leg squat touchdown
To perform a single-leg squat touchdown, the client stands straight up, with hands on hips and one leg raised off the ground in front of the body approximately six inches off the ground. With the client maintaining proper form, have him or her squat down on the standing leg, reach across the body with the opposite arm, and touch the standing foot while maintaining balance. Have the client keep their balance by pulling in the core muscles and tightening the buttocks. Perform ten repetitions on each side. Make sure the knees are aligned with the toes to maximize the benefits of the stretch.

### Medicine ball chop and lift
To perform the medicine ball chop and lift dynamic stretch, you will need a medicine ball of a size and weight appropriate for the particular client. The client begins standing straight up with feet a bit more than shoulder-width apart. He or she turns one leg inward, so the toes point perpendicular to the other foot and bends the knee of that leg. Have the client bend over the straight leg with the medicine ball extending toward the floor. The client straightens all the way up while twisting the ball across the body and above the head. The client returns to the original position and repeats ten times for each side.

<u>Tube walking</u>

Tube walking is a dynamic stretching exercise performed using a length of rubber exercise tubing. To perform tube walking from side to side, begin by having the client place tubing around both legs just above the ankles. The client stands straight up with hands on hips and feet shoulder-width apart. The knees should be slightly bent and pliable, and the toes should face straight forward. Keeping good body alignment, the client pulls in the core muscles and then takes ten little steps to the side. Be sure the knees do not rotate inward and the toes point forward. Have the client repeat the exercise in the opposite direction.

## Specific stretching technique and strengthening exercises

If the client exhibits a feet-turning-out compensation when viewed from behind, it is likely that he or she has the following tight or overactive muscles:
- Biceps femoris
- Soleus
- Lateral gastrocnemius

Additionally, the following muscles are likely weak, or underactive:
- Popliteus
- Gracilis
- Soleus
- Medial gastrocnemius
- Medial hamstring

Performing self-myofascial release and static stretching on the biceps femoris and the gastrocnemius—and performing single-leg balance reaches as a strengthening exercise—can help alleviate these problems.

If the client exhibits a knees-moving-inward compensation when viewed from behind, it is likely that he or she has the following tight or overactive muscles:
- Biceps femoris
- Tensor fascia lata
- Adductor complex
- Vastus lateralis

Additionally, the following muscles are likely weak or underactive:
- Gluteus maximus
- Gluteus medius
- Vastus medialis oblique

Performing self-myofascial release and static stretching on the tensor fascia lata/iliotibial (TFL/IT) band and the adductors and performing side-by-side tube walking as a strengthening exercise can help alleviate these problems.

If the client exhibits an excessive forward lean in the lumbo-pelvic-hip (LPH) complex when viewed from the side, it is a sign of a muscle imbalance that must be addressed by the CPT. It is likely that he or she has the following tight or overactive muscles:
- Abdominals
- Hip flexors

- 112 -

- Soleus
- Gastrocnemius

Additionally, the following muscles are likely weak or underactive:
- Erector spinae
- Gluteus maximus
- Anterior tibialis

Performing self-myofascial release and static stretching on the hip flexor complex and the piriformis and performing ball squats as a strengthening exercise can help alleviate these problems.

If the client exhibits a low-back-arching compensation in the lumbo-pelvic-hip (LPH) complex when viewed from the side, it is a sign of a muscle imbalance that must be addressed by the CPT. It is likely that he or she has the following tight or overactive muscles:
- Hip flexor complex
- Latissimus dorsi
- Erector spinae

Additionally, the following muscles are likely weak or underactive:
- Core stabilizers
- Hamstrings
- Gluteus maximus

Performing self-myofascial release and static stretching on the erector spinae, hip flexors, and the hip flexor complex and performing ball squats as a strengthening exercise can help alleviate these problems.

If the client exhibits an arms-slumping shoulder compensation when viewed from the side, it is likely that he or she has the following tight or overactive muscles:
- Teres major
- Pectoralis major
- Latissimus dorsi

Additionally, the following muscles are likely weak or underactive:
- Rhomboids
- Mid trapezius
- Lower trapezius
- Rotator cuff

Performing self-myofascial release and static stretching on the thoracic spine and the latissimus dorsi and performing squat-to-row exercises for strengthening can help alleviate these problems.

If the client exhibits a scrunching-up-of-the-shoulders compensation when a pushing/pulling assessment is viewed from the side, it is likely that he or she has the following tight or overactive muscles:
- Levator scapulae
- Upper trapezius
- Upper scalene

Additionally, the following muscles are likely weak or underactive:
- Rhomboids
- Mid trapezius
- Lower trapezius
- Rotator cuff

Performing self-myofascial release and static stretching on the upper scalene and the upper trapezius and performing ball cobra exercises for strengthening can help alleviate these problems.

If the client compensates by jutting the head forward when a pushing/pulling assessment is viewed from the side, it is likely that he or she has the following tight or overactive muscles:
- Levator scapulae
- Upper trapezius
- Upper scalene

Additionally, the following muscles are likely weak or underactive:
- Deep cervical flexors

Performing self-myofascial release and static stretching on the upper scalene and the upper trapezius can help alleviate this problem. Keeping the head soft and in a neutral position when performing all activities can help strengthen the weak muscles.

# Cardiorespiratory Training

Integrated cardiorespiratory training is any activity that places positive, controlled stress on the cardiorespiratory system. Integrated cardiorespiratory training is any activity that places positive, controlled stress on the cardiorespiratory system. Because this is a very simple definition, nearly any activity can be considered integrated cardiorespiratory training. Walking, running, sports activity, and lifting weights are examples of integrated cardiorespiratory training. Activities also include exercises that require mechanical implements such as a treadmill (often a foundation of the gym experience).

Cardiorespiratory training can be used as a separate component of a workout when incorporated as a warm-up or cool-down and as the main part of the workout itself.

## Warm-up

A warm-up is a preparatory action taken that readies the body to perform physically. There are two types of warm-ups:
1. A general warm-up consists of low-level activity meant to get the body prepared for general activities. Running around a track or on a treadmill before weight training is considered a general warm-up
2. A specific warm-up focuses on the activity that follows and prepares the body for the specific stresses it will be placed under. Performing some isometric exercises such as push-ups before weight training is considered a specific warm-up.

### Benefits of a warm-up
A warm-up benefits a cardiorespiratory workout in the following ways:
1. Mentally prepares a person for physical activity.
2. Increases the temperature of the body and its tissues, which increases the body's metabolism in preparation for physical activity and makes soft tissue more amenable to stretching.
3. Increases the activity level of the heart and lungs, which prepares these organs for more activity, and increases blood flow and oxygen flow.

It has not been conclusively demonstrated that warm-ups prevent injury, but they have benefits and should be performed before an activity is undertaken. It has been demonstrated that warm-ups have the potential to reduce neuromuscular fatigue. When a person exercises, lactic acid builds up in the muscles and can accumulate over subsequent training sessions. Warm-ups may help inhibit the buildup of lactic acid in the muscles, thereby reducing neuromuscular fatigue.

### Length of warm-up
Ideally, a warm-up should last around ten minutes, although this time can be shortened or lengthened depending on the particular client and the activity that will be undertaken. The warm-up should include general and specific elements, engaging the body in cardiorespiratory activity and taxing some of the main muscle groups that the main workout will target.

For novice clients, the warm-up may last for a good portion of the entire workout for the first several sessions as they become accustomed to some of the exercises used for stabilization. After the client gets used to these introductory exercises and techniques, he or she can do them on his or her own before working with the trainer each session. This can usually commence after three sessions at the discretion of the health and fitness professional. This will leave more time to work on more-substantive fitness areas one-on-one.

<u>Warm-up routines</u>
A warm-up for an individual at the *stabilization level* includes the following:
- Five to ten minutes of cardiorespiratory training, such as running on a treadmill, pedaling on a stationary bike, or walking on a stair climber.
- Five to ten minutes of static stretching, focusing on the leg muscles.
- Five to ten minutes of self-myofascial release exercises.

A warm-up for an individual working at the *strength level* includes the following:
- Five to ten minutes of cardiorespiratory training, such as running on a treadmill, pedaling on a stationary bike, or walking on a stair climber.
- Five to ten minutes of active-isolated stretching, focusing on the leg muscles.
- Five to ten minutes of self-myofascial release exercises.

A warm-up for an individual at the *power level* includes the following:
- Five to ten minutes of dynamic stretching, such as tube walking or prisoner squats.
- Five to ten minutes of self-myofascial release exercises.

**Cool-down**

A cool-down is a low-intensity activity performed after a training session that helps transition the body back to regular heart and breathing rates. An ideal cool-down lasts from five to ten minutes.

Benefits of a cool-down include:
- Slows the cardiorespiratory system
- Decreases the body's temperature
- Restores the proper muscle length and tension
- Decreases the risk of light-headedness or feinting
- Facilitates the return to the body's normal functionality

A cool-down should include a reduction in activity level, taking a higher-rate cardiorespiratory training activity down to approximately half the heart rate level for a few minutes. This reduces the stress on the body on a gradient and also helps prevent blood from collecting in the lower extremities, which can lead to a client becoming dizzy and perhaps even fainting.

A cool-down should also incorporate static stretching and self-myofascial release to maximize muscle extensibility and release lactic acid from the muscles after a workout to reduce soreness.

A client should be able to perform his or her own cool-down after approximately three sessions, at the discretion of the health and fitness professional. This will allow more time for the client and trainer to focus on the substantive portion of the workout one-on-one.

## Benefits of cardiorespiratory training

Cardiorespiratory training can increase general fitness levels and help control weight. It can decrease many chronic problems and give a person an emotional outlet that helps improve mental well-being and sleep patterns.

Cardiorespiratory training increases the following:
- Muscle extensibility
- General performance of all activities, from daily activities to sports and fitness activities
- Immune system function
- Glucose tolerance
- Blood work
- Bone density

Cardiorespiratory training decreases the following:
- General tiredness
- Overweight
- Mental stress symptoms, from depression to anxiety
- Chronic illnesses
- Diabetes
- High blood pressure
- Heart disease

## Health- vs. fitness-related benefits

Cardiorespiratory activity has health-related benefits as well as fitness-related benefits. Moderate cardiorespiratory can produce marked improvement in overall health, even if it is not accompanied by measurable gains in fitness level. Cardiorespiratory training needs to be more intense to confer fitness benefits.

Cardiorespiratory training can have a positive cumulative effect in the following areas:
- Decrease in the resting and exercising heart rate
- Increase in VO2 maximum, cardiac volume, stroke output, and the ability of muscles to process oxygen

## F.I.T.T.E. Factors

The acronym F.I.T.T.E. stands for the following:
- Frequency—the number of training sessions conducted within a specific time, (e.g., one week)
- Intensity—how physically demanding an activity is. For improved health, moderate level activity is recommended. For improved fitness levels, a higher intensity level is recommended.
- Time—duration of time spent engaged in an activity. For improved health, 30 minutes a day is a good time frame. For increased fitness levels, more time is recommended.
- Type—the precise activity being undertaken
- Enjoyment—how fun or pleasant a given activity is

Enjoyment (the E in NASM's F.I.T.T.E. Factors for cardiorespiratory training) is often overlooked when putting together a cardiorespiratory routine for a particular client. It is important to create a program that considers the needs and interests of the individual client to encourage the client to stick with the program. When the activities are geared toward the client's personality, likes, and dislikes, he or she is more likely to continue with the training regimen and derive full benefit from the consistent application of training. It can also ensure that the client is happy with the CPT's work, leading to potential referrals.

Improved health fitness parameters

NASM recommends the following cardiorespiratory-training guidelines for improved general health:
- Frequency—Five to seven sessions per week
- Intensity—Moderate
- Time—Up to 30 minutes daily, which can be broken into shorter segments
- Type—Any activity that will get heart and respiratory rates up, such as walking or jogging, or even working around the house
- Enjoyment—The more enjoyable the activity, the better

NASM recommends the following cardiorespiratory-training guidelines for improved fitness:
- Frequency—Three to five sessions per week
- Intensity—Measured by heart rate maximum (between 60 and 90 percent) or VO2 maximum (40 to 85 percent)
- Time—Twenty minutes to an hour per session
- Type—Any activity that will increase heart and respiratory rates
- Enjoyment—The more enjoyable the activity, the better

**Fat-burning zone**

The law of thermodynamics states that body fat can only be burned when the body is using more energy than it is consuming. This is important because many clients begin exercising with a goal of improving their aesthetic appeal (e.g., they seek to lose fat and look better). The idea of a fat-burning zone is a misconception based on a misunderstanding of metabolism. While it is true that during lower intensity exercise the body burns a greater percentage of calories from fat than it does from carbohydrates, this does not constitute an ideal fat-burning zone. As exercise intensity increases, a greater percentage of calories will be burned from carbohydrates, but a greater number of calories will be burned overall, including more calories from fat.

**Calorie usage**

Measuring respiratory gasses with a metabolic analyzer by way of indirect calorimetry can reveal the amount of oxygen and carbon dioxide exchanged in the lungs, which usually correlates with the amounts of the same gasses used by body tissues. This shows a person's respiratory exchange ratio (RER), which could then be used to determine the percentage of carbohydrates being burned versus the percentage of fat being burned. The RER represents a comparison of the carbon dioxide produced to the amount of oxygen taken in. The higher the RER, the higher is the level of carbohydrates being burned.

## EPOC

EPOC stands for Excess Postexercise Oxygen Consumption—the increased need for oxygen after exercise, which raises metabolism, resulting in more calories burned. This phenomenon is a result of the body working to return to its initial state: lowering the heart rate, refilling energy stores, and cooling off body tissue. The intensity of a workout has a direct impact on EPOC, and breaking a workout into two sessions may also help maximize the effects of this phenomenon.

## Fat-burning regimen

Because of the law of thermodynamics, the overall expenditure of calories is the most important factor to consider when a health and fitness professional implements into a training regimen. A person must burn more calories than he or she consumes.

Because the body attempts to conserve energy as a general rule, it is important to maximize calorie burning to maximize excess post exercise oxygen consumption (EPOC), which encourages the body to continue to burn calories after the training session is over through increased metabolic activity.

## General adaptation syndrome and the principle of specificity

When designing a cardiorespiratory program for a client, it is important to remember general adaptation syndrome—the body's ability to cope gradually with stresses placed upon it. The principle of specificity is an important concept that a CPT must understand to enact the desired change in a client. The body will adapt in response to the particular stresses it is subjected to. Cardiorespiratory exercises must be varied in type, intensity, and frequency to prevent the body from adapting to a routine and to force the body to progress through a fitness program. This is especially relevant if fitness goals, and not just general health goals, are the client's primary objective. Stage training and circuit training are good ways to incorporate varied cardiorespiratory training into a client's exercise routine.

## Stage training

Stage training is a systematic approach to cardiorespiratory training that gives the body enough time to heal and recuperate while varying the routine enough to avoid general adaptation syndrome (the stage in which the body becomes used to an exercise routine and fails to continue progressing toward fitness goals).

NASM's stage-training progression is presented in three stages based on a person's heart rate and RER. These three stages go with the three phases of the OPT model (stabilization, strength, and power). Each stage is meant to act as a platform for the next progressive stage.

### Heart rate zones
Zone one encompasses an RER of 0.80 to 0.90, representing a 65- to 75-percent heart rate maximum. The aerobic energy system is engaged and burning fatty acids and glycogen to perform at this level. Lighter exercise, such as walking, falls under zone one.

Zone two encompasses an RER of 0.95 to 1.0, representing a 76- to 85-percent heart rate maximum. The aerobic and anaerobic energy systems are engaged and burning glycogen and lactic acid to perform at this level. Moderate exercise, such as jogging, falls under zone two.

Zone three encompasses an RER of 1.1, representing an 86 to 90 percent heart rate maximum. The anaerobic energy system is engaged and burning glycogen and adenosine triphosphate/creatine phosphate (ATP/CP) to perform at this level. Higher-intensity activity, such as running sprints, falls under zone three.

| Zone | RER | % of HR Max | Energy System | Examples |
|---|---|---|---|---|
| One | .8-.9 | 65-75% | Aerobic | Walking, light jogging |
| Two | .95-1.0 | 76-85% | Aerobic/Anaerobic | Group exercise, spinning |
| Three | 1.1 | 86-95% | Anaerobic | Sprinting |

Stage I, which correlates with zone one, is best for a relatively new client still in the stabilization level of OPT. Stage I increases blood flow to the body and creates a platform from which the client can progress.

Stage II, which correlates with zone two, is best for a client who has progressed to the strength level of OPT. Stage II pushes the body to burn more calories and raises the anaerobic threshold to meet advanced fitness goals.

Stage III, which correlates with zone three, is best for a client that has progressed to an advanced level of training. Stage III increases the amount, intensity, and speed of the workout.

Implementing stage I (stabilization level) cardiorespiratory training
Stage I is a beginning phase and should follow a gradual progression. The goal is for the client to be able to perform up to 30 minutes of exercise at 65 to 75 percent of maximal heart rate, keeping the body in an aerobic state and taxing only the target system.

Some beginning clients may only be able to handle this workload for a few minutes at a time. Start the client off in five-minute increments until he or she can handle thirty-minute sessions three times a week. This could take a few months' time, but it is important to progress a client at a manageable rate to achieve the desired effects and properly prepare the body for stage II.

Implementing stage II (strength level) cardiorespiratory training
Stage II is a median phase designed for those who have progressed beyond the beginning workloads of stage I. The ideal goal is for the client to be able to push their body to work in aerobic and anaerobic states, as revealed by the client's heart rate.

Intervals are added to the workout to change the intensity of the workout periodically to accomplish this. Work the client through zone one, with the heart rate at 60- to 75-percent of maximum capacity, and then zone two, with the heart rate at 80- to 85-percent of maximum capacity.

*Adding stage II interval training to a client's workout regimen:* To begin stage II interval training, a client starts with a five- to ten-minute cardiorespiratory training warm-up in zone one. The trainer pushes the client into a higher heart rate zone—zone two—by gradually increasing the workload or intensity of the activity over the course of one minute. After this one-minute interval, the client should return to zone one for another five-minute period. This pattern should be repeated until three one-minute, zone-two intervals have been performed. A short cool-down of a few minutes ends the session.

If a client is unable to reach a zone-two heart rate or maintain it for the entire minute-long interval, modified interval training can be used until the client can perform the standard progression.

If the client cannot hit the higher heart rate zone, take the highest number he or she was able to attain and calibrate this as an 85-percent heart rate. Subtract 5 percent from this number and use this as the target zone-two heart rate until the client can eventually achieve the higher number.

If the client's heart rate exceeds the target heart rate, but he or she can recover when the interval is over, adjust the target rate by adding a few beats to the target number.

## Implementing stage III (power level) cardiorespiratory training

Stage III is an advanced phase designed for those who have progressed beyond the intermediate workloads of stage II. The ideal goal is for the client to be able to push their body to work primarily in the anaerobic system, as revealed by the client's heart rate.

Intervals are added to the workout to change the intensity of the workout periodically to accomplish this. Progressively work the client through zones one through three, with the heart rate being pushed to up to 85- to 90-percent maximum capacity through the use of specific intervals.

*Adding stage III interval training:* To begin with stage III interval training, the client starts with a five- to ten-minute cardiorespiratory warm-up in zone one. The trainer pushes the client into a higher heart rate zone (zone two) by gradually increasing the workload or intensity of the activity over the course of two minutes. The trainer then takes the client directly into zone three with a one-minute interval at an increased intensity. A three-minute interval at a lower intensity should be used to transition the client back to his or her zone-two heart rate, followed by a ten-minute cool down in zone one.

## Coordinating stages

Stage training should be approached in a systematic and staggered manner, so the client's body does not adapt to the routine and fail to continue progressing toward fitness goals. This means that a rotation of stage I, stage II, and stage III should be employed. This ensures that the client will not overtrain or become burned out, and the risk of injury is minimized.

The client's metabolism will increase as they are able to perform varying levels of activity and intensity. A monthly plan might include stage I, stage II, and stage III on alternating days, two days of rest, followed by a downward progression consisting of stage II, stage I, and stage III on alternating days finishing with two days of rest. The cycle is then repeated.

## Circuit training

Circuit training is a weight-training method that involves performing different types of weight training in rapid succession, so the heart rate stays elevated throughout the routine. A client can perform weight training and a cardiorespiratory workout without spending twice as much time doing each component separately. Circuit training is a very effective workout regimen that can improve a person's level of fitness and increase metabolism by boosting excess post-exercise oxygen consumption (EPOC) and increasing muscle mass.

Some common circuit-training exercises include chest presses, triceps extensions, biceps curls, and overhead presses.

A client who may respond to circuit training the best is one who is averse to traditional forms of cardiorespiratory training, such as running or aerobics, but enjoys weight training. By capitalizing on the client's enjoyment of weight training and stacking the exercises in a rapid-fire sequence, the client can get still get the benefits of a cardiorespiratory workout without even noticing. This goes hand in hand with NASM's F.I.T.T.E. Factors, which stress finding activities the client enjoys to maximize compliance with the program and overall mental and emotional benefits.

Rest period
Studies have shown that waiting 20 seconds between circuit-training sets can produce higher levels of excess post-exercise oxygen consumption (EPOC), while waiting 60 seconds between sets results in a higher overall calorie burn for the circuit-training session. However, this could be misleading, as the higher calorie burn may result from the training session being longer in duration. Whichever rest period a CPT chooses when designing a circuit-training routine for a client, he or she should be careful not to extend the rest period; resting for more than three minutes can negate the beneficial effects of circuit training entirely.

Circuit training and stage training
A systematic approach to a client's workout regimen can be used, incorporating stage training and circuit training for maximum results.

For a *beginner client*, this could include a warm-up and cool-down consisting of about 10 minutes of flexibility work (self-myofascial release and stretching exercises) with about 10 minutes of stage I cardiorespiratory training, followed by 20 minutes of circuit-training cardio, and another 10 minutes of stage-training cardio.

Time ranges can be determined by the trainer, with sections of the routine cut down to five minutes if, for example, the client's heart rate is exceeding the target maximum during stage training.

For an *intermediate client* who is past the basic level of training, this could include a warm-up and cool-down consisting of ten minutes of flexibility work (self-myofascial release and stretching exercises), about 10 minutes of stage II cardiorespiratory training, followed by 20 minutes of circuit-training cardio, and another 10 minutes of stage-training cardio.

Time ranges can be determined by the trainer, with sections of the routine cut down to five minutes if the client's heart rate is exceeding the target maximum during stage training, for example.

For an *advanced-level client*, include a warm-up and cool-down of about 10 minutes of flexibility work (self-myofascial release and stretching exercises) with about 10 minutes of stage III cardiorespiratory training, followed by 20 minutes of circuit-training cardiorespiratory training, and finally 10 minutes of stage II cardiorespiratory training.

Time ranges can be determined by the trainer, with sections of the routine cut down to five minutes if, for example, the client's heart rate is exceeding the target maximum during stage training.

**Cardiorespiratory activities for specific situations**

Because all cardiorespiratory exercises and activities require the client to move, it is important to consider how this movement occurs and whether it is ideal for that particular client.

For a client who exhibits rounded shoulders or a protruded head postural distortion, it is important to keep an eye on the following and troubleshoot when necessary:

- Do not allow a client to lean forward excessively on cardiorespiratory training equipment such as a treadmill; watch for overreliance on handles, which can lead to further postural problems.
- Watch for proper form on all equipment, including bikes and elliptical trainers.
- Make sure watching television or using electronic equipment (e.g., MP3 player) is not affecting the client's posture as he or she works.

For a client who exhibits an excessive lower-back-arch postural distortion, it is important to keep an eye on the following and troubleshoot when necessary:

- Keep running or walking at a manageable speed, so the client does not attempt to compensate by extending his or her stride, aggravating this postural distortion.
- Consider avoiding stair steppers or stationary bicycles when beginning to train with that client, because these may exacerbate the postural distortion from the outset.
- Add extra flexibility exercises that target this particular area.

For a client whose feet rotate out and knees bend in, it is important to keep an eye on the following and troubleshoot when necessary:

- Watch for proper form on all cardiorespiratory machines, as it will be easy for the ankle and knee joints to flex improperly during use.
- Consider alternate cardiorespiratory exercise sources other than stair steppers or treadmills on incline mode when beginning to train with this client, because these may exacerbate the postural distortion from the outset.
- Add extra flexibility exercises that target these particular areas.

# Core Stabilization Training

The core is the center of the human body. It is composed of skeletal components such as the lumbo-pelvic-hip (LPH) complex, the lower spine, and the corresponding musculature which consists of twenty-nine muscles that attach to the LPH complex.

The core musculature is composed of two sets of muscles: the movement and stabilization systems. As the name of each implies, the movement system is the primary source of core motion, while the stabilization system helps maintain the structural integrity of the LPH complex and cervical spine.

The core acts as the center of motion and gravity for the entire body; much of the body's power is generated from this region.

## Stabilization system and movement system

The core musculature systems work together to stabilize the central skeletal system, act as the center of gravity, and initiate much of the body's motion. This is accomplished by absorbing shock and distributing weight appropriately among other functions. It is important to address the stabilization system first to create the groundwork from which to build to train these muscles to work synergistically. This will strengthen a client's core and allow further strengthening of the movement-system muscles.

The stabilization system, divided into the local and global systems, keeps the core skeletal systems in place and working properly. The local stabilization system provides support to the abdomen by providing variable tension between structural (skeletal) components. The local stabilization system is composed of the following muscles:
- Transversus abdominis
- Internal oblique
- Lumbar multifidus
- Pelvic floor muscles
- Diaphragm

The global stabilization system supports the dynamic connection of the pelvis to the spine. The global stabilization system is composed of the following muscles:
- Quadratus lumborum
- Psoas major
- External oblique
- Parts of the internal oblique
- Rectus abdominis
- Gluteus medius
- Adductor magnus
- Adductor longus
- Adductor brevis
- Gracilis
- Pectineus

The stabilization system of the core musculature is made up mainly of slow-twitch muscles that work best under a sustained stress (up to 20 seconds) to get the desired result of heightened intramuscular coordination, which is the ability of the nervous system to effectively and efficiently communicate within the muscle. This is important to promote stabilization of the LPH complex.

The movement system, which acts as the primary source of core motion and action, is composed of the following muscles, which lie lower in the hips and upper legs:
- Hip muscles
  - Adductors
  - Abductors
- Hamstrings
- Quadriceps
- Latissimus dorsi

The movement system works in concert with the stabilization system to move the LPH complex. This means that there must be high levels of intermuscular coordination, which is the ability of the nervous system to communicate effectively and efficiently between different muscles so they can work together properly.

Many people may have strong movement system muscles working with weak stabilization muscles. It is the job of the stabilization system to hold the skeletal system in proper position. If the powerful muscles acting on top of the skeletal system are not fully controlled, a person is vulnerable to injuries, compensations, postural distortions, and improper muscle interactions (such as synergistic dominance). These can lead to improper movement and, ultimately, injury. It is important to train and strengthen these deep-stabilization muscles to ensure optimal kinetic-chain communication and function.

## Core musculature

The core musculature is vital because it helps insulate the spine from external forces and injury, and it is the source point of most major movement of the body. Training these muscles is important to increase strength, flexibility, body stability, and force production. This requires a systematic approach that follows NASM's Optimum Performance Training (OPT) model of stability, strength, and power phases.

The stability phase of core training aims at creating a supporting musculature system for the lumbo-pelvic-hip (LPH) complex. The strength phase of core training aims to improve strength by addressing how the muscles communicate and move efficiently. The power phase of core training aims to increase how much explosive force the muscles can produce at a given time by the muscles of the LPH complex.

## Chronic back pain

Approximately 8 percent of American adults suffer from chronic back pain. This is often caused by limited strength and control of the stabilization muscles such as the diaphragm, pelvic-floor muscles, transversus abdominis, and internal obliques.

Performing abdominal exercises to strengthen the movement system muscles without proper stabilization strength, can stress the underlying structures by increase pressure and exerting force on the spine. This can lead to damaged spinal disks and spinal ligaments. The solution is to make sure that the stabilization muscles are trained in a progressive manner along with the movement system muscles so that they can begin to work synergistically.

## Drawing-in maneuver

Performing two simple exercise—the drawing-in maneuver and bracing— before core training increases pelvic stabilization. The drawing-in maneuver improves the performance of the local stabilization system. The easiest way to perform the exercise in a controlled and measurable manner is to have the client get on the floor on all fours, with knees and hands shoulder-width apart. Have the client concentrate on the abdominals at the belly button, and then pull in the abs from the belly button toward the spine. Bracing strengthens the global movement system. Bracing stabilizes the body by contracting the core (abdomen), lower back, and buttocks muscles simultaneously.

Performing these exercises before other abdominal work will help maintain the lumbo-pelvic-hip (LPH) complex in a neutral position during a training session.

## Training the core musculature systems

The core musculature has several important functions, including protecting the spine from the stresses and forces of everyday life. A training program should focus on increasing strength and power in the LPH complex to meet the demands placed on the body. Greater muscle control and increased strength make for a more efficient kinetic chain with ideal neuromuscular efficiency.

Stabilization training follows the OPT model, consisting of three levels of core training exercises including stabilization, strength, and power levels.

## Stabilization training exercises

### Marching exercise
To perform the marching exercise, the client lies on the floor with knees bent at a 90-degree angle. Feet should be flat on the floor, and arms should be straight down at the side of the body.

Using the drawing-in maneuver, the client lifts one foot off the floor while maintaining perfect form. The client holds this position for a few seconds and then lowers the foot back to the floor. Repeat the exercise while using the opposite foot.

The key to this exercise is to make sure the client stays drawn-in during the exercise this targets muscles that ensure the core stabilization muscles are being worked.

### Two-leg floor bridge exercise
Have the client lie on the floor with knees bent at a 90-degree angle. Feet should be flat on the floor, and arms should be straight down at the side of the body. Make sure toes are pointing forward.

The client should perform the drawing-in maneuver and shift the hips up off the ground, lifting the rear end off the ground, creating a plank with the torso, in which the shoulders, hips, and knees are aligned. Have the client slowly lower back to the starting position.

The key to this exercise is to make sure the client does not overextend the hips and thrust the lower back into an overextended position, which places the wrong kind of stress on the spine.

### Prone cobra floor exercise

Begin the prone cobra floor exercise by having client lie face down on the floor with arms extended at the sides of the body and the palms of the hands down.

Have the client perform the drawing-in maneuver and press down toward the floor with contracted gluteal muscles. While contracting the shoulder muscles together, lift the chest off the floor and raise the arms. Have the client hold for a few seconds, and then lower the chest, chin, and arms back to the ground.

The key to this exercise is to make sure the client does not overextend the chest and arms and put the lower back into an overextended position, which places the wrong kind of stress on the spine.

### Prone iso-ab exercise

The prone iso-ab exercise is also known as a plank. The client lies flat on the floor as if preparing for a push-up, and then performs the drawing-in maneuver. Contracting the gluteal muscles, have the client push up off the ground, leaning on arms bent at a 90-degree angle. Have the client hold for a few seconds, and then return the entire body to the floor.

If this position is too advanced, the exercise can also be performed in a full push-up position, or a modified push-up position with the knees bent on the ground.

## Strength-training exercises

### Ball crunch exercise

For the ball crunch exercise, a large stability ball is used. The client lays on the ball with his or her back on the ball and legs bent over the edge at a right angle. Have the client bend the arms at the elbow and place the hands behind the head. The client should perform the drawing-in maneuver to prepare the core. He or she performs an abdominal crunch, lifting up off the ball with a movement that emanates from between the shoulder blades, and then returns to starting position.

To maximize the benefit from this exercise and maintain proper form, be sure the client presses the chin toward the chest during the exercise.

### Back extension exercise

For the back extension exercise, a back extension bench is used. The client positions him- or herself over the bench with the body facing downward. Have the client bend the arms at the elbow and place the hands behind the head. The client should perform the drawing-in maneuver to prepare the core, slowly pull the torso up, so the body comes to a straight-line position, and then return to the starting position.

To maximize the benefit from this exercise and maintain proper form, be sure that the client keeps all major points of the body aligned—from the knees to the hips to the shoulders—watching to prevent hyperextension of the lower back.

### Reverse crunch exercise

For the reverse crunch exercise, a weight bench is used. The client lays on his or her back on the bench with the legs bent at a right angle at the hip and a 45-degree angle at the knees. Have the client grip the weight bench with both hands at about ear level. The client should perform the drawing-in maneuver to prepare the core muscles. He or she then slowly pulls the hips upward off the bench, pulling the knees in toward the torso. The client slowly returns to the starting position in a controlled manner.

To maximize the benefit of this exercise and maintain proper form, be sure the client maintains control of the legs throughout the exercise, taking care not to use the legs to create momentum; rather, the movement should emanate from the core muscles. This will help ensure the safety of the lower back.

### Cable rotation exercise

For the cable rotation exercise, a cable machine is used. The client stands with feet shoulder-width apart and both arms extended out from the body at waist level. Have the client hold the cable in one hand, and then cross the other hand over the body to also hold the cable, without twisting the torso. The client should perform the drawing-in maneuver to prepare the core muscles and then twist at the hips, allowing the knee to rotate in as the body twists. The core muscles and gluteus maximus should be the primary working muscles. The client returns to the starting position in a slow and controlled manner.

To maximize the benefit from this exercise and maintain proper form, be sure that the client maintains extension in the hips, knees, and ankles. This will protect the lower back from hyperextension and unnecessary stress.

**Power-training exercises**

### Rotation chest pass exercise

For the rotation chest pass exercise, a weighted medicine ball and a partner are needed. The client stands with feet shoulder-width apart and knees bent. Have him or her hold the medicine ball at chest level, with the elbows bent out evenly at each side. The client should perform the drawing-in maneuver to prepare the core muscles, and then have the client pivot one leg as he or she pushes the ball out to the side rapidly with power to the partner (or at a wall if no other person is available). The core muscles and the gluteus maximus should be the primary muscles used during this exercise. The partner can perform the same exercise or just toss the ball back so the exercise can be repeated.

To maximize the benefit from this exercise and to maintain proper form, be sure that the client maintains extension in the hips, knees, and ankles. This will protect the lower back from hyperextension and unnecessary stress.

### Stability ball/medicine ball pullover throw

For the stability ball/medicine ball pullover throw exercise, a stability ball, and a weighted medicine ball will be needed along with a partner, if available. Have the client lie back on the stability ball with knees hanging over the edge at a right angle and feet resting on the floor. The client extends the arms over the head, holding the medicine ball in both hands. The client should perform the drawing-in maneuver to prepare the core muscles and tuck the chin into the body as he or she does a rapid crunch, pulling the medicine ball forward over the head and tossing it with power to a partner or at a wall if no partner is available. All of the core muscles and the gluteus maximus are activated during this exercise.

Make sure the client keeps the lower back supported during this exercise and uses the core muscles, not momentum from the arms, to perform this exercise to protect the lower back from hyperextension.

### Front medicine-ball oblique throw exercise

For the front medicine-ball oblique throw, a weighted medicine ball and a partner will be needed. Have the client stand facing either the partner or a wall, with feet shoulder-width apart. Have the client bend the knees and hold the medicine ball with both hands on the outside of one knee. The torso should be slightly twisted to that side. The client should perform the drawing-in maneuver to prepare the core muscles. In a rapid lifting motion, the client straightens and throws the ball forward with force, with arms extending straight out at about ear level.

This exercise can be performed in repetitions on each side or in an alternating fashion. Be sure that the client keeps the hips, knees, and ankles properly flexed and that the back is not hyperextended.

### Woodchop throw exercise

For the woodchop throw exercise, a weighted medicine ball will be needed. Have the client stand with their feet shoulder-width apart. The client holds the medicine ball in both hands and raises it over the head to one side, pivoting the opposite foot and twisting the torso at the hips. The client should perform the drawing-in maneuver to prepare the core muscles. In a rapid descending motion, the client crosses the body with the medicine ball and throws it down toward the opposite foot, shifting from one foot to the other.

This exercise can be performed in repetitions on each side or in an alternating fashion.

### Soccer throw exercise

The soccer throw requires a weighted medicine ball. Have the client stand with their feet shoulder-width apart. The client holds the medicine ball in both hands and raises it overhead. The client should perform the drawing-in maneuver to prepare the core muscles. In a rapid descending motion, the client tosses the medicine ball to the floor and allows the arms to follow through.

## Balance

Balance is the ability to maintain the body in a particular position, which is essential to all movement activities. Balance is not a singular ability, but it is a component of all motion and works in conjunction with the kinetic chain and movement systems of the body.

While balance is often approached as a static process, it is a dynamic one. Balance requires that a person is able to increase or decrease force to the correct location in the body at the correct moment and in the correct plane of motion. The ability to accomplish this is directly related to a person's stability, strength, and power capabilities.

To maintain balance, a person must use all parts of the kinetic chain and many different neurological avenues that require optimal force-couple relationships and length-tension relationships, joint stability and efficiency, and muscular and neurological coordination.

# Balance Training

Effective balance training continually challenges a person's ability to maintain equilibrium and balance threshold. The balance threshold is how far the body can move away from the center of gravity while still maintaining equilibrium. The best way to challenge this is through all planes of motion and through activities that keep the client a little off kilter, thus encouraging the correct neural pathways to increase communication, ultimately resulting in increased reaction time and neuromuscular coordination.

It is very important that challenges to the client's balance be controllable and progressive. The client should be challenged by a combination of factors which will increase in difficulty. Some factors involved are:
- The number of arms or legs in use
- The stability of the client's support (e.g. floor, balance beam, or half foam roll)
- The speed of the exercise
- The complexity of the exercise

For example, the basic progression for proprioceptive exercise is:
- Position the client on the floor with no implements
- The client uses half of a foam roll, placed rounded-side-down on the floor
- The client uses an Airex balance pad placed on the floor
- The client uses a balance disc placed on the floor

<u>Scientific rationale</u>
Balance training is essential to the improvement of dynamic joint stabilization, which is the body's ability to support a joint during any given movement. This can be accomplished by introducing multisensory conditions while a client is performing basic exercises. This helps the client become aware of his or her body balance and also helps the body start to program in biomechanically correct movement patterns. A proper progression through the Optimum Performance Training (OPT) levels is vital to avoid movement compensations and poor form during particular exercises.

The posterior tibialis and the peroneus longus stabilize the foot and ankle complex. The glutes and the adductor complex stabilize the hip joint. The rotator cuff stabilizes the humerus on the glenoid fossa.

## Multisensory conditions

Multisensory conditions refer to a training environment that provides varying sensory input to stimulate the body's mechanoreceptors and proprioceptors. This provides a wealth of input to the body's neurological system, increasing the communication between the neurological and muscular systems. The body's ability to rapidly respond to balance challenges increases, allowing a person to maintain a high degree of balance even when equilibrium is challenged.

Controlled instability refers to the manner in which challenges to a client's balance should be introduced. By creating an environment that offers a progression of instability, starting with the flat floor and ending with a balance disc, a health and fitness professional gives the client a little bit of instability at a time. This allows the client to approach exercises and increase stability gradually, in a controlled manner, while maintaining proper form and avoiding movement compensations that might otherwise result.

## Balance and joint dysfunction

When an individual suffers from joint dysfunction, there will be an accompanying balance problem. This is because joint dysfunction is symptomatic, as well as a cause, of a host of other problems that affect balance. These include an unfortunate cycle of injury: basic muscle inhibition, which leads to injury to the joint itself, which in turn leads to swelling of the joint and ultimately to altered ability of the body to translate sensory input to proper movement. This can all lead to dysfunction in the kinetic chain, creating faulty movement patterns that disrupt not only basic movement, but also overall ability to maintain body equilibrium or balance. This can result from many different issues, including synergistic dominance or slow prime mover activation.

## Levels of balance training

Like all aspects of a systematic, progressive fitness-training regimen, the three basic levels of NASM's OPT fitness model—stabilization, strength, and power—are built into balance training.

Stabilization balance exercises include:
- Single-leg lift and chop
- Single-leg hip rotation (internal and external)
- Single-leg balance
- Single-leg throw and catch
- Single-leg balance reach

Strength balance exercises include:
- Single-leg Romanian deadlift
- Single-leg squat
- Single-leg squat touchdown
- Multiplanar Lunge to balance
- Multiplanar Step-up to balance

Power balance exercises include:
- Multiplanar Single-leg box hop-down with stabilization
- Multiplanar Single-leg box hop-up with stabilization
- Multiplanar (transverse, frontal, and sagittal) hop with stabilization

## Balance-training: stabilization-level exercises

Single-leg balance exercise
To perform the single-leg balance exercise, have the client stand up straight with the feet positioned shoulder-width apart and the toes facing straight forward. Hands should be placed on the hips, and upper-body posture should include chest lifted and the shoulders back. The client should perform the drawing-in maneuver to prepare the core muscles. He or she then slightly lifts one leg up off the floor by bending the leg at the knee. Have the client balance on one foot for up to 20 seconds, keeping the shoulders, hips, and ankles in alignment, returning the foot to the floor in a slow, controlled manner.

To maximize the effectiveness of this exercise, have the client keep the gluteus maximus of the balancing leg in contracted mode for the duration of the balancing time.

### Single-leg balance reach exercise

To perform the single-leg balance reach exercise, the client stands up straight with the feet shoulder-width apart and the toes facing straight forward. Hands should be placed on the hips. Upper-body posture includes chest lifted and shoulders back. Have the client perform the drawing-in maneuver to prepare the core muscles, slightly lift one leg up off the floor by bending the leg at the knee, and then straighten the leg, so it is stretched directly in front of the body. He or she holds this position for two beats then slowly returns to the original position. This exercise can be repeated without setting the foot down.

This exercise can also be progressed to different planes of motion. To work in the frontal plane, have the client extend the leg out to the side of the body; to work in the transverse plane, have the client reach behind the body with the leg, turning the torso in the direction of the extended leg.

### Single-leg hip internal and external rotation exercise

To perform the single-leg hip internal and external rotation exercise, the client stands up straight with the feet shoulder-width apart and facing straight forward. Hands should be placed on the hips; upper-body posture includes chest lifted and shoulders back. The client should perform the drawing-in maneuver to prepare the core muscles, and then slightly lift one leg up off the floor by bending the leg at the knee. Have the client turn the body at the hip, first inward then outward, for two beats in each direction, and then slowly return to the original position. This exercise can be performed in a set on one leg, or by alternating legs.

Make sure the client maintains a neutral hip position to avoid unnecessary strain to the lower back.

### Single-leg lift and chop exercise

For the single-leg lift and chop exercise, a weighted medicine ball is used. The client stands up straight with the feet shoulder-width apart and the toes facing straight forward. Hands should be placed on the hips. Upper-body posture includes chest lifted and shoulders back. The client should perform the drawing-in maneuver to prepare the core muscles, and then slightly lift one leg up off the floor by bending the leg at the knee. Have the client hold the medicine ball in both hands, extended over the head to the same side as the raised leg, and then swing the ball downward to the opposite side of the body, holding there for two beats.

To maximize the effectiveness of this exercise, have the client keep the knee in line with the toes of the raised leg.

### Single-leg squat touchdown exercise

For the single-leg squat touchdown, a weighted medicine ball is used. Have the client stand up straight with the feet shoulder-width apart and the toes facing straight forward. Hands should be placed on the hips, and upper-body posture should include chest lifted and shoulders back. The client should perform the drawing-in maneuver to prepare the core muscles, and then slightly lift one leg up off the floor by bending it at the knee. From this position, the client should squat and reach down diagonally with the hand from the same side as the lifted leg and touch the opposite ankle. He or she then returns to the starting position, using the core muscles and gluteus maximus to maintain balance on the way up.

If the ankle proves too difficult for the client to reach, have him or her reach to a point higher up on the leg and work lower as they progress.

## Balance-training: strength-level exercises

### Single-leg squat exercise

For the single-leg squat exercise, the client stands up straight with the feet shoulder-width apart and the toes facing straight forward. Hands should be placed on the hips; upper-body posture includes chest lifted and shoulders back. The client should perform the drawing-in maneuver to prepare the core muscles, and then slightly lift one leg up off the floor by bending at the knee. Have the client slowly perform a squat on one leg, just to the point where alignment starts to go out; hold for two beats.

To maximize the effectiveness of this exercise, the client should keep the knee in line with the toes of the raised leg.

### Single-leg Romanian deadlift exercise

For the single-leg Romanian deadlift exercise, a weighted medicine ball is used. The client stands up straight with the feet shoulder-width apart and the toes facing straight forward. Hands should be placed on the hips. Upper-body posture includes chest lifted and shoulders back. The client should perform the drawing-in maneuver to prepare the core muscles, and then slightly lift one leg up off the floor by bending the leg at the knee, to about ankle level. Have the client reach directly down and touch the top of the lifted foot. He or she should return to the starting position, using the core muscles and gluteus maximus to maintain balance on the way up.

If the top of the foot proves too difficult for the client to reach, have him or her reach to a point higher up on the leg and work lower as they progress.

### Multiplanar Step-up to balance exercise

For the step-up to balance exercise, an exercise step is needed. Have the client begin by facing the exercise step, with feet placed shoulder-width apart. Hands should be placed on the hips. Upper-body posture includes chest lifted and shoulders back. The client should perform the drawing-in maneuver to prepare the core muscles, and then step up onto the exercise step with one foot. With toes pointing forward and hips straight, the client balances over the one foot, with the other foot up, leg bent at a 90-degree angle at the knee. After holding for two beats, the client slowly returns the lifted foot to the ground and returns to the original starting position.

### Multiplanar Lunge to balance exercise

To perform the lunge to balance exercise, have the client stand up straight with the feet positioned shoulder-width apart and the toes facing straight forward. Hands should be placed on the hips. Upper-body posture includes chest lifted and shoulders back. The client should perform the drawing-in maneuver to prepare the core muscles. He or she lunges forward in a deep lunge, with the back knee bending to the ground. Pushing off hard from the front leg, the client should return to an upright position, balancing on the back leg alone, while the formerly front leg is bent at a 90-degree angle.

This exercise can also be performed in different planes, with a side lunge to work in the frontal plane, and a turning lunge to work in the transverse plane.

Make sure the client's back is not hyperextended during these lunges. If the hip muscles are overactive, a shallower lunge is advisable.

## Balance-training: power-level exercises

### Multiplanar hop with stabilization exercise
For the multiplanar hop with stabilization exercise, an agility ladder is used. Place the agility ladder flat on the ground, and have the client stand at one end, with the feet positioned shoulder-width apart. Hands should be placed on the hips. Upper-body posture includes chest lifted and shoulders back. Have the client perform the drawing-in maneuver to prepare the core muscles, and then slightly lift one leg by bending at the knee. The client hops forward with the raised foot into the first slot of the agility ladder, landing on the balancing leg, and holds this position for up to five beats. Then have the client hop backward, again switching the feet.

This exercise can be performed in all planes of motion. To work in the sagittal plane, have the client begin with his or her back facing the agility ladder and hop backward. To work in the transverse plane, have the client stand next to the agility ladder and hop sideways.

### Multiplanar Single-leg box hop-up with stabilization exercise
For the single-leg box hop-up with stabilization exercise, an exercise step will be used. Have the client begin by facing the exercise step, with the feet positioned shoulder-width apart. Hands should be placed on the hips. Upper-body posture should include chest lifted and shoulders back. The client should perform the drawing-in maneuver to prepare the core muscles, and then slightly lift one leg by bending at the knee. From that position, have the client jump up onto the box with both feet, landing with knees bent slightly and feet pointing forward. Repeat the exercise using either the same start foot or by alternating feet.

This exercise can also be performed in the transverse and frontal planes.

### Multiplanar Single-leg box hop-down with stabilization exercise
For the single-leg box hop-down with stabilization exercise, an exercise step is used. The client begins by standing atop the exercise step, with the feet positioned shoulder-width apart. Hands should be placed on the hips. Upper-body posture includes chest lifted and shoulders back. The client should perform the drawing-in maneuver to prepare the core muscles, and then slightly lift one leg by bending at the knee. From that position, have the client jump down to the floor from the box, landing on both feet, with knees bent slightly and feet pointing forward. Repeat the exercise by using the same start foot or by alternating the feet.

This exercise can also be performed in the transverse and frontal planes.

## Implementing balance-training regimens

The best way to implement a balance-training regimen is by following NASM's Optimum Performance Training (OPT) model. Usually, the correct balance-training level will correspond to the current overall training level the client is in (e.g., a stability-level client should work on stability-level balance exercises).

Three sets of stabilization balance exercises should be performed for as many as four exercises; each set should include 12 to 20 repetitions. The pace of the exercises should be slow and controlled, with up to 90 seconds of rest between each set.

Select as many as four strength balance exercises and perform two to three sets of each, with eight to twelve repetitions per set. The exercises should be performed at a medium pace, with up to a minute of rest between each set.

Power balance exercises should be performed in two or three sets of up to two exercises, with between eight to a dozen repetitions each. The pace of the exercises should be fully controlled, holding the end pose for up to five beats, with up to a minute of rest between each set.

| OPT Level | Phase | Balance Exercise | Reps | Sets | Rest |
|---|---|---|---|---|---|
| **Stabilization** | 1 | 1 – 4 balance stabilization | 12 – 20<br>6 – 10 (SL) | 1 - 3 | 0 – 90 s |
| **Strength** | 2 | 1 – 3 balance strength | 8 - 12 | 2 - 3 | 0 – 60 s |
| **Hypertrophy** | 3 | 0 – 4 balance strength | 8 - 12 | 2 - 3 | 0 – 60 s |
| **Maximal Strength** | 4 | 0 – 3 balance strength | 8 - 12 | 2 - 3 | 0 – 60 s |
| **Power** | 5 | 0 – 2 balance power | 8 - 12 | 2 - 3 | 0 – 60 s |

# Reactive Training

Reactive or power training is the third level on NASM's OPT model. Reactive training comprises rapid-fire exercises that increase the body's ability to produce maximum force quickly. Before a client attempts reactive-training exercises, he or she should have progressed through the first two levels of the OPT model, stabilization, and strength. Once the client builds sufficient strength and balance, he or she can engage in power-level activities.

To increase a person's ability to create explosive muscle force, a trainer must incorporate plyometric exercises that have an eccentric contraction coupled with a powerful concentric contraction. Plyometrics will increase the ability of the nervous system and muscular system to communicate efficiently and produce maximum force.

## Integrated performance paradigm

Reactive training gives a person the ability to program rapid, correct movement patterns into their muscles and neural pathways. This gives all components of the kinetic chain, including the muscles, ligaments, and tendons, the ability to become stronger for all activities, whether daily living or athletic in nature. A body can only react as quickly as its level of coordination will allow. The outcome is to improve a person's ability to react quickly in an efficient, high-energy way; this is commonly called rate of force production. Due to the perception that reactive training increases injury risk, it is often left out of a traditional training program. However, if the client properly progresses through the first two levels of the OPT model, and his or her particular needs are assessed and built into the training routine, power-level training can be effectively and safely incorporated into that client's overall goals.

## Levels of reactive training

Like all aspects of a systematic, progressive fitness training regimen, the three basic levels of NASM's OPT fitness model—stabilization, strength, and power—are built into reactive training.

Stabilization reactive exercises include:
- Multiplanar jump with stabilization
- Squat jump with stabilization
- Box jump-down with stabilization
- Box jump-up with stabilization

Strength reactive exercises include:
- Tuck jump
- Squat jump
- Power step-up
- Butt kick.

Power reactive exercises include:
- Proprioceptive plyometrics
- Single-leg power step-up
- Ice skater

## Reactive-training: stabilization-level exercises

<u>Squat jump with stabilization</u>
The client begins the squat jump with stabilization exercise by standing with the feet positioned shoulder-width apart and the toes facing straight forward. The client should perform the drawing-in maneuver to prepare the core muscles and to tighten the gluteus maximus. Have the client bend as though sitting down in a chair, with arms straightened behind the body. Then the client jumps straight up, with arms going straight up over the head and legs extending straight. Have the client land in the same knees-bent position, with arms returning to the starting position, and hold for up to five seconds.

<u>Box jump-up with stabilization exercise</u>
For the box jump-up with stabilization exercise, an exercise step is used. The client begins by facing the exercise step with the feet positioned shoulder-width apart. Arms should be straight and held in line with the torso. Upper-body posture includes chest lifted and shoulders back. The client should perform the drawing-in maneuver to prepare the core muscles and then bend the knees deeply as though sitting down in a chair. From that position, the client jumps up onto the box with both feet, landing with knees bent and feet pointing forward. Repeat the exercise using either the same starting foot or by alternating the feet.

This exercise can also be performed in the transverse and frontal planes.

<u>Box jump-down with stabilization exercise</u>
For the box jump-down with stabilization exercise, an exercise step is used. The client begins standing atop the step; feet are placed shoulder-width apart. Arms should be straight and held in line with the torso. Upper-body posture includes chest lifted and shoulders back. The client should perform the drawing-in maneuver to prepare the core muscles and then bend the knees deeply as though sitting down in a chair. From that position, have the client jump down off of the box with both feet, landing with knees bent and feet pointing forward. Repeat the exercise using either the same starting foot or by alternating feet.

This exercise can also be performed in the transverse and frontal planes.

<u>Horizontal jump with stabilization exercise</u>
The client begins the horizontal jump with stabilization exercise by standing atop the exercise step, with the feet positioned shoulder-width apart. Arms should be straight and held in line with the torso. Upper-body posture includes chest lifted and shoulders back. The client should perform the drawing-in maneuver to prepare the core muscles and then bend the knees deeply as though sitting down in a chair. From that position, have the client jump straight ahead as far as he or she can. The client finishes with knees bent, feet facing forward, and arms straight and held parallel to the bent knees. Have the client hold the end position for up to five beats.

This exercise can also be performed in the transverse and frontal planes. Make sure that the client lands gently to help the body properly absorb the shock of the exercise.

## Reactive-training: strength-level exercises

### Squat jump exercise

The client begins the squat jump exercise by standing with the feet positioned shoulder-width apart and the toes facing straight forward. The client should perform the drawing-in maneuver to prepare the core muscles and to tighten the gluteus maximus. The client bends as though sitting down in a chair, with arms straightened behind the body. The client jumps straight up, with arms going straight up over the head and the legs extending straight. Have the client land in the same knees-bent position, with arms returning to the starting position. As soon as the client has landed, he or she should perform another squat jump, again ending in the starting position.

### Tuck jump exercise

The client begins the tuck jump exercise by standing with the feet positioned shoulder-width apart and the toes facing straight forward. The client should perform the drawing-in maneuver to prepare the core muscles and to tighten the gluteus maximus. The client bends as though sitting down in a chair, with arms straightened behind the body. Have the client jump straight up with the body and arms staying in the same position, but keep the legs bent in and under the body. The client lands in the same knees-bent position, with arms returning to the starting position. As soon as the client has landed, he or she should perform another tuck jump, again ending in the starting position.

Make sure the client maintains proper form throughout the exercise and lands gently to avoid unnecessary shock to the body.

### Butt kick jump exercise

For the butt kick jump, the client begins by standing with the feet positioned shoulder-width apart and the toes facing straight forward. The client should perform the drawing-in maneuver to prepare the core muscles and to tighten the gluteus maximus. Have the client bend as though sitting down in a chair, with arms straightened behind the body. The client jumps straight up, with the body and arms straightening up and the legs bending in rapidly under the buttocks. He or she lands in the same knees-bent position, with arms returning to the starting position. As soon as the client has landed, he or she should perform another butt kick jump, again ending in the starting position.

Make sure the client maintains proper form throughout the exercise and lands gently to avoid unnecessary shock to the body.

### Power step-up exercise

For the power step-up exercise, an exercise step will be needed. The client begins facing the step, with the feet positioned shoulder-width apart and the toes facing straight forward. The client should perform the drawing-in maneuver to prepare the core muscles and to tighten the gluteus maximus. Have the client step up onto the box with one foot, and then push up off of the box with force, extending both legs straight while in the air. The client lands in the starting position and performs another step up right away.

To maintain proper alignment and maximize the effectiveness of the exercise, make sure the client keeps the knees and feet lined up before the step-up motion and during landing.

## Reactive-training: power-level exercises

### Ice skater exercise

For the ice skater exercise, an agility ladder is used. Lay the agility ladder flat on the floor, and have the client begin by standing in front of the ladder, facing away from it with the feet positioned shoulder-width apart. The client bends the knees deeply and leans the torso forward, lifting the inside leg slightly in a posture resembling that of a speed skater. The client should perform the drawing-in maneuver to prepare the core muscles, and then jump from the balancing leg to the raised leg in a sideways motion, parallel to the agility ladder. The client jumps back and forth in the same manner as quickly as he or she can while maintaining proper form.

### Single-leg power step-up exercise

For the single-leg power step-up exercise, an exercise step will be needed. The client begins facing the step, with feet shoulder-width apart and the toes facing straight ahead. The client should perform the drawing-in maneuver to prepare the core muscles and to tighten the gluteus maximus. Have the client step up onto the box with one foot then push up off of the box with force and extend both legs straight while in the air. The client lands on the stepping leg and then performs another step up right away.

To maintain proper alignment and maximize the effectiveness of the exercise, make sure the client keeps the knees and feet lined up before the step-up motion and during landing.

### Proprioceptive plyometrics exercise

For the proprioceptive plyometrics exercise, five disc cones are needed. (If no disc cones are available, any relatively flat item, even masking tape, can be used.) Lay the disc cones in a T formation on the ground, and have the client stand by them with feet shoulder-width apart. The client should perform the drawing-in maneuver to prepare the core muscles and to tighten the gluteus maximus, and then bend the knees slightly. Instruct the client to either hop on a single leg or jump on both feet in various patterns over, across, and through the cone formation. Be sure that the client maintains proper alignment of the knees and ankles, and there is no hyperextension of the lower back.

## Implementing reactive-training regimens

The best way to implement a reactive-training regimen is by following NASM's OPT model. Usually, the correct reactive-training level will correspond to the current overall training level the client is in (e.g., a stability-level client should work on stability-level balance exercises).

Stabilization reactive exercises are performed in up to three sets of up to two exercises, with from between five to eight repetitions each. The pace of the exercises should be slow and controlled, with up to 90 seconds of rest between each set.

Strength reactive exercises are performed in two or three sets of up to four exercises, with from between eight to ten repetitions each. The pace of the exercises should be medium, with up to a minute of rest between each set.

Power reactive exercises are performed in two or three sets of up to two exercises, with from between eight to a dozen repetitions each. The pace of the exercises should be as quick as possible while maintaining control, with up to a minute of rest between each set.

# SAQ Training

SAQ refers to speed, agility, and quickness training. It follows NASM's OPT model.

Speed is a term used to describe a person's aptitude for straight-ahead swiftness. Speed includes front side and backside mechanics, which refer to the triple flexion of the front and back legs, respectively.

Agility is a term used to describe a person's aptitude for beginning or stopping motion quickly.

Quickness is a term used to describe how fast a person can react to external stimulus and alter his or her position in response.

## Positioning

Proper running mechanics are essential to optimal kinetic chain efficiency. Consider the following kinetic chain checkpoints:
- Head—The head should remain in alignment with the hip complex and be maintained in a neutral position, without extension or compensation.
- LPH complex—The lumbo-pelvic-hip (LPH) complex should remain neutral, with a slight lean ahead when accelerating.
- Knees—The knees should always face forward. If the knee rotates inward, an increase in stability exercises and a decrease in activities that may lead to injury are required.
- Feet/ankles—The feet should always face forward and be in a dorsiflexed position upon impact with the ground. Watch for improper internal rotation, which can lead to injury.

## Implement SAQ training regimens

The best way to implement an SAQ-training regimen is by following NASM's OPT model. Usually, the correct SAQ training level will correspond to the current overall training level the client is in—for example, stability-level clients should work on stability-level exercises.

Stabilization SAQ exercises are performed in up to two sets of up to six exercises, of half an agility ladder, with up to 60 seconds of rest between each ladder drill and up to 90 seconds for cone drills.

Strength SAQ exercises should be performed in up to four sets of up to nine exercises, of half an agility ladder, with up to 60 seconds of rest between each ladder drill and up to 90 seconds for cone drills.

Power SAQ exercises should be performed in up to six sets of up to nine exercises, of half an agility ladder, with up to 60 seconds of rest between each ladder drill and up to 90 seconds for cone drills.

| OPT Level | Drills | Horizontal inertia | Unpredictability | Example Exercises | Sets | Reps | Resting period |
|---|---|---|---|---|---|---|---|
| **Stabilization** | 4-6 | limited | limited | Cone Shuffles, Agility ladder drills | 1-2 | 2-3 | 0-60 s |
| **Strength** | 6-8 | moderate | limited | 5-10-5, T-Drill, Box drill, Stand Up to Figure 8 | 3-4 | 3-5 | 0-60 s |
| **Power** | 6-10 | maximal | moderate | Modified Box Drill, Partner Mirror Drill, Timed drills | 3-5 | 3-5 | 0-90 s |

## SAQ training: strength level exercises

One-ins exercise
The one-ins exercise requires a speed ladder and is one of a series of NASM speed-ladder drills specifically designed to improve speed, agility, and quickness.

To perform this exercise, lay the speed ladder down on the ground. The client begins at either end of the ladder. The client should perform the drawing-in maneuver to prepare the core muscles. The client quickly runs through the speed ladder, with one foot stepping in each of the squares. Be sure the client maintains proper form, with feet, knees, hips, and shoulders all facing forward and arms bending at the elbows for each step.

Two-ins exercise
The two-ins exercise requires a speed ladder and is one of a series of NASM speed-ladder drills specifically designed to improve speed, agility, and quickness.

To perform this exercise, lay the speed ladder down on the ground. The client begins at either end of the ladder. The client should perform the drawing-in maneuver to prepare the core muscles, and then he or she quickly performs the following progression: Step with one foot into a square, and then land with both feet in the same square. Step with the same beginning foot into the next square, and then land with both feet in the same square. Repeat to the end of the ladder, and then do another set beginning with the opposite foot.

Side shuffle exercise
The side shuffle exercise requires a speed ladder and is one of a series of NASM speed-ladder drills specifically designed to improve speed, agility, and quickness.

To perform this exercise, lay the speed ladder down on the ground. The client begins at either end of the ladder, facing forward. The client should perform the drawing-in maneuver to prepare the core muscles, and then take a sideways step into the first square of the ladder with the foot closest to the ladder. The other foot should follow into the same square. Then a sideways step with the leading foot is taken into the next square, with the other foot following. Repeat to the end of the ladder, and then do another set in the opposite direction.

## In-in-out-out exercise

The in-in-out-out exercise requires a speed ladder and is one of a series of NASM speed-ladder drills specifically designed to improve speed, agility, and quickness (SAQ).

To perform this exercise, lay the speed ladder down on the ground. The client begins at either end of the ladder. The client should perform the drawing-in maneuver to prepare the core muscles. He or she quickly performs the following progression: Hop forward into the first square with both feet together, into the second square with both feet together, and then hop with both feet apart, straddling the ladder, for two sections. Repeat to the end of the ladder, and then perform another set in the opposite direction. Repeat as quickly as possible while maintaining proper form.

## In-in-out exercise

The in-in-out exercise requires a speed ladder and is one of a series of NASM speed-ladder drills specifically designed to improve speed, agility, and quickness.

To perform this exercise, lay the speed ladder down on the ground. The in-in-out exercise is also known as a zigzag due to the motion the feet make along the speed ladder.

The client begins standing next to the ladder. The client should perform the drawing-in maneuver to prepare the core muscles, and then quickly perform the following progression: Step with the foot closest to the ladder into the square diagonal to the starting position, and then bring the other foot into that square as well. Have the client step out of the opposite side of the ladder to a position diagonal to the starting point with the first foot and then with the second foot. Repeat this progression to the end of the ladder as quickly as possible while maintaining proper form.

## Ali shuffle (washing machine) exercise

The Ali shuffle requires a speed ladder and is one of a series of NASM speed-ladder drills specifically designed to improve speed, agility, and quickness.

To perform this exercise, lay the speed ladder on the ground.

The client begins by standing on the ladder, with the squares running to the right. The client should perform the drawing-in maneuver to prepare the core muscles, then quickly perform the following progression: In a jogging motion step with the right foot into the first square, and then follow with the left. Step with the right foot into the square to the right, followed by the left. Step with the right foot backward out of the ladder, followed by the left. Step sideways to the right with the right foot, followed by the left. Repeat this progression to the end of the ladder as quickly as possible while maintaining proper form.

## SAQ training: strength-level drills

## 5-10-5 drill

The 5-10-5 drill requires three cones and is one of a series of NASM cone drills specifically designed to improve speed, agility, and quickness.

Place three cones an equal distance apart in a straight line across 10 yards of floor space. The client begins at the middle cone, which will be designated as the start and finish point for the drill.

First, have the client sprint from the center cone to one far cone. Then the client sprints from that cone to the cone at the far end. Lastly, the client sprints back to the center cone. Repeat this progression as the client's template dictates, making sure that the client maintains proper form throughout the exercise.

## Box drill

The box drill requires four cones and is one of a series of NASM cone drills specifically designed to improve speed, agility, and quickness.

Place four cones in a square, with each side ten yards in length. The client begins at the lower-right corner and performs a different action along each side of the square. First, have the client perform a sprint straight forward to the top-right cone. Then the client side shuffles (hopping with feet open, then closed, then open, then closed) to the top-left cone. The client then backpedals to the bottom-left cone. Lastly, the client performs a grapevine motion (step right, step over with the left, step right, step behind with the left) back to the starting cone. Repeat this drill in the opposite direction, making sure the client maintains proper form throughout the exercise.

## T-drill

The T-drill exercise requires four cones and is one of a series of NASM cone drills specifically designed to improve speed, agility, and quickness.

Place the cones in a T formation: the start/end cone will be the bottom-center point. Place the second cone five yards straight ahead, and then place the last two cones five yards to each side of the second cone.

The client begins at the start cone and sprints forward to cone two. The client then side shuffles to the left-hand cone. The client performs a grapevine all the way to the other side to the right-hand cone. Then the client side shuffles back to the center cone. Finally, have the client sprint back to the start position.

Repeat this drill in the opposite direction, making sure that the client maintains proper form throughout the exercise.

## L.E.F.T. drill

The L.E.F.T. drill requires two cones and is one of a series of NASM cone drills specifically designed to improve speed, agility, and quickness.

Place two cones ten yards apart. This exercise consists of having the client travel back and forth between the two cones performing different movements. Beginning with the left-hand cone, the client first sprints straight across to the other cone. Next, have him or her backpedal to the starting cone. The client side shuffles to the far cone and side shuffles back to the start cone. The client performs a grapevine to the far cone and back again to the starting cone. Finally, the client finishes the exercise with one more sprint to the far cone.

Make sure the client maintains proper form throughout the exercise.

# Integrated Resistance Training

## Final component

The final component of an integrated training program is resistance training—weight lifting and other similar exercises. Building muscle is an important component of a fitness regimen because it improves a person's ability across the OPT spectrum, increasing stabilization, strength, and power-producing capabilities. It is also the part of the training routine most often associated with the typical workout.

While this aspect of training is often viewed as the central element, it is but one part of an overall fitness scheme. To properly program resistance training into a fitness regimen, the trainer must understand how to get results, which requires knowing common barriers such as the principle of adaptation and general adaptation syndrome.

## Principle of adaptation

The principle of adaptation may be the most important physiological concept for a health and fitness professional to know and understand. This principle outlines how the human body will change (adapt) to meet additional demands placed upon it from outside stresses to the best of its ability. Because training is usually used as a means of achieving adaptation, whether in the form of weight loss, increased strength or endurance, this principle is the key to all training activities.

It is also important to understand the flip side of this principle: Because the body will adapt to additional stresses, a trainer must vary the method in which stresses are applied, so the body will continue to adapt and not hit a performance plateau.

## Benefits

A resistance-training program can offer a host of benefits derived from the body's ability to adapt to the additional stimuli placed upon it. These adaptations are a function of the general adaptation syndrome and the principle of specificity, which dictate that the body will adapt to the specific forces placed upon it.

Performance benefits include:
- Additional endurance
- Additional explosive strength (power)
- Additional strength in the tissues (muscle, ligament, and tendon)

Physiological benefits include:
- Heightened metabolism
- Improved bone density
- Heightened cardiovascular ability
- Improvements to the hormonal (endocrine) system
- Less body fat
- More lean muscle

## General adaptation syndrome

Stages
The alarm reaction stage, resistance development stage, and exhaustion stage are the three stages of general adaptation syndrome. Each causes a very specific reaction in the body, and they must be understood to maximize training gains.

- The alarm reaction stage is the body's first response to new stimuli. An alarm reaction related to fitness training might be increased oxygen intake or blood flow to the stressed site.
- The resistance development stage is the stage in which the body specifically adapts to a particular stimulus, meaning the body learns to cope without making any significant gains. The takeaway from this stage is that the body needs to be continuously challenged to reach new levels of fitness
- Exhaustion refers to the body's inability to cope properly with repeated stimuli over time, causing a breakdown in proper function.

| Stage | Reaction |
|---|---|
| **Alarm reaction** | Initial reaction to stressor such as increased oxygen and blood supply to the necessary areas of the body |
| **Resistance development** | Increased functional capacity to adapt to stressor such as increasing motor unit recruitment |
| **Exhaustion** | A prolonged intolerable stressor produces fatigue and leads to a breakdown in the system or injury |

Alarm reaction stage
Exercise places stress on bones, joints, muscles, connective tissues, and the nervous system. When a deconditioned individual begins exercising, the body undergoes a number of physiological changes in response. Increased supply of blood and oxygen and, improved neural recruitment are examples of the body's physiologic responses to exercise. This is referred to as the alarm reaction stage.

Resistance development stage
In the resistance-development phase of general adaptation syndrome, the body becomes accustomed to a new stress placed upon it and creates a generalized response to handle this stress. After the initial response, which will manifest as a gain in fitness training (such as being able to run a lap more quickly), the body will not increase in ability unless further stress is placed upon it.

Although many fitness professionals are aware of GAS, they don't always address it properly when designing a program for a client. Often in resistance training, a trainer will merely add more weight to an exercise. While this is one way of changing the stress placed on the body, it is not the only way. It is important to change the number of repetitions and the tempo at which they are performed, along with other elements that are addressed under NASM's program-design parameters.

Exhaustion stage
When there is an ongoing stress on the body, even a positive one, as is the case with fitness training, the body will adapt to a certain extent and then potentially become exhausted or incapable of continuing to cope with the stress. This can lead to a variety of problems such as stress fractures, tears and strains, joint weakness, and general tiredness.

Exhaustion can disrupt a training regimen due to injury as well as through client apathy: A client who is not experiencing ongoing improvement may become disinterested and lose the motivation to continue.

*Reducing incidence:* it is important for a trainer to recognize that there are many tissues used in a given workout and take steps to prevent exhaustion and its related injuries in resistance training. These fibers have differing levels of blood flow and therefore may adapt to increased stimulus at different rates. To reduce repetitive stress and increase the range of stress placed on the different tissues, whether muscle, ligament, or tendons, varying weights and tempos should be used as well as different exercises that span all of the planes of movement.

## Principle of specificity

The principle of specificity is frequently referred to by an alternate name, the specific adaptation to imposed demands (SAID) principle, which simply states that a person's body will learn to cope with added stresses placed on it.

The take away from this principle is that the body will adapt to meet the demands that are placed on it. The trainer must design a program that challenges the client's body to adapt in the desired fashion.

The OPT model is used to address this issue. It includes stabilization (which includes stabilization endurance), strength (which includes strength endurance, hypertrophy, and maximal strength), and power (which includes the power phase).

### Metabolic, mechanical, and neuromuscular specificity
Metabolic, mechanical, and neuromuscular specificity refer to different types of stimuli that can be placed on the body to cause an adaptation reaction.
- Metabolic specificity describes the amount of energy demanded of the body—how much energy a workout requires, which can vary depending on the length of time spent training or the intensity at which training is performed.
- Mechanical specificity describes the amount of weight or the types of activities demanded of the body—how much resistance is being applied and in what number of repetitions.
- Neuromuscular specificity describes how fast a given exercise is performed.

### Achieving goals
The principle of specificity can be used to help a client achieve specific goals based on the fact that the body adapts to the specific demands that are placed on it. That is, doing specific exercises and activities ultimately makes it easier to perform those same activities as the body meets the specific demands placed upon it. As an example, if a client is training to run a marathon, incorporating running into their training regimen would be essential to prepare the body to adapt to it.

However, the principle of specificity also tells us that repeating the same activity over and over without adding systematic training to help complementary body tissues (such as ligaments and tendons) adapt can lead to injury or exhaustion. This creates a barrier for a client attempting to achieve a specific goal.

## Goal of resistance-training

The primary goal of resistance training is to create adaptations in the body relating to strength. This, and more, can be accomplished by increasing the client's overall endurance, creating more lean muscle mass, or by assisting in reducing overall body fat.

With a systematic, integrated approach, the health and fitness professional can help a client maximize the adaptations of all different types of body tissues and minimize exhaustion resulting from general adaptation syndrome, allowing the client to train longer without injury or kinetic-chain compensations.

## Strength

Strength is defined as the ability of the body to overcome an exterior force through internal tension. This can come in the form of stabilizing, enduring, balancing, or creating explosive power.

Traditional training programs have focused too much on single-muscle hypertrophy, or building muscle in a single muscle group, working only in one plane of motion. For example, a classic resistance-training program might include a large number of biceps curls. This approach fails to recognize that muscles work in more than one way (e.g., concentrically, isometrically, and eccentrically).

NASM's approach differs in that it works in multiple planes of motion, uses multiple exercises, varies repetitions, changes tempo, and works not only the specific muscle but also the supporting tissues to create overall adaptations while minimizing injury or exhaustion.

## Maximizing strength gains

As with all elements of NASM's integrated training regimen, the OPT model should be followed when creating a resistance-training routine to maximize gains in strength. Exercises should follow the order of the OPT model (stabilization, strength, and power) to create the sought-after neuromuscular adaptations. Each phase focuses on exercises designed to have a specific effect on the neuromuscular system.

For the stabilization phase, specific adaptations include muscular endurance and overall stability. For the strength phase, specific adaptations include strength-endurance, building muscle mass (hypertrophy), and creating the highest amount of strength possible (maximal strength). For the power phase, there are no additional specific adaptations other than creating explosive power (Power can be understood as a force over a time.)

## Stabilization level

The stabilization level of training is vital to help strengthen the underlying musculature and create a strong foundation for all movement. Stabilization is the key to a novice client's success because it addresses the communication of the neuromuscular system—how the brain and nerves tell the muscles to move.

Muscular endurance and stability are the two specific adaptations of this level:

- Endurance refers to the length of time a muscle can work. This is important because if the body cannot endure ongoing stressors, form and function will deteriorate, potentially leading to injury.
- Stability refers to the body's ability to maintain proper postural form while working or moving. This requires muscle endurance (which is why the endurance phase precedes the stability phase) and proper neuromuscular communication to assure the correct muscles are being called upon to perform a given task.

## Strength level

The strength level of the OPT model focusses on achieving higher levels of strength capability and neuromuscular efficiency. There are three specific adaptations to the strength level of resistance training: strength-endurance, hypertrophy, and maximal strength. Each phase should be approached in order as the stages are progressive. Strength endurance refers to the length of time a person can maintain a given level of force. Hypertrophy refers to building the size of muscles, exercising them isometrically, concentrically, and eccentrically in all planes of motion. Maximal strength refers to training that encourages the top number of muscle fibers and motor units to work to create top levels of force.

## Power level

The power level of the OPT model is designed to help the client achieve explosive force production as quickly as possible. This requires completion of the stabilization and strength levels to establish a proper muscular foundation and the amount of strength needed for such tasks, while concurrently training the neuromuscular system to communicate efficiently enough to handle the demands of power movement.

The power phase improves the body's ability to produce force by activating more motor units, improving the synchronization between them, and increasing the activation speed. The primary goal is to increase the speed at which movement occurs, so the client is better equipped to handle daily activities or sports-related or other functional activities. This can be accomplished by adding either more speed, velocity, force, or weight.

## Types of resistance-training systems

There are many different types of resistance-training systems. Resistance-training systems were initially appealing to people looking to maximize hypertrophy, such as bodybuilders. Systems include:

- Single-set—doing one set of a given exercise
- Multiple-set—doing multiple sets of a given exercise
- Vertical loading—progressing through the exercises that have been programmed on the OPT template in a vertical fashion
- Horizontal loading—performing all the desired sets of each exercise before going on to the next exercise
- Circuit training—performing all exercises one after another without stopping in between
- Superset—doing two sets of the same exercise without stopping in between
- Pyramid—adding more weight, or taking weight off, with each set
- Drop sets—Perform a set to failure, remove a small amount of weight, continue with the set

- Peripheral heart action—Modified circuit training that alternates between upper and lower body exercises
- Split routine—focusing on different areas of the body for separate training sessions

## Single-set resistance-training system

As the name implies, the single-set resistance-training system involves performing one set of each given exercise. A set includes eight to twelve repetitions performed at a moderate pace. The single-set training routine is seen as appropriate for a beginning-level client and may not provide enough challenge for an intermediate- or advanced-level client to attain desired strength goals.

While single-set training is sometimes dismissed within the health and fitness industry, it can be ideal for beginner clients who need simple training exercises that do not overtax their bodies as they move through the stabilization level of the OPT model. This method can help avoid overtraining and injury for these clients.

## Multiple-set resistance-training system

The multiple-set resistance-training system involves performing several sets of several different exercises over the course of a workout. This training approach has been in vogue since the 1940s. The number of sets and repetitions depends on the training level of the client and his or her ultimate goals. While a client at any level can be placed in a multiple-set resistance-training routine, it is particularly beneficial for advanced clients looking for significant strength and hypertrophy gains.

Health and fitness professionals should be cautious with multiple-set resistance training, taking care not to over-train a client through overuse of areas of the body, leading to exhaustion and possible injury. This is especially likely with novice clients whose body tissues have not been fully conditioned through the steps of the OPT model.

## Pyramid resistance-training system

The pyramid resistance-training system involves increasing or decreasing the weight after each set. When adding weight, anywhere from ten to twelve repetitions per set are recommended. Weight should be added incrementally until the client can only perform a few repetitions at that level.

When subtracting weight, fewer repetitions per set are recommended; the heaviest sets should involve about two repetitions, and the lightest set should include four to six repetitions.

This system can also be adapted to a higher number of repetitions (up to 20) by correspondingly decreasing the overall starting and ending weights.

## Superset resistance-training system

A superset involves performing two or more exercises in succession. This can be accomplished in two ways: by using compound sets or by using tri-sets. A compound set works the antagonist muscles of a muscle group one right after the other. This is an effective way to maximize training time. A tri-set uses three different exercises to work the same muscle group or body area. Tri-sets can also be modified as a bi-set, or two exercises to work one area.

Supersets should be performed in rapid succession without a rest between sets. Usually, supersets entail eight to twelve repetitions per set, although this can be modified by performing a higher number of repetitions at a lighter weight load. Superset training is very effective for those seeking maximal hypertrophy and strength gains, such as Olympic weight lifters or competitive bodybuilders.

### Circuit-training resistance-training system

The circuit-training resistance-training system involves many different exercises performed in rapid succession. The short rest between sets gives not only weight-training benefits but also a cardiovascular workout. In the workout programming, the number of sets, the number of repetitions, and the amount of rest between sets can all be adjusted. Sets can be single, double, or triple; repetitions can range from eight to a dozen. Rest periods can be short (10 to 15 seconds—just long enough to set up the next exercise) but should be no longer than one minute.

Because this is a rapid workout that provides weight training and cardiorespiratory benefits, it is a very good option for those with limited time to train.

### PHA resistance-training system

The peripheral heart action (PHA) resistance-training system is circuit training that alternates between upper body and lower body exercises. PHA training can improve circulation because it distributes blood flow through the upper and lower extremities. The client can perform a wide range of repetitions depending on the ultimate training goal (8 on the low end and 20 on the high end). This may be an ideal part of a program aimed at changing body composition.

### Split-routine system

The split-routine training system splits the body into different regions to be trained during different training sessions. This can be ideal for athletes that have specific track and field events, such as shot-putters, or those seeking maximum hypertrophy, such as bodybuilders. Adequate recovery time is need for each body region trained.

### Vertical and horizontal loading resistance-training systems

Vertical loading, a resistance-training system favored by NASM, travels down the NASM training template in a vertical manner and cycles through body parts in the following manner: whole body, pectoral area, back area, upper arms/shoulders, front arm (biceps), back arm (triceps), and lower extremities. A full rotation is performed, and then the client can begin at the top again. If the exercises are done in rapid succession, this can also become a circuit-style resistance-training routine.

Horizontal loading exhausts one region of the body at a time before working out another region. This is a very popular method of resistance training, but it can waste time with extended rest between sets. If minimal rest is used, horizontal loading can be an effective method of maximizing strength and hypertrophy gains.

## Total-body: stabilization-level exercises

### Ball squat/curl-to-press exercise

For the ball squat/curl-to-press, a stability ball and dumbbells are used.

Have the client stand facing away from a wall, with the stability ball pressed up against the wall by his or her lower back. The client holds the dumbbells in both hands and then rolls down the wall in a squat. The toes should be pointed forward, and the feet are placed shoulder-width apart.

As the client rolls up on the ball and straightens the legs out of the squat, he or she curls the dumbbells up by bending the arms fully at the elbow, and then continues to lift the dumbbells into full extension over the head, with the palms facing away from the wall.

Be sure that the core musculature is engaged at all times and the feet, knees, and hips stay in proper forward alignment.

Multiplanar step-up balance to overhead press exercise

For the multiplanar step-up balance to overhead press, an exercise step and dumbbells are used. The client stands in front of the step with the dumbbells in both hands. Have the client place one foot on the step, so the leg is bent at the knee. The client should step up onto the box with the raised leg, fully straightening it as the other leg is brought up and bent at a right angle at the knee, resulting in the client balancing on the stepping leg. At the same time, the client curls the dumbbells up by bending the arms fully at the elbow and then continues to lift the dumbbells into full extension over the head, with the palms facing forward.

Be sure that the core musculature is engaged at all times and the feet, knees, and hips stay in proper forward alignment.

## Total-body: strength-level exercises

Lunge to two-arm dumbbell press exercise

For the lunge to two-arm dumbbell press, two dumbbells will be needed.

The client stands with the legs shoulder-width apart and the dumbbells in both hands at the sides of the body. The hands should be turned in toward the body. Have the client step into a deep lunge with one foot forward. Both legs should be bent at right angles. From there, the client pushes hard back into the starting position, while moving the arms through a full curl, and then straightening them up fully overhead. Repeat and lunge with opposite foot.

Be sure the core musculature is engaged at all times and the feet, knees, and hips stay in proper forward alignment to engage the correct muscle groups and avoid unnecessary strain on the lower back.

Squat to two-arm press exercise

For the squat to two-arm press, two dumbbells are used.

The client stands with the feet shoulder-width apart and the dumbbells in both hands, which should rest at the client's sides. The client should activate the core muscles by performing the drawing-in maneuver. Keeping the back straight, have the client bend the knees as if he or she is sitting in a chair. Using the gluteal muscles, the client straightens into a standing position while bending the arms at the elbows into a full curl. This motion is then continued with the arms fully extended over the head.

Be sure that the core musculature is engaged at all times and the feet, knees, and hips stay in proper forward alignment to engage the correct muscle groups and avoid unnecessary strain on the lower back.

## Total-body: power-level exercises

<u>Two-arm push press exercise</u>
For the two-arm push press, two dumbbells are used.

Have the client stand with the feet shoulder-width apart and the dumbbells in both hands, which should rest at his or her sides. The client should activate the core muscles by performing the drawing-in maneuver. Keeping the back straight, the client raises the dumbbells up to his or her ears, with the elbows bent and the palms of the hands facing forward. As the client fully extends the arms up over the head, he or she steps forward with one leg. The forward leg should remain bent, and the back leg should be rotated inward at the hip and knee. The foot should be flexed with the heel off the ground.

Be sure that the core musculature is engaged at all times and the feet, knees, and hips stay in proper forward alignment to engage the correct muscle groups and avoid unnecessary strain on the lower back.

<u>Barbell clean exercise</u>
For the barbell clean, a lightly weighted barbell will be needed.

Have the client bend behind the barbell, with knees fully bent and hands gripping the barbell with knuckles facing forward. The feet should be shoulder-width apart. The client should activate the core muscles by performing the drawing-in maneuver. Keeping the back straight, the client raises the barbell by bending straight up at the elbow (not in a curl). When the bar is at chest level, the elbows fully bend, so the barbell is under the chin. This is a reverse curl: The palms should be facing forward, not in toward the client.

Be sure that the core musculature is engaged at all times and the feet, knees, and hips stay in proper forward alignment to engage the correct muscle groups and avoid unnecessary strain on the lower back.

## Vertical-loading: stabilization-level exercises

<u>Ball dumbbell chest press</u>
For the ball dumbbell chest press, a stability ball and dumbbells are used.

Place the ball on the ground, and have the client lie face up on the ball, with the upper back resting on the ball and the lower body bent at a right angle at the knees, feet facing forward. The client holds the dumbbells straight up, which will be directly in front of him- or herself at chest level. Palms should be pointed forward or down to the client's recumbent position.

The client bends the arms at the elbows, lowering the dumbbells into a press position, and then straighten them back out in front of the body.

Be sure the core musculature is engaged at all times and the feet, knees, and hips stay in proper forward alignment to engage the correct muscle groups and avoid unnecessary strain on the lower back.

## Push-up exercise

The client starts in a classic push-up position: The legs are closed, the feet are together, the arms are shoulder-width apart, and the palms are flat and pointing up. The client should perform the drawing-in maneuver, tightening the core musculature to maintain a strong plank position to challenge these muscles and to avoid unnecessary stress to the lower back. Have the client bend his or her arms at the elbows and lower down as far as possible while maintaining proper form.

To make this exercise easier, have the client position on the knees or press off of a bench or wall instead of the ground.

To make this exercise harder, have the client position the feet on a stability ball or place the hands on medicine or stability balls.

## Standing cable row back exercise

A cable machine is used for the standing cable row.

The client stands facing the cable machine with the feet shoulder-width apart and one foot about eighteen inches in front of the other foot. Both knees should be slightly bent. Have the client grip the cables with arms fully extended straight in front at chest height. The hands should face inward. The client pulls straight back, bends the elbows, and presses the shoulder blades down. Have the client slowly release and return to the original position. Be sure that proper posture is maintained; do not allow the shoulders to rise or the head to press forward.

This exercise can be performed in a seated position to make it easier. The arms can be alternated while standing on two feet or the exercise could be performed on one foot to make this exercise more challenging.

## Ball dumbbell row back exercise

For the ball dumbbell row, a stability ball and a set of dumbbells are used.

Have the client lie on his or her stomach on the ball. The body should be in a plank position, with the core musculature activated and the body flat and extended. The client holds the dumbbells just off the ground in front of him- or herself, with arms fully extended straight ahead at shoulder level. The palms of the hands should face the ground. Have the client perform a row motion by pulling the dumbbells straight back toward his or her body, bending the elbows and pressing the shoulder blades down.

To make this exercise easier, the client bends over the ball instead of laying on it. To make this exercise more difficult, try alternating the arms or performing the exercise one arm per set.

## Single-leg dumbbell scaption shoulder exercise

For the single-leg dumbbell scaption, two dumbbells are used.

The client stands in a neutral position, with hips, knees, and feet facing front. Have the client hold the dumbbells in both hands, which should be facing forward and held in a low V slightly away from the body. The client should perform the drawing-in maneuver to activate the core musculature and gluteals. Then have him or her raise one foot slightly off the ground and balance on the other foot.

The client slowly raises the dumbbells out to either side by lifting the arms so the body is in a T pose. The thumbs should face the ceiling. Have the client slowly release and return to the starting position.

To make this exercise easier, the client performs the exercise sitting down or standing on both feet. To make this exercise more difficult, the client alternates arms or uses only one arm per set.

## Seated stability-ball military press shoulder exercise

For the seated stability-ball military press, a stability ball and two dumbbells are used.

The client sits on the ball in a neutral position, with hips, knees, and feet facing forward. Have the client hold the dumbbells in both hands, which should be raised to form right angles at the elbows, with the dumbbells at ear level; the hands should face forward.

The client should perform the drawing-in maneuver to activate the core musculature. Make sure the client maintains proper posture to avoid unnecessary stress to the lower back. Have the client raise the dumbbells over his or her head by straightening the arms; the hands should continue to face forward throughout the motion. The client slowly releases and returns to the starting position.

To make this exercise easier, the client sits on a stable surface. To make this exercise harder, the client alternates arms or uses only one arm per set.

## Seated dumbbell shoulder press exercise

For the seated dumbbell shoulder press, a weight bench and two dumbbells are used.

The client sits in a neutral position, with hips, knees, and feet facing forward, on a weight bench that has the seat back raised. Knees are bent at right angles, and feet are flat on the floor. Have the client hold the dumbbells in both hands, which should be raised to form right angles at the elbows, with the dumbbells at ear level; the hands should face forward.

The client should perform the drawing-in maneuver to activate the core musculature. Make sure the client keeps proper posture to avoid unnecessary stress on the lower back. Have the client raise the dumbbells over his or her head by straightening the arms; the hands should continue to face forward throughout the motion. The client slowly releases and returns to the starting position.

Watch out for postural compensations, especially the head protruding forward; correct this immediately.

## Single-leg dumbbell curl biceps exercise

For the single-leg dumbbell curl, a set of dumbbells is used.

The client begins in a neutral position, with the hips, knees, and feet facing forward. Have the client hold the dumbbells in a low V formation, with the arms held slightly away from the body. The hands face forward and slightly outward. The client should perform the drawing-in maneuver to activate the core musculature and to tighten the gluteals. The client raises one foot slightly off the ground and balances on the opposite leg while bending at the elbow and lifting the dumbbells into full curls. The client slowly releases and returns to the starting position. Be sure the client keeps the shoulder blades pressed down during the exercise.

To make this exercise easier, the client stands on both feet. To make this exercise more difficult, the client alternates arms or uses only one arm per set.

### Single-leg barbell curl biceps exercise
For the single-leg barbell curl, a weighted barbell is used.

The client begins in a neutral position, with the hips, knees, and feet facing forward. Have the client hold the barbell with arms fully extended and resting near the tops of the thighs. The palms of the hands face forward. The client should perform the drawing-in maneuver to activate the core musculature and tighten the gluteals. The client raises one foot slightly off the ground and balances on the opposite leg while bending at the elbow and lifting the barbell into a full curl. Have the client slowly release and return to the starting position. Be sure the client keeps the shoulder blades pressed down during the exercise.

To make this exercise easier, the client stands on both feet. To make this exercise more difficult, the client alternates arms or uses only one arm per set.

### Supine ball dumbbell triceps extension exercise
For the supine ball dumbbell triceps extension, a stability ball and set of dumbbells are used.

The client lies on the stability ball with the mid-back resting on the ball, the lower torso balanced off the edge of the ball, and the legs bent at the knee in a right angle. Have the client hold the dumbbells in both hands, which should be held straight up, or in front in the recumbent position, with arms fully extended at shoulder level. The palms should face inward, toward each other.

The client should perform the drawing-in maneuver to activate the core musculature; make sure proper posture is maintained to avoid unnecessary strain on the lower back. The client bends the elbows toward the head, making a right angle. Have the client slowly release and return to the original position.

To make this exercise easier, the client performs it on a stable surface. To make this exercise harder, the client alternates arms or uses one arm per set.

### Prone ball dumbbell triceps extension exercise
For the prone ball dumbbell triceps extension, a stability ball and a set of dumbbells are used.

The client lies on his or her stomach on the stability ball, with the legs straight back and toes resting on the floor. Have the client hold the dumbbells in both hands with the upper arms held close to the body and bent at a right angle at the elbow. The palms should face inward, toward the stability ball.

The client should perform the drawing-in maneuver to activate the core musculature; make sure proper posture is maintained to avoid unnecessary strain on the lower back. The client straightens the arms straight back, so they are in a straight line with the body. Have the client slowly release and return to the original position.

To make this exercise easier, the client performs it standing up. To make this exercise harder, the client alternates arms or uses one arm per set.

## Ball squat leg exercise

For the ball squat, a stability ball and a set of dumbbells are used.

The client presses the stability ball up against a wall with his or her mid-back. Have the client stand in a neutral position, with hips, knees, and feet facing forward. The dumbbells are held at the client's sides, with the hands facing inward. The client should perform the drawing-in maneuver to activate the core musculature. The client rolls down the wall on the ball by bending at the knees until they are almost at a right angle. Have the client slowly roll back up to the starting position.

To make this exercise easier, the client bends less or holds on to a fixed object while squatting. To make this exercise more difficult, the client omits the stability ball; observe for kinetic-chain compensations and correct immediately.

## Multiplanar step-up to balance

For the multiplanar step-up to balance, an exercise step and a set of dumbbells are used.

The client stands in front of the step in a neutral position, with hips, knees, and feet facing forward. Have the client hold the dumbbells at his or her sides, with arms fully extended and hands facing in. The client should perform the drawing-in maneuver to activate the core musculature and also to ready the gluteals. The client steps up with one foot, pushes upward, and balances on that foot while the other foot is brought up by fully bending the opposite leg. The second foot should never touch the step. Have the client balance for a beat then return to the original starting position.

To make this exercise easier, the client can use a lower step. To make this exercise more difficult, the client can step up in different planes of motion.

## Vertical-loading: strength-level exercises

### Flat dumbbell chest press

For the flat dumbbell chest press, a weight bench and two dumbbells are used.

The client lies down flat on the weight bench with his or her knees hanging over the edge, bent at a right angle, toes pointed forward. Have the client hold the dumbbells straight in front of him- or herself, with arms fully extended at shoulder level. The hands should be facing down from the client's recumbent perspective. The client should perform the drawing-in maneuver, tightening the core musculature and making sure not to hyperextend the lower back.

Have the client bend the arms at the elbows, opening the arms, so the upper part is level with the body and the arms are bent at right angles. The client presses back up to the starting position. Be sure the arm muscles contract during the movement and the shoulders retract and press down.

### Barbell bench press chest exercise

For the barbell bench press, a weight bench and weighted barbell are used.

Have the client lie down flat on the weight bench with his or her knees hanging over the edge bent at a right angle; toes pointed forward. The client grips the barbell with the arms spaced wider apart than the shoulders. The client should perform the drawing-in maneuver, tightening the core musculature and making sure not to hyperextend the lower back. The client lifts the barbell from the stand, and then lowers it to the chest in a slow, controlled motion. Have the client press the bar back upward, fully straightening the arms.

### Seated cable row back exercise
For the seated cable row, a cable machine is used.

The client sits facing toward the cable machine, placing the feet on the steps shoulder-width apart, knees slightly bent. Have the client grip the cables and fully extend the arms out front. The client should perform the drawing-in maneuver to activate the core musculature. Be sure the core muscles are in proper alignment to avoid unnecessary strain on the lower back. Have the client pull back on the cables, bending the elbows and pressing the shoulder blades down. Make sure no postural distortions occur, particularly the head-jutting-forward compensation, and have the client keep his or her torso stabilized and still. The client slowly releases the cables and returns to the starting position.

### Lat pull down back exercise
For the seated lat pull down, the client must use a lat machine.

Have the client sit facing in toward the lat machine. Hips, knees, and feet should face forward. The client should perform the drawing-in maneuver to activate the core musculature. The client grips the handles of the machine at a point wider than the shoulders; the hands should face forward, toward the machine. Leaning back just slightly, have the client pull the handles down in a slow, controlled manner so the arms are completely bent at the elbow, and the bar is in front of the chest. Have the client slowly release and return to the original position.

Make sure the client maintains proper posture to avoid placing unnecessary stress on the lower back. NASM recommends against lat exercises that pull the weight behind the head instead of in front of the head because these exercises add stress to the upper back and neck musculature.

### Seated shoulder press exercise
For the seated shoulder press, a shoulder press machine is used.

The client sits on the shoulder press machine in a neutral position, with hips, knees, and feet facing forward. Knees are bent at a right angle, and feet are flat on the floor. Have the client grip the handles, with hands positioned wider than shoulder-width apart.

The client should perform the drawing-in maneuver to activate the core musculature. Make sure the client keeps proper posture to avoid unnecessary stress to the lower back. Have the client pull down slowly on the handles, bending at the elbow, until reaching the lowest point the handles will go. The client slowly releases and returns to the starting position.

Watch postural compensations, especially the head protruding forward; correct this immediately.

### Biceps curl exercise
For the biceps curl, a curl machine will be needed. Be sure the machine is calibrated to fit the client.

The client sits at the curl machine in a neutral position, with the hips, knees, and feet facing forward. Have the client grip the handles of the machine with the palms facing forward. The client should perform the drawing-in maneuver to activate the core musculature; make sure proper posture is maintained to avoid unnecessary strain on the lower back.

The client bends the arms at the elbow and brings the handle up in a full curl. Have the client slowly release and return to the original position. Be sure the client keeps the shoulder blades pressed down during the exercise and the movement is fully controlled all the way up and down to avoid strain on the elbow joint.

## Seated two-arm dumbbell biceps curl

For the seated two-arm dumbbell biceps curl, a weight bench and a set of dumbbells are used.

The client sits in a neutral position, with the hips, knees, and feet facing forward on the weight bench, which should be in the seat back position. The client holds the dumbbells in both hands in a low V formation, with arms fully extended; the palms are facing forward. The client should perform the drawing-in maneuver to activate the core musculature; make sure proper posture is maintained to avoid unnecessary strain on the lower back.

Have the client bend the arms at the elbow and bring the dumbbells up in a full curl. The client slowly releases and returns to the original position. Be sure the client keeps the shoulder blades pressed down during this exercise.

## Cable pushdown triceps exercise

For the cable pushdown, a cable machine is used.

The client stands in front of the cable machine in a neutral position, with hips, knees, and feet facing forward. Have the client grip the handles on the machine; the arms should be bent at right angles. The client should perform the drawing-in maneuver to activate the core musculature. The client pulls down on the handles, fully extending the arms, so they are in a straight line with the body. The client slowly releases and returns to the original position. Be sure the client fully controls motion, so the elbow is not strained.

## Supine bench barbell triceps extension exercise

For the supine bench barbell triceps extension, a weight bench and a weighted barbell are used.

The client lies flat on the weight bench in a neutral position. The knees hang off the edge of the bench and bend at a right angle; knees and feet face forward. Have the client grip the barbell with both hands, spaced shoulder-width apart. The palms should face down, from the client's recumbent perspective. The client slowly bends the arms at the elbows, so the bar is being moved toward the face. The hands should face straight up. Have the client slowly release and return to the starting position.

Be sure that the client does not hold the barbell with too wide of a grip, because this can increase the stress on the elbow joint.

## Leg press exercise

For this exercise, a leg press machine is needed.

The client sits on the leg press machine in a neutral position. Be sure the machine is calibrated for the client's height.

The client places the feet on the plate a shoulder-width distance apart, with knees and feet pointing forward. The client should perform the drawing-in maneuver to activate the core musculature and ready the gluteals then push the weight slowly away. Observe for kinetic-chain compensations and correct immediately. The client maintains the exercise for as long as the proper form can be maintained, and then slowly returns to the starting position.

Barbell squat

For the barbell squat, a weighted barbell is used.

The client stands in a neutral position, with feet evenly spaced under the shoulders. The hips, knees, and feet are pointing straight ahead. Have the client rest the barbell across the back of his or her shoulders. The hands should grip the barbell further apart than the shoulders.

The client should perform the drawing-in maneuver to activate the core muscles; be sure he or she maintains proper posture to avoid unnecessary strain on the lower back. The client squats by bending at the knee and slowly lowering down. Have the client continue to the point where postural compensations are seen, and then have the client slowly return to the original position.

As the client increases his or her strength and stability, he or she will be able to squat further without compensations.

## Vertical-loading: power-level exercises

Two-arm medicine ball chest pass

For the two-arm medicine ball chest pass, a weighted medicine ball is used.

The client stands facing a wall that is about five to ten feet away. The shoulders, hips, and feet should face forward, with the knees slightly bent. The client holds the medicine ball in front of his or her chest, with the elbows slightly bent. The client should perform the drawing-in maneuver to activate the core musculature. Making sure the client's body maintains proper posture, have him or her throw the ball at the wall by pushing it forward in an explosive motion, using the arm and chest muscles.

This exercise can also be performed on equipment if a medicine ball is not available.

Two-arm rotation chest pass exercise

For the two-arm rotation chest pass, a weighted medicine ball is used.

The client stands next to a wall that is about five to ten feet away. The shoulders, hips, and feet should face forward, with the knees slightly bent. The client holds the medicine ball in front of his or her chest, with the elbows slightly bent. The client should perform the drawing-in maneuver to activate the core musculature. Making sure the client's body maintains proper posture, have him or her twist sideways, pivoting the foot and inverting at the hip and knee joints as he or she throws the ball at the wall by pushing it forward in an explosive motion, using the arm and chest muscles, particularly using the arm farthest from the wall. This motion is much like a side pass in basketball.

Medicine ball pullover throw-back exercise

For the medicine ball pullover throw-back, a stability ball and weighted medicine ball are used.

Have the client lie on the stability ball with his or her mid-back pressed against the ball and legs hanging over the edge; knees bent at a right angle and feet pointing forward. The client should perform the drawing-in maneuver to activate the core musculature. Make sure the client maintains proper posture to avoid placing unnecessary stress on the lower back. The client holds the medicine ball in both hands; the arms should be fully extended over his or her head.

Focusing on using the abdominals, the client contracts up, bends forward, and throws the medicine ball forward in a strong, quick motion. Make sure the chin remains pressed into the chest during the exercise.

### Medicine-ball scoop pass exercise
For the medicine-ball scoop pass, a weighted medicine ball is used.

The client stands in a neutral position, with hips, knees, and feet facing forward. The feet are shoulder-width apart. The client should perform the drawing-in maneuver to activate the core musculature. Make sure the client keeps proper posture to avoid unnecessary stress to the lower back.

Have the client bend at the knees, keeping the back straight and core muscles pulled in, and hold the medicine ball with both hands on the outside of one knee. In a strong, explosive motion using the core muscles and gluteals, the client tosses the ball forward. The hands should be fully extended in front of the body at approximately shoulder level at the end of the movement. The client can toss the ball at a wall or work with a partner who tosses the ball back. Have the client repeat the exercise, alternating sides.

### Medicine-ball side oblique throw shoulder exercise
For the medicine-ball side oblique throw, a weighted medicine ball is used.

The client stands in a neutral position, with hips, knees, and feet facing forward. The feet are shoulder-width apart. The client should perform the drawing-in maneuver to activate the core musculature. Make sure proper posture is maintained to avoid unnecessary stress to the lower back.

Have the client bend at the knees, keeping the back straight and core muscles pulled in, and hold the medicine ball with both hands on the outside of one knee. In a strong, explosive motion using the core muscles and gluteals, the client tosses the ball sideways. The hands should be fully extended to the side of the body at approximately shoulder level at the end of the movement. The opposite hip, knee, and foot should fully rotate inward. The client can toss the ball at a wall or work with a partner who tosses the ball back. Have the client repeat the exercise, alternating sides.

### Squat jump leg exercise
To perform the squat jump, the client stands in a neutral position with feet shoulder-width apart, and hips, knees, and feet are facing forward. The client bends slightly at the knees and pulls the arms straight down and back in alignment with the torso. The client should perform the drawing-in maneuver to activate the core muscles and maintain proper posture to avoid unnecessary strain on the lower back. In a quick, explosive movement, have the client bend even further in the squat, and then jump straight up, extending arms and legs straight. On landing, the client returns both arms and legs to the starting position.

Be sure the client keeps the body controlled and lands in a gentle manner to avoid unnecessary strain on the joints.

## Tuck jump leg exercise

The client stands in a neutral position with feet shoulder-width apart and hips, knees, and feet facing forward. The client bends slightly at the knees and pulls the arms straight down and back in alignment with the torso. The client should perform the drawing-in maneuver to activate the core muscles and maintain proper posture to avoid unnecessary strain on the lower back. In a quick, explosive movement, have the client bend even further in the squat, and then jump up, pulling the knees into a tight tuck, but keeping the back straight. On landing, the client returns both arms and legs to the starting position.

Be sure the client keeps the body controlled and lands in a gentle manner to avoid unnecessary strain on the joints.

# Client Relations and Behavioral Coaching

## Stages of Change Model

People naturally resist change. Resistance to change is one of the biggest obstacles preventing clients from achieving their fitness goals. A trainer can help a client overcome their resistance to change by using NASM's stages of change model. There are five stages in the model, each with defining characteristics and strategies for success. When a trainer identifies the client's location in the change model, they can apply the appropriate strategy to help the client reach their goal.

The first stage is pre-contemplation, defined by an unwillingness to change. These people rarely seek out a trainer. The best strategy for working with a prospective client in this stage is supportive myth dispelling. When a client is considering exercise but not actively exercising, they are in the contemplation stage. Education is the best tool for a client in this stage. In the preparation stage, a client exercises infrequently but would like to begin a more rigorous and consistent program. Designing a realistic program and setting SMART goals are important methods used to help clients in this stage. The fourth stage is the action stage. In this stage, the client is exercising, but has not reached the six-month mark. It is important to identify any obstacles to success and develop a strategy to overcome the barrier. The last stage is the maintenance stage. When a client has exercised for six months or more they are in this stage. The best way to assist a client in this stage is to help them evaluate their progress and set new goals.

# Client Goal Setting

## Positive vision

When a person has direction and purpose, activities focus on attaining those goals. When a person only has a vague idea of what he or she may want to accomplish, actions may likewise be vague and meandering, never really adding up to any forward progress. These people are much more likely to have negative effects and to:
- Spend too much time thinking about what he or she wants to accomplish
- Spend less time working toward accomplishing these goals
- Be distractible and put things off
- Be less satisfied with life
- Be unhappy or depressed
- Have a higher incidence of illness

## Clarity and detail

A health and fitness professional must take responsibility in guiding the client's overall experience in the fitness setting. This starts with helping the client come up with a specific vision instead of a vague goal to set sights on a solid target and to avoid letdowns from the perception of not accomplishing a too-general goal.

For example, if a person says they want to lose weight, the health and fitness professional should press further for a more-specific vision. A person can work out with a great deal of success, lose inches from the waistline and build muscle, which weighs more than fat, thus revealing no actual weight loss. If the client's goal is merely to lose weight, he or she may perceive the efforts to have failed.

Instead, the trainer should inquire further as to what the client's underlying goals and motivations are and set more specific targets, such as losing inches from the waistline or reducing BMI.

## Root cause analysis

Root cause analysis is the process of continuing to ask a person "Why?" until the most basic motivation for an action is uncovered. When asking a client their goal or goals in the fitness setting, simply ask "Why?" when he or she gives a response. For example, if a client says she wants to lose weight, ask why. Her response may be that she wants to fit into her old jeans. Then ask why. Her response may be that she has a high school reunion coming up. It is always helpful to you and the client to understand the underlying motivation.

NASM also has a short list of alternative questions that help accomplish the same goal. Clients may find these queries unusual, so encourage the client to remain open minded as you create goals together. These questions include:
- The lottery scenario: What would you do if you won?
- The superman scenario: If you could do anything well, what would it be?
- Who do you admire and why?
- What are your favorite activities?

## Psychological aspect

A vision is an overarching picture of the goal or set of goals a client wants to achieve. However, just having this picture in mind will not put him or her on the road to achieving it. For that, there must be a strategy, or a defined method, of working toward those goals.

Developing a strategy is essential because a client can become discouraged if he or she feels the goals are not being met. By defining steps, the client can engage in activities and measure success in smaller increments. This allows the client to see that progress is being made; although the ultimate goals may not be realized right away, they are attainable.
NASM uses the acronym SMART to help the health and fitness professional and the client come up with a specific strategy for achieving fitness goals.

For many clients, fitness goals are not difficult because of the physical challenges they present, but because a person has behavioral issues that must be changed or negative attitudes about fitness, nutrition, or his or her own body that must be addressed to succeed.

As a health and fitness professional, it is important to know how to help a person accomplish their fitness goals not only from a training standpoint, but also from a psychological standpoint. This is necessary because trainers must continually motivate the client not only for the client's own good but also to help themselves achieve goals and retain clients.

### Maximizing psychological approach
There are five steps recommended by NASM to motivate clients, outline realistic goals, and put the client in the right frame of mind to overcome barriers and accomplish their goals:
1. Vision—encompasses looking at the big picture and creating an ideal scenario that the client is working toward
2. Strategy—breaks down exactly how the vision will be achieved, using measurable goals and methods
3. Belief—focuses on overcoming nonphysical barriers to success—specifically fear, uncertainty, and doubt (FUD)
4. Persistence—details how to maintain focus and determination even when the actions are difficult.
5. Learning—deals with tweaking the overall approach to learn from the good and the bad. Positive steps should be further explored, while missteps or negative aspects can be curtailed.

## SMART

SMART is an acronym used by NASM to guide health and fitness professionals and assist in creating a strategy for each client to achieve his or her fitness goals. The letters stand for the following:
- Specific—A specific goal clearly identifies what is to be achieved. Specific goals offer clear direction and level set expectations.
- Measurable—Measurable goals can be quantified and tracked. Without the ability to track goals, it is difficult to determine success or failure.
- Attainable—An attainable goal follows the Goldilocks principle (not too easy not too hard). It is challenging enough that the client must work hard to achieve it, but not so difficult that the client loses hope. Clients do not progress when goals are too easy and lose motivation when goals are not attainable.

- 164 -

- Realistic—A goal is realistic if a client is willing and able to achieve it.
- Timely— Time-bound goals have clearly defined time frames which provide structure and set priorities.

## Belief

Belief is essential when working toward goals. No matter how specific a person's vision is and what strategy is undertaken to accomplish it, it will never come to fruition if the client does not believe that it is possible to accomplish the goals. Sometimes, a person may say they want something, but he or she will have an underlying fear of achieving it. These conflicting attitudes can lead to apathy or self-sabotage.

As a health and fitness professional, it is important to work toward minimizing what NASM refers to as FUD: fear, uncertainty, and doubt. Identifying these elements with the client is the first step. Small, achievable goals should be used to build the client's confidence. Any negative feelings can also be indulged in a controlled manner; for example, the client may be allowed one minute in the locker room to verbalize his or her fears or impediments and then leave these feelings at the door for the duration of the workout.

### Research
There is a great deal of scientific information available relating to how a sense of believing in oneself can have a great positive impact on a person's life. These impacts include:
- Having a better work ethic
- Being more content
- Tackling problems in a positive manner
- Recovering from setbacks more easily
- Coping better and learn from mistakes
- Having better goal-setting skills

## Fears and anxieties

NASM encourages several different methods to help a client overcome fears and doubts. These include:
- Making time for the negative—Sometimes clients have a hard time keeping the voice quiet within that tells them they can't. Instead of forcing this noise to be quiet, allow the client to indulge, but only at a set time and place. By verbalizing fears, the client may be able to leave these feelings behind when beginning a workout.
- Visualizing success—Instead of picturing failure, the client visualizes success. This positive visualization is linked to better performance.
- Take it one step at a time—Even though a big-picture vision has been set, it is essential for clients to remember that goals are achieved one step at a time. Define some of these small steps, and work toward them to bolster confidence.

## Persistence

Long-term success requires persistence, or the ability to continue on a path even in the face of problems or challenges. This holds true for fitness goals as well—not only accomplishing the goals in the first place but also maintaining the results over time. By addressing this reality with clients, it increases the likelihood that they will be able to accept that setbacks are part of a realistic journey toward the goal, and will help the client realize their ultimate goals.

Research has shown that even among people who can keep their annual resolutions for two years, they admit to more than a dozen cheats in that period. However, instead of becoming completely demoralized, they viewed this as a realistic part of life and resumed their drive to maintain the goal.

<u>Bolstering levels of persistence</u>
When it comes to achieving fitness goals, it is important that a client is able to persevere through minor setbacks in pursuit of the ultimate goal. NASM recommends three different approaches to promoting perseverance:
1. Plan for challenges—When developing a strategy for accomplishing goals, account for occasional setbacks. If a client anticipates potential setbacks and there is a strategy in place for handling them, they may be easier to cope with.
2. Give rewards—NASM espouses the deposit-and-refund technique, where the client gives money to a friend and gets a partial refund for each increment of success (for example, losing a pound). This works very well in group training, too.
3. Build a support group—Help the client build a network of friends, family, and workout buddies who can act as a support system. Not only will this inspire high performance but these people can also help the client get through challenging times with love and encouragement.

**Learning**

Learning deals with how a client can gain knowledge from the positives and negatives he or she has experienced on the road to meeting goals. NASM advocates self-monitoring, which simply means that the client monitors his or her progress, honestly viewing and recording the good and the bad. Studies have shown that people who engage in self-monitoring are better able to meet their goals.

Recording helps the client see progress or slipups more clearly. Once the client sees progress objectively, corrective action can be taken. The client should make adjustments to strategy and execution, tweaking the routine to incorporate what works and to eliminate things that are not working.

<u>Methods of learning</u>
It is vitally important for a client to identify actions or activities that are not conducive to accomplishing a goal. Once the potential detractors are identified, the client must make the necessary changes to correct them. If a client continues with activities that are contrary to accomplishing a goal, progress may be slow or nonexistent, and the client may become discouraged or feel like they are failing. NASM recommends the following:
- Change what you can—It is important to work on things that can be changed and let go of what cannot. Look at actions, not measurements, when beginning a fitness regimen.
- Look at the record—When habits are examined, patterns (positive and negative) emerge. Use this information as a tool to develop improved strategies.
- Rate it—Have clients rate their daily progress on a 0–10 scale.
- Look at progress—Review clients' training records with them to monitor progress toward fitness goals.

# Customer Service

Instead of viewing personal training solely as a source of income, a health and fitness professional should focus on improving people's lives and promoting healthy lifestyles. This viewpoint helps underscore the main goal of a trainer's business—to maintain a happy, healthy clientele. When the trainer focuses on the client, better service (and the resulting benefits) is provided. Continued education with a focus on the ability to offer a wide array of tools to the client is part of the client-focused approach. NASM recommends continuing education through its certification training, which includes its Foundations for the Health and Fitness Professional course, the Certified Personal Trainer certification course, and numerous continuing education courses that give trainers tools to work with special populations or with specialized exercise techniques.

## Uncompromising customer service

Fitness training is a very competitive business. Thousands of gyms offer personal training sessions with independent trainers. This means that it is essential for a trainer to build an excellent reputation based not only on skill as a trainer and ability to get results, but also on the level of customer service offered.

Uncompromising customer service encompasses not only the quality of the training but also the level of attention and how valued the client feels. This can come from such features as promptly returned calls, timeliness of workouts, and professional billing practices. It is also important for the trainer to make sure the client feels comfortable in the workout environment—whether it is a health club or other locale. A trainer should remember that spending decisions are in large part emotional. By offering the very best customer service, a trainer improves the way a client feels about the entire training experience.

## Six guidelines for customer service

A health and fitness professional should act in a manner that reflects the idea that his or her entire business could depend on how each person he or she interacts with rates that interaction. Some guidelines for extending the best customer service are:
1. Present oneself professionally, consider appearance and in manner.
2. Speak to everyone at a health club and work toward making positive contacts.
3. Speak in a professional, educated manner that elicits confidence.
4. Answer and encourage all questions and respond respectfully.
5. Work to promote professional work relationships.
6. Learn from mistakes or complaints.

Maintaining positive relationships with coworkers and potential clients, continuing to educate oneself, increasing the services offered, and behaving in a professional manner are all essential components of excellent customer service.

# Acquiring Clients

## Potential customers

Nearly everyone is a potential customer. As people consume foods laden with calories and lead increasingly sedentary lifestyles, adding daily fitness activities is crucial for improving health and wellness. Research has shown that people in special populations can benefit from regular exercise, making children, seniors, pregnant women, and even those with heart and lung problems potential clients in need of health and fitness trainers with specific and specialized knowledge.

In the past, personal training was viewed as a luxury, in modern life, it is becoming a necessity. Personal trainers are needed to help people stay fit and to prevent potential health problems that result from postural distortions and sedentary living.

There are a variety of motives driving people to seek a trainer. Motives may include a desire to look and feel better, a need to perform physical tasks more effectively, and improved overall health. Because nearly everyone wants to accomplish at least one of these goals, the number of potential customers is substantial.

## Approach potential customers

When a trainer is not working with a client, the focus should be on building clientele, making approach techniques essential. Adopting a policy of saying hello to every person, sprucing up the gym area, and offering water or towels to members, are examples of simple customer service gestures that will help the trainer build a reputation as a conscientious professional and attract potential clients.

Approach the client in a very friendly, neutral manner the first time. Introducing yourself or asking the client's name and leaving it at that until a future encounter is a good move. Upon meeting that person again, calling them by name will help you stick out in the customer's mind.

## Building rapport

After breaking the ice, you may feel more comfortable offering a small bit of advice to a client who is working out independently. Proceed tactfully; focus on maximizing the exercise rather than correcting the client, and use the opportunity to share information, rather than offer instruction.

Many people have firm ideas about how to exercise and may perceive corrective language as admonishing or even rude. A negative approach may rub the client the wrong way, which is not the intent. Avoid correcting or offering a better way. Even the seemingly innocuous "can I suggest something?" can come off as offensive.

## Increasing value of services

Just because a person wants to get in shape or lose weight does not mean that he or she will. Before a person commits to working with a trainer, he or she must feel that there is adequate value for the money and time invested.

It is extremely helpful for a trainer to be well versed in all NASM's systematic tools to demonstrate that the services offered have a high value. These include performing assessments, programming the Optimum Performance Training (OPT) template, having a wide knowledge of different exercises that target various muscle groups, the ability to help a client achieve performance goals, and being able to discuss fluently the OPT model and how it can benefit a specific client.

Being able to show clients that you are proficient with many specific tools for success gives them confidence that working with you will provide the value that they are seeking for their money.

## READ system

NASM teaches CPTs to employ a specific system to acquire new clients. To help describe the steps in a memorable way, NASM uses the acronym READ. The letters stand for the following:
- Rapport—the essential relationship building that a trainer must establish with a new client.
- Empathy—the sense of understanding that must go hand in hand with physical training skills, in which the trainer learns to uncover and cater to the emotional reasons a person seeks training.
- Assessment—the process of determining what the client is trying to accomplish.
- Development—the ability of the trainer to build a plan for success.

### Rapport
Rapport is the first step required for trainers to obtain new clients; it is the foundation of a professional relationship based on communication, pleasant interaction, and commonality of purpose. This foundation is essential to establish trust and build common ground from which to work.

It is necessary to maximize communication to build rapport with a potential client. This comes not only in the form of verbal communication but also in actions and nonverbal cues, such as body language. These communications convey an overall impression to potential clients that reflects positively on the trainer and the training environment. Because people make decisions based on how they feel about a certain situation, establishing rapport in these subtle interactions is vital.

*Developing a presence:* Developing rapport with a potential client is an essential first step to eventually closing the sale. To maximize the level of positive nonverbal communication, a trainer can work on developing a certain presence that inspires confidence and respect.

According to NASM, presence is typified by three elements: professionalism, enthusiasm, and confidence.
- Professionalism can be conveyed by the style of dress and appearance, friendliness, and manner of behavior (never gossiping or bad-mouthing the health club, its staff, or other clients).
- Enthusiasm is displaying a positive outward attitude about training and clients. This shows that the trainer is happy to be working with clients and values their goals and business.
- Confidence is necessary to build the trust of a potential client and show that the trainer is competent and can deliver the results he or she promises.

## Empathy

Empathy is being able to understand someone else's point of view and the emotions that result. This is important because it is a potential client's motivation—not his or her goals—that is key to gaining them as a client. The trainer must understand the client's motivation to build empathy.

Motivation is why someone does something, feels a certain way, or acts in a particular manner. It is essential for a trainer to understand motivation not only to develop a rapport with a potential client but also to understand how to inspire a current client to stick with his or her training program by encouraging them based on these emotional triggers.

Empathizing with a client helps the trainer navigate the psychology associated with helping people accomplish fitness goals. If a trainer can understand where a person is coming from and what negative associations, fears, or doubts the person is dealing with, the trainer can be more sensitive and tactful while helping the person accomplish his or her goals.

*Building empathy:* People behave in large part based on how they feel about things, not necessarily on what they think. This is based on a person's life experiences and observations. To build empathy and understanding with a client, the trainer must ask four questions:
1. What is your goal?
2. When did you set this goal?
3. Why is this goal important to you?
4. What have been prior roadblocks to accomplishing this goal?

The answers will help the trainer uncover how the client feels about fitness, working out, and his or her body. Once a trainer knows the answers to the four questions, he or she can establish whether the person is motivated by the positive (feeling healthy or looking good) or the negative (avoiding illness or being fat). This will allow the trainer to empathize with the client and provide insight into how to motivate that particular person.

## Enthusiasm

Once a health and fitness professional understands why a person wants to achieve certain fitness goals, he or she can tailor motivational efforts to match the person's specific needs. Clients can be motivated by the positive (feeling healthy or looking good), or the negative (avoiding illness or being fat).

To build enthusiasm among those who are motivated by the positive, trainers should:
- Remind the client that working out today will pay off in the future.
- List the potential benefits of each exercise for the client.
- Give praise that emphasizes accomplishment, pride, and noticing small improvements.

To build enthusiasm among those who are motivated by the negative, trainers should:
- Remind the client that skipping a workout today will have negative effects in the future.
- List the negative aspects of not performing a certain exercise for the client.
- Speak to the client's emotional issues: fear, being fat, and not being accepted.

## Assessment

In the assessment phase of closing a sale with a potential client, the health and fitness professional puts the technical aspects of his or her NASM training into action. The trainer has already established a relationship of trust (rapport) and gotten to understand why the client wants to achieve certain goals (empathy).

Now is the time to find ways to accomplish those goals, utilizing the OPT model and all of the other assessment tools contained in the NASM CPT course. By detailing some ideas and concrete techniques to accomplish these fitness goals, the trainer will make the value of his or her services clear to the client, making it easier to close the sale. This will be accomplished by asking the right questions, and then making the features and benefits of a training program clear.

*Asking questions:* To assess how to help a client achieve goals, it is vital to engage in a question-based dialogue. This not only helps identify what the client is trying to accomplish, but it also engages the client in the process. NASM recommends following these steps:
1. Ask directive and nondirective questions.
2. Engage closely when listening to the client's response.
3. Rephrase the response to show you understood and to clarify.
4. Jot things down to refer to later.

Directive questions result in short answers, preferably yes or no. Nondirective questions are leading in nature, resulting in a more detailed response.

## Development
The last step in closing a sale with a potential client is development. The health and fitness professional applies the knowledge gained from that particular client and crafts an action plan using techniques from NASM's CPT course.

This is the opportunity for the trainer to use his or her technical skills by showing the client the features of the program and its ultimate benefits. Features of a program include the number of workouts, the specific exercises that will be used, the set of assessments that will be employed, and any other technical aspects. Benefits refer to the positive results that come from using the features.

Clients tend to be more interested in benefits than in features. While it is good to discuss features to show proficiency in training techniques, don't go overboard just to hear yourself talk. Clients are more interested in how the features translate into benefits.

## OPT features

### Improving overall fitness
If a client's main goal is to improve general conditioning to improve daily function, incorporate the following features:
- Balance will improve through better neuromuscular control and efficiency.
- Core strength is increased; therefore, external forces will be guided away from the spine.
- Synergistic dominance is decreased.
- Flexibility will increase through improved arthrokinematics.
- Relative flexibility and reciprocal inhibition will be lessened.
- The OPT model is used to increase stability and functional strength, progressing through to the power stage: high-velocity strength training.

The program will focus on flexibility, stability, and increased strength. The benefits to the client (which they're more concerned with) will include the ability to accomplish daily tasks effectively and stave off chronic injury cycles. There will be a lower risk for injury and chronic illness, which translates into less time lost from work and more time for healthy engagement with loved ones. There will also be less pain resulting from sedentary work and lifestyle habits.

## Changing body composition

If a client's main goal is to improve his or her general body tone, incorporate the following features:
- The balance stage will focus on higher motor unit communication.
- The core strength phase will focus on building the transversus abdominis.
- Strength aspects will start first with stabilization, then core strength, and then endurance.
- The client will build a base that will lead to a more-responsive neuromuscular system that is prepared for power training.
- Flexibility training will lower reciprocal inhibition and arthrokinematic inhibition.

The program will focus on improving flexibility and target tight areas that prevent major muscle groups from working properly (such as the gluteals). The benefit to the client (which they're more concerned with) will include better overall muscle tone.

## Building muscle mass

If a client's main goal is to improve his or her level of strength and muscle size, incorporate the following features:
- Increased neuromuscular efficiency, which increases balance and stabilization.
- Core exercises maximize the efficiency of the kinetic chain.
- Strength exercises first stabilize, then provide more everyday strength, and ultimately progress into optimal strength through muscle hypertrophy.
- Power exercises focus on neuromuscular improvement to target prime mover and synergist muscle function.

The program will focus on stabilizing the kinetic chain and getting the muscles and nervous system to communicate more efficiently, making it easier for those muscles to get a workout. The benefits to the client (which they're more concerned with) will include building joint strength so the joints can handle the stress necessary to build larger muscles.

## Maximizing client performance

The benefits of an OPT program aimed at improving performance for a specific sport or athletic activity is easy to describe to a client: Work will be aimed at better performance and reducing injury risk by improving speed, strength, and control over the body.

The features of such a program are more technical:
- The core musculature will be maximized and the kinetic chain balanced and strengthened.
- Flexibility will be enhanced through better tissue extensibility.
- Balance will be improved by stabilizing joints and by training on the neuromuscular level (mechanoreceptors and proprioceptors).
- All levels of strength training will be used to improve function, protect joints under higher levels of work and strain, and build muscle mass.
- Power levels will be explored to maximize the explosive power necessary in sporting events and athletic endeavors.

## Losing fat and decreasing BMI

The benefits of a fat-loss program are easy for a potential client to understand. The main purpose is to lose fat while building lean muscle. These activities will increase the body's base metabolism level, burn more calories, and result in visible changes to the figure, including lost inches and slimmer appearance.

The features of such a program are more technical:

- The OPT model will first focus on stabilizing the core musculature and increasing the neuromuscular communication throughout the body. This is necessary so that exercises will target the correct muscle groups. If these muscles are worked properly, muscle mass and metabolism will increase.
- Flexibility exercises will aim at increasing neuromuscular efficiency.
- Strength training will aim to increase lean muscle mass and rev up metabolism.

## Selling services

Health and fitness professionals must be highly proficient in the technical aspect of what they do, and they must also possess business acumen to make a living. For some, the selling aspect of the job can be challenging because selling might be perceived as being pushy, or it might open the trainer up for personal rejection that he or she finds unpalatable. To be successful, the trainer will have to deal with these aspects of the job and find a way to view them positively.

The best way to approach selling is by developing a positive attitude about the service that is being provided. If the trainer is competent, there is an absolute value in the service. By approaching customers with care and concern for their health and goals, a trainer can feel that he or she is sincerely providing a beneficial service and not attempting to sell a person something without value.

## 10 Steps to Success formula

NASM developed a list of 10 Steps to Success designed to help a health and fitness professional understand what is necessary to handle the business side of a training practice:

1. Annual income—What is the trainer's annual income goal?
   This should be based on actual personal expenses, not some lofty number. It should reflect what other successful trainers in the area make, and be sufficient to provide a reasonable lifestyle.

2. Weekly income—How much income is needed per week to meet the annual goal?
   This is simply the annual income figure divided by 52 (or a lower number of weeks to reflect either an annual vacation or a slow period that may occur at holiday time).

3. Weekly sessions—How many sessions are needed per week to earn the weekly income goal?
   Once weekly income is figured, the number of sessions needed to accomplish this income goal can be deduced. The weekly income is divided by the cost of a training session. For example, if the weekly goal is $500, and the trainer charges $50 per hour, then 500 ÷ 50 = 10 one-hour training sessions per week.

4. Closing percentage—What percentage of client interactions result in a completed sale?
   The closing percentage refers to how many sales are made out of how many are attempted. For example, if a trainer speaks to 100 people and signs 10 up for training sessions, the closing percentage is 10%.

5. Time frame—What are some time goals?

> To determine how to build a clientele to meet the ultimate annual income goals, there must be reasonable time frames built in. The time frame must be attainable and provide a sense of urgency.

6. People contacted—How many potential clients must be approached to meet the closing percentage goals?

> Divide the desired number of clients by the closing percentage to determine how many clients must be approached to retain the desired number of clients. Divide the total number of clients to be contacted by the desired time frame to determine the number of contacts per week.

7. People contacted daily—How many people must be communicated with every day to reach this closing percentage goal?

> Divide the weekly target by the number of days worked to get the daily goal. As an example, if a trainer must speak to 90 people over three weeks and works five days a week, this works out to six potential clients each day: $90 \div (3 \times 5) = 6$

8. People contacted hourly—How many people must be communicated with every hour to reach this closing percentage goal?

> Divide the daily goal by the number of hours worked to calculate the hourly goal. As an example, if the trainer works a six-hour shift, at least one potential client must be spoken to every hour.

9. Contact information—Has the trainer obtained the person's contact information?

> After a certain level of rapport has been established, the trainer should make an effort to get a potential client's contact information. The trainer could offer to design a few specific exercises for that person and contact the person to implement these in the future.

10. Follow up—Has the trainer contacted the person after the initial communication?

> Following up is extremely important when selling one's training services. Not only does it help to build rapport but it also develops relationships with people who may not be in a position to hire a trainer at the present but may want to do so in the future. It also creates a positive impression among people who may recommend others to the trainer.

## Losing sales

Most trainers who struggle with sales, do so because they are reluctant to ask for the sale. The primary reason a sale is not made is there is no direct attempt to ask for the sale. To overcome this hesitation, the trainer should practice making it a part of every dialogue with potential clients. With practice, a comfort level will be developed, and the aversion to sales will fade.
At times, the sale is asked for prematurely. There may not be enough rapport with the potential client for him or her to feel comfortable saying yes. Work on developing rapport before trying to sell the person.

It is also important to effectively communicated level of value of the service. If the potential client is unsure about the benefits of training, the trainer must educate him or her for a true understanding of value received.

Sometimes the client may not be able to afford a trainer. This situation cannot be changed by the trainer. The trainer can follow up and foster the relationship so that if the person's financial circumstances change trainer will be well positioned to make the sale.

The sale is not complete when a trainer closes a new client. The time immediately following a sale is vital for the trainer. The trainer must back up the sales talk and actively demonstrate the value of the service to the client.

The first meeting should be scheduled within two days of closing the sale. Send the client a thank-you via mail or email, to show your appreciation for their time and to confirm the time of the appointment. Call before the appointment to confirm and take a moment to review to avoid cutting into workout time. Sincerely congratulate the client on taking action to accomplish his or her goals.

## Declining services

A potential client who resists signing up for training today is not a lost cause, and may be a future client or a source of other clients. Always maintain a high level of professionalism and friendliness. Thank the individual for his or her time, and get that person's contact information to check in with them at a later date.

Become a resource for that person. Place a follow-up phone call in 10-14 days to ask if he or she has any questions regarding the fitness regimen that you may be able to help with. Send an article or Web link that might be of interest to the person after approximately one month. Record each interaction in a daily journal or day planner.

Communication will help demonstrate your professionalism, commitment to your work, and convey the value of your services. Effective communication may eventually turn a no answer into a yes response.

# Professional Development and Responsibility

## Code of Ethics

A code of ethics represents some basic guidelines for behavior that members of a given profession adhere to. All major professions maintain ethical guidelines and require some manner of compliance to ensure the quality of practitioners in the field, and to keep the profession in good repute among the general public. This helps all members of the profession deliver the best services to its clients.

NASM has a fourfold approach to its code of ethics. This includes a section on general standards of professionalism, some tenets of confidentiality, legal and ethical aspects of fitness training, and a section on general business practices.

### Professionalism section

The professionalism section of NASM's code of ethics contains 11 tenets:
1. To abide by the code
2. To conduct oneself professionally
3. To treat clients and colleagues with respect
4. To not be judgmental of clients and colleagues
5. To communicate professionally
6. To provide a safe environment for clients:
    a. By not making medical diagnoses or treating nonemergency conditions when not licensed to do so
    b. By ensuring clients see a physician before undertaking a workout regimen
    c. By reviewing a medical history form filled out by the client
    d. By holding emergency certifications
7. To tell the client to seek medical attention when:
    a. The client's health significantly changes
    b. You discover the client has an illness, injury, or risk factor
    c. The client is in unexpected, unusual, or unwarranted pain
8. To recommend the services of a nutritionist or dietitian and to not offer advice without training
9. To maintain personal hygiene
10. To maintain professional dress
11. To maintain certification and continuing education

## Confidentiality section

Three code of ethics tenets pertain to confidentiality. Clients provide a great deal of personal and medical information to health and fitness professionals, and it is imperative that trainers protect the clients' privacy. Trainers should follow these ethical guidelines:
1. Keep all confidences of the client, and do not discuss the client with others. Do not mention clients in promotional materials advertising the trainer's services unless there is express permission to do so. Only divulge information when it is necessary for professional or emergency medical reasons.
2. Remember that minors do not have the legal capacity to consent to how their personal information is being used, so seek permission from their legal guardian.
3. Protect client records and make sure they are not accessible to others.

## Legal and ethical section

Four code of ethics tenets describe the legal and ethical responsibilities of CPTs. By following all applicable laws and rules, trainers protect themselves and keep the profession in good repute. NASM's rules include:
1. Follow all applicable laws for each jurisdiction in which the trainer resides (federal, state, and local)
2. Accept responsibility for everything he or she does
3. Keep records that are true and complete. It is also important to keep these records in a secure place to maintain client confidentiality
4. Make sure to respect copyrights and trademarks as they apply to the trainer's practice

## Business practices section

Seven code of ethics tenets pertain to business practices and responsibilities of its CPTs. NASM's rules include:
1. Obtain appropriate insurance
2. Keep accurate notes about each client's work and progress
3. Represent services and capabilities honestly to the general public
4. Represent training and certifications honestly
5. Advertise in a professional way without using prurient images or language
6. Keep meticulous financial and tax records
7. Keep current with all laws on sexual harassment

## Compliance with NASM's code of ethics

NASM members, whether currently certified or not, are expected to conform to the code of ethics to maintain the highest level of personal conduct and to keep the health and fitness professional profession in excellent repute.

Members that fail to comply with the code of ethics will be subject to a list of progressive disciplinary actions. Punishment range from minor sanctions to expulsion from the National Academy of Sports Medicine. Other punishments include temporary suspension and revocation of current certifications.

Additionally, all members are ethically bound to report instances of breaches of the code of ethics by other members.

# Emergency Aid

CPR is an acronym that stands for cardiopulmonary resuscitation. This is an emergency aid procedure given when a person has stopped breathing and has gone into cardiac arrest. Adult CPR is appropriate for people older than eight years old.

Be sure any immediate danger to oneself or the unconscious person is removed before commencing CPR. Call 911 to summon help, and follow instructions given by the dispatcher.

The ABCs of CPR stand for: Airway, Breathing, and Circulation. Clear the airway, and make sure there are no obstructions that might be causing the person to choke. Check for breathing; if there is no respiration, mouth-to-mouth must be given to introduce air into the body manually. Air must circulate through the body, which must also be done manually, by compressing the chest to get the heart to pump oxygenated air. These compressions can pump around 30 percent of the blood that the heart can normally.

**Muscle strain, bone fracture or dislocation, or ligament strain or sprain**

It is not uncommon for a health and fitness professional to see strains or sprains in his or her line of work. Symptoms will include an immediate pain to the area, difficulty putting weight on that muscle or joint, swelling, and bruising. Immobilize the affected area, and apply ice packs to help reduce inflammation. If the person loses feeling to the area or has any indication of reduced blood flow, it will be necessary to get the person immediate medical attention.

If it is suspected that a person has broken a bone, it will be necessary to get immediate medical attention. Depending on the severity of the injury, an ambulance can be summoned, or the person can be driven by car. Immobilize the affected area, and watch for signs of shock. If there is a spinal injury, move the person only if there is an absolute need to get out of harm's way, and then call for emergency assistance.

**Bleeding**

When a person bleeds, it can be as minor as a paper cut or as serious as a life-threatening emergency, depending on the situation. If a person begins to bleed, apply direct pressure to the wound to encourage the body's clotting response. If this does not stanch the blood flow, a pressure dressing should be used. If this does not work, try putting the injured area above the heart while continuing to apply pressure. If this doesn't work, apply a tourniquet.

Use precautions for your health when dealing with someone who is bleeding. Avoid touching the blood directly, and use gloves to minimize the chance of contracting a blood-borne illness.

**Shock**

When a person goes into shock, it is a serious medical emergency. Shock can occur for a variety of reasons, including blood loss, sudden stress, or cardiac or lung problems. The person will become clammy, fatigued, light-headed, possibly sick to his or her stomach, and might lose consciousness.

Help the person to a comfortable, prone position, with the feet higher than the heart. Bundle the person up to keep him or her warm. Watch the person carefully for signs of unconsciousness. Give cardiopulmonary resuscitation (CPR) if needed. If the person is breathing but loses consciousness, roll him or her onto the side to prevent choking due to potential vomiting.

Seek medical attention while carefully monitoring the person's condition.

## Seizures

A seizure can be a sudden and frightening episode in which a person loses control of his or her body. For many seizure sufferers, a single seizure is part of a long-term problem, such as epilepsy, that he or she manages on a regular basis. If this is the case, a health and fitness professional should be made aware of this condition. Have a physician-approved workout regimen and an emergency plan for a seizure episode.

If a person has a seizure, immediately make sure that he or she is in the safest position—on the floor and away from anything that he or she could hit with the body, especially the head. Do not put anything in the person's mouth.

Note when the seizure started, how long it lasts, and when it ends. If the person loses consciousness and begins to seize again, call 911 right away.

## Insulin shock

Insulin shock is a problem that can occur for people with diabetes, which is a condition that the trainer should be made aware of if it exists in his or her clients. Symptoms can include irritability and irrational behavior, extreme and sudden fatigue up to unconsciousness, and clammy skin. Insulin shock is extremely serious and can lead to death if not attended to.

To help correct insulin shock, a health and fitness professional can provide something to eat that is high in sugar: juice, a sugary soda, a piece of candy, or the like. Do not give the person anything if he or she is unconscious, but do call for help immediately.

Unlike many other emergency conditions, insulin shock can in large part be avoided by careful monitoring of the blood sugar. If a client has diabetes, be sure that you and the client have a physician-approved workout regimen and an emergency plan for blood sugar issues that may occur.

## Asthma attacks

An asthma attack is an umbrella term for several lung problems that result in difficulty breathing. This can be as mild as a general wheezing or as serious as a life-threatening inability to breathe. Symptoms can include difficulty breathing, loud breathing (wheezing), turning purple or blue, and anxiety or a feeling of claustrophobia. The person's ability to speak can be a good indicator of how distressed the person is—an inability to speak or to only be able to speak a word or two at a time indicates serious trouble breathing.

Make sure the person is not choking or having an allergic reaction. Then put the person in a comfortable position. Call for help and follow the instructions given by the dispatcher. If the person has taken any medication, do not allow them to exceed the recommended dose without further instruction.

## Heart attack

A heart attack is a very serious medical condition that occurs when the heart muscle malfunctions, causing a lack of blood, and therefore oxygen, to the heart muscle. The damage can range from mild and self-correcting to that which requires immediate medical intervention.

Symptoms of a heart attack include pain and pressure in the chest that may also be felt in the arms, especially the left arm, or the jaw. The person may be cold and clammy, may sweat profusely, have trouble catching his or her breath, and may become ill.

If a heart attack is suspected, put the person in a safe, relaxed position and administer aspirin if possible to thin the blood so it can travel through restricted arteries. Help keep the person calm and breathing as normally as possible, and ask if he or she took nitroglycerin, as this information may be relevant to emergency personnel later.

## Stroke

A stroke is a serious medical condition with effects that range from mild and temporarily debilitating, to fatal. If a client is having a stroke, it is important to recognize it as soon as possible and get the person medical attention.

A stroke is the result of a problem with a blood vessel in the brain; the vessel could have a blockage, it could leak, or it could burst. Symptoms include a sudden and serious headache, slurring when speaking, paralysis on one side of the body, hallucinations, becoming delirious, or passing out.

Put the person in a safe position and call for medical assistance immediately, or take the person to an emergency room if practicable.

## Choking

Choking is a highly serious situation in which a person cannot take in oxygen because something is blocking the airway. A person who is choking will not be able to speak or cough, so they must be observed for physical cues. A person may wave their arms, point to their throat, clutch their throat, and, in the absence of oxygen, may even turn purple or blue.

Perform the Heimlich maneuver to remove the airway obstruction. Standing behind the person, place a fist over the belly button and below the rib cage, with the other hand resting on top of the fist. Quick, upward motions should be made to force air from the lungs up to dislodge the obstruction.

If the person passes out, lay him or her on the floor, try to open the mouth, look in for an obstruction, and remove it. If this doesn't work, a flat variation of the Heimlich can be tried by straddling the person's waist and placing the heel of the hand above the belly button and pressing down rapidly several times.

## Heat stroke/exhaustion

Heat exhaustion and heat stroke are two very serious medical conditions that must be monitored in hot outdoor environments as well as in cooler indoor settings, given that the rigors of a workout can raise body temperature, especially in people with known risk factors.

Heat exhaustion is characterized by clammy skin that is cool or normal in temperature. The person may be extremely fatigued, sweating profusely, and experience lightheadedness and a lowered pulse rate. Cramping may also be an issue. Get the person into a cooler environment, put his or her head between the knees if dizzy, and loosen any restricting garments. Fan the person and allow him or her to drink water or an electrolyte beverage.

Heat stroke is characterized by very hot skin. The person may feel extremely fatigued, but will likely have no sweating and an elevated pulse rate. They may even seem delirious. The person should be taken to a cool environment and cooled down slowly. Remove restricting clothing and apply cool (but not cold), wet cloths and cold packs in the armpits.

## AEDs

A defibrillator is a device that can be used to jump-start the heart when it is in cardiac arrest. It is only to be used in an emergency situation, but it can be very effective in restoring a heartbeat with an electrical charge.

A manual defibrillator is a complex piece of equipment meant for emergency personnel with more qualifications for handling the machine and the circumstances under which it might be necessary. Other, less-qualified, people may use an automated defibrillator, which may be fully automated or partially automated. A fully automated machine needs only to be attached properly to work, while a partially automated machine may require the operator to activate it.

An adult automated external defibrillator (AED) is not appropriate for small children (younger than 8 years old or less than 60 pounds). It should only be used for a person who is in cardiac arrest—that is, someone with no heartbeat and who is not breathing.

### Cardiac arrhythmias:

The body has an electrical impulse system that controls the brain's communication with the muscles (via the nerves) as well as the efficient pumping of the heart. When the electrical pattern is disrupted or not working properly, it can lead to the heart stalling out, so to speak. This is referred to as cardiac arrhythmia or abnormal rhythm.

Several issues can lead to problems with the heart pumping:
- Ventricular fibrillation
- Pulseless ventricular tachycardia
- Pulseless electrical activity
- Asystole

The first two, ventricular fibrillation and pulseless ventricular tachycardia, will respond to the electrical current provided by an AED; the other two, pulseless electrical activity and asystole, will not respond to AED treatment.

# Practice Test

## Practice Questions

1. The joint movement that results in an increase of the joint angle is called a(an):
   a. Abduction
   b. Adduction
   c. Extension
   d. Flexion

2. Which of these muscles is not part of the Rotator cuff?
   a. Supraspinatus
   b. Infraspinatus
   c. Teres minor
   d. Teres major

3. Which of the following should be considered a life-threatening medical emergency?
   a. Anterior cruciate ligament tear
   b. A dislocation of the cervical spinal cord
   c. An Achilles' tendon rupture
   d. A hip fracture in an elderly individual

4. Which of the following can cause pain in the lumbar area?
   a. Strain of the tibialis anterior muscle
   b. Strain of the longissimus thoracis muscle
   c. Strain of the gastrocnemius muscle
   d. Strain of the sternocleidomastoid muscle

5. When working with a trainer, an individual lifts a 10-pound weight straight over her head through a distance of 2.5 feet. How much linear work has been generated?
   a. 4 pound-feet
   b. 7.5 pound-feet
   c. 25 pound-feet
   d. 50 pound-feet

6. For average groups of people represented below, which order represents the lowest resting heart rate to the highest resting heart rate?
   a. Men, women, children, elderly individuals
   b. Children, women, elderly individuals, men
   c. Elderly individuals, women, men, children
   d. Elderly individuals, men, women, children

7. The body recruits type I muscle fibers for activities of
   a. long duration and low intensity
   b. long duration and high intensity
   c. short duration and high intensity
   d. none of the above

8. All of the following classes of nutrients provide sources of energy EXCEPT
   a. proteins
   b. vitamins
   c. fats
   d. carbohydrates

9. A nonathlete who weighs 80 kg would require _____ grams per day of protein.
   a. 50 grams
   b. 80 grams
   c. 64 grams
   d. 100 grams

10. A deficiency of which vitamin can lead to difficulty seeing at night and an increased susceptibility to infections?
    a. vitamin B1
    b. vitamin B3
    c. vitamin E
    d. vitamin A

11. You are exercising outdoors and become concerned that your client may be dehydrated. At what point would her condition be considered a medical emergency?
    a. When she complains that her leg muscles are cramping
    b. When she seems to be confused and doesn't know where she is
    c. When she becomes dizzy and light-headed
    d. When she begins complaining of a headache

12. What food information is NOT present on a food label?
    a. amount of protein in a serving
    b. amount of cholesterol in a serving
    c. amount of calories in a serving
    d. amount of caffeine in a serving

13. When meeting with a client for the first time, all of the following can be helpful comments to make to a client EXCEPT
    a. "How would you like this work to help you?"
    b. "Can you tell me about your daily routine?"
    c. "What health problems do you have?"
    d. "Do you think you have clinical depression?"

14. A client in the precontemplation stage of behavior might think to himself:
    a. "I just can't lose weight."
    b. "I have a plan to lose weight."
    c. "I am really thinking about how to lose weight."
    d. "I am so proud I lost weight!"

15. An example of a substitution behavioral change that you might suggest to a client is
    a. "Call your best friend to walk with you every day."
    b. "Take the stairs instead of the elevator at work."
    c. "If you reach this goal we set up, you can have a reward of your choosing."
    d. "Put your running shoes right by your bed, so you are motivated to run first thing in the morning."

16. Your client is in the maintenance stage of behavior and is exercising regularly. One day she cancels her appointments with you, claiming she has too much to do at work. If she abandons her exercise routine completely, it is called a(an):
    a. lapse
    b. self-change
    c. relapse
    d. self-challenge

17. All of the following can help the client-trainer relationship EXCEPT
    a. Accepting your client for what she can do, even if others her age can do more
    b. Asking your client about his week
    c. Answering a text or phone call during a session
    d. Keeping information between the two of you confidential

18. An example of active listening is
    a. "Why didn't you do this exercise this week?"
    b. "Great job with your exercises this week!"
    c. "How did your big project at work turn out?"
    d. "So you are saying that you didn't understand how this exercise was supposed to feel?"

19. The interactive tool that can lead to change by creating an equal partnership between the client and the trainer is called
    a. Motivational interviewing
    b. Generative moments
    c. Appreciative inquiry
    d. Change talk

20. Goals that a trainer helps a client set should be all of the following EXCEPT
    a. Time-limited
    b. Action-based
    c. Broadly defined
    d. Measurable

21. Active listening, building rapport, and showing understanding of a client's situation are all components of:
    a. Nonverbal communication
    b. Intrinsic motivation
    c. Extrinsic motivation
    d. Client-centered techniques

22. As a prelude to creating a personal training package for a client, a trainer should obtain all of the following EXCEPT
    a. Approval and signature of a physician
    b. Informed consent from the client
    c. Permission to post the client's photo on the trainer's Web site
    d. Health history of the client

23. Several atherosclerotic cardiovascular disease risk factors exist. A client who has which of the following would be considered to have a positive risk factor for hypertension?
    a. Systolic blood pressure ≥ 140 mm Hg on two separate occasions
    b. Diastolic blood pressure ≥75 mm Hg on two separate occasions
    c. Systolic blood pressure ≥ 140 mm Hg and diastolic blood pressure ≥ 100 mm Hg on one occasion
    d. Having taken an antihypertensive medication in the past

24. Shortness of breath at rest is called
    a. Ischemia
    b. Dyspnea
    c. Syncope
    d. Orthopnea

25. All of the following are true of intermittent claudication EXCEPT
    a. People with diabetes have a greater risk of having intermittent claudication.
    b. Intermittent claudication does not usually occur when a client stands or sits.
    c. Intermittent claudication usually goes away within 10 minutes of stopping an exercise.
    d. Symptoms associated with intermittent claudication are reproducible.

26. Which of the following pulses is not commonly used to determine an individual's heart rate?
    a. Carotid
    b. Brachial
    c. Radial
    d. Popliteal

27. Normal systolic and diastolic blood pressure measurements (in mm Hg) include which of the following?
    a. Systolic 110, diastolic 75
    b. Systolic 130, diastolic 70
    c. Systolic 140, diastolic 85
    d. Systolic 110, diastolic 85

28. An individual weighs 80 kg and is 1.75 meters tall. What range does his BMI fall into?
    a. Normal
    b. Overweight
    c. Obese class I
    d. Obese class II

29. The Rockport is a field test that involves
    a. Running continuously for 1.5 miles
    b. Walking intermittently for 2 miles
    c. Stepping up and down continuously for 3 minutes
    d. Walking as fast as possible for 1 mile

30. An individual's flexibility can be assessed by which of the following?
    a. A one-repetition bench press
    b. A sit-and-reach test
    c. A push-up test
    d. A curl-up test

31. The hip joint is what joint type?
    a. Ball-and-socket joint
    b. Hinge joint
    c. Cartilaginous joint
    d. Pivot joint

32. The primary function of the respiratory system is
    a. Delivering nutrients to tissues in the body
    b. Regulating the body's pH level
    c. Facilitating the exchange of oxygen and carbon dioxide
    d. Maintaining fluid volume to prevent dehydration

33. Stretching that requires assistance from a personal trainer is called
    a. Active stretching
    b. Passive stretching
    c. Ballistic stretching
    d. Static stretching

34. All of the following are benefits of increased flexibility EXCEPT
    a. Improved circulation
    b. Increased range of motion
    c. Improved coordination
    d. Increased chance of muscle injury

35. The condition that involves a rapid breakdown of muscle tissue due to too much exercise, which can potentially result in kidney failure, is called
    a. Myoglobinuria
    b. Rhabdomyolysis
    c. Dialysis
    d. Proteinuria

36. Benefits of nonlinear periodized training programs include all of the following EXCEPT
    a. Using a progressive increase in the workout intensity
    b. Allowing for variation in the workout intensity
    c. Having a "power" training day
    d. Training both power and strength of muscles within one week

37. What is the approximate target heart rate for a 50-year-old man in beats per minute (bpm)?
    a. 75 to 120
    b. 85 to 110
    c. 85 to 145
    d. 120 to 160

38. An effective cardiorespiratory training program session should include all of these basic components EXCEPT
    a. Power phase
    b. Cool-down phase
    c. Warm-up phase
    d. Endurance phase

39. The "talk test" refers to
    a. The practice of speaking with your client before a training session to check in with the client
    b. The practice of talking with your client during the cool-down phase to see how the session felt.
    c. The ability of an individual while exercising to talk or respond to a trainer's questions without gasping for breath.
    d. The comfort level of a client to let a trainer know when an exercise is too hard.

40. Individuals with osteoporosis
    a. Should not do flexibility training exercises
    b. Should avoid twisting or flexing of the spine
    c. Should not worry about proper breathing techniques
    d. Are not more likely to develop fractures

41. Which of the following inhibits a person's joint flexibility?
    a. Having cold muscles
    b. Being a woman
    c. Having more relaxed muscles
    d. Having a more physically active lifestyle

42. Older adults should engage in an aerobic exercise program that provides which of the following?
    a. 25 minutes, 3 days a week of mild-intensity aerobic activity
    b. 30 minutes, 3 days a week of moderate-intensity aerobic activity
    c. 20 minutes, 5 days a week of vigorous-intensity aerobic activity
    d. 30 minutes, 5 days a week of moderate-intensity aerobic activity

43. Which of the following conditions is an absolute contraindication for exercising during pregnancy?
    a. Poorly controlled seizure disorder
    b. Ruptured membranes
    c. Heavy smoker
    d. Poorly controlled hypertension

44. Common complications of diabetes include all of the following EXCEPT
    a. Kidney problems
    b. Vision problems
    c. Hearing problems
    d. Peripheral nerve problems

45. How much weight loss is appropriate for an obese individual with a BMI greater than 30?
    a. 1 kg a week
    b. 2 kg a week
    c. 3 kg a week
    d. 4 kg a week

46. Which of the following is not covered when obtaining informed consent from a client?
    a. Benefits that the client should expect to gain
    b. Risks and discomfort that may be associated with the training program
    c. Purpose of the training program
    d. How much the training program will cost

47. The end of a bone is called the
    a. Epiphysis
    b. Periosteum
    c. Endosteum
    d. Diaphysis

48. All are true of a synovial joint EXCEPT
    a. The synovial cavity is filled with synovial fluid.
    b. A synovial joint can flex and extend.
    c. A synovial joint may be supported by ligaments.
    d. A synovial joint never contains any other structures inside of it.

49. Leg raises are an example of a(an):
    a. Hip extension
    b. Knee flexion
    c. Hip flexion
    d. Hip abduction

50. Which function does the autonomic nervous system NOT regulate?
    a. Digestion
    b. Breathing
    c. Running
    d. Secretion of hormones

# Answers and Explanations

1. C:  When a joint is extended, the angle of the joint is increased. Flexion is the opposite of extension and causes the joint angle to decrease. Abduction refers to movement that is directed away from the midline of the body. The opposite of abduction is adduction. Adduction describes movements that are made toward the midline of the body.

2. D: The Supraspinatus is an abductor of the arm. The Infraspinatus and Teres minor are external rotators. The Subscapularis is the missing muscle of the rotator cuff.

3. B:  Any trauma to the neck (or cervical spine) should be considered a medical emergency. When the cervical vertebrae are dislocated or fractured, the spinal column can become unstable. This can potentially lead to paralysis or death. While an Achilles' tendon rupture or anterior cruciate ligament tear is a serious leg/knee injury, respectively, and may be career ending for athletes, either one is not life threatening. A hip fracture or a fracture of the neck of the femur can cause permanent disability, especially in the elderly. However, these are also not usually life threatening.

4. B:  The longissimus thoracis muscle is located in the posterior lumbar region. It is part of the erector spinae group. These muscles help maintain posture and provide stability to the spine. Lumbar pain, also called low back pain, is one of the most common causes of disability. About 60 to 80% of the general population will experience it at some point in their lives. Determining the specific cause of lumbar pain may be difficult, but muscle strain, an intervertebral herniated disc, and joint inflammation can all cause lumbar pain. The other muscles are not located in the lumbar region. The sternocleidomastoid muscle is located in the cervical region. Strain to this muscle occurs with "whiplash" injuries. The tibialis anterior muscle is located on the anterior and lateral part of the lower leg. The gastrocnemius muscle is located on the posterior part of the lower leg.

5. C:  Multiplying the force times the distance through which the force travels will result in the linear work generated. Ten times 2.5 equals 25.

6. D:  Heart rate is the number of times that the heart beats per minute and can be measured by taking a pulse. Average people have a resting heart rate of 60 to 80 beats per minute (bpm). The elderly have a lower resting heart rate than adult men and women. Men have a resting heart rate that is about 10 bpm lower than that of adult women. Children have resting heart rates that are higher than those of adults. When comparing fit to unfit individuals, fit individuals have a lower resting heart rate.

7. A:  The body has two types of muscle fibers: type I and type II. Together, these muscle fibers can do all types of tasks. However, the body recruits each type during different activities and at specific times, depending on the type and duration of motion required. Type I muscle fibers, also called slow-twitch fibers, are used for activities of long duration and low intensity, such as those involving endurance. In contrast, type II muscle fibers are employed for high-speed, high-power tasks. These muscle fibers are capable of generating force more quickly than type I muscle fibers.

8. B:  Carbon is critical for the energy production process. Proteins, fats, and carbohydrates—which are all sources of carbon—contribute to several functions in the body. They help provide energy so that muscles, nerves, and metabolic processes work normally. Energy is measured in calories (cal) or kilocalories (kcal). When individuals exercise, they can "burn" energy more quickly. Vitamins

and minerals are critical for providing essential nutrients that the body needs to maintain normal function; however, they are not a source of energy.

9. C:  The average person's daily requirement for protein is 0.8 g/kg. In other words, multiplying 0.8 by the person's weight in kilograms will give the daily amount of protein in grams needed. For this individual, that would be $80 \times 0.8 = 64$ grams. Athletes require more protein each day (about 1.2 to 2 g/kg of body weight) than sedentary individuals. If this individual were an athlete, he or she would require between 96 and 160 grams of protein per day. In addition to these specific recommendations, it is also recommended that protein accounts for about 12 to 15% of the total calories a person eats each day.

10. D:  Vitamin A, known as retinol, is found in foods such as fish liver oils, butter, and egg yolks. It is critical for red blood cell and embryo development and normal functioning of the eyes, the immune system, and the skin. Vitamin $B_1$ is also called thiamin. A deficiency of this vitamin can lead to beriberi. Symptoms of beriberi can include cardiovascular problems, peripheral neuropathy, and cognitive and psychiatric problems. Vitamin $B_3$ is also known as niacin; a deficiency of this vitamin can cause a disease called pellagra. Pellagra can cause a skin rash, gastrointestinal symptoms, or cognitive difficulties. If untreated, it can also lead to death. Vitamin E is an antioxidant that augments the immune system. It can help prevent cell membranes from being destroyed by harmful free radicals.

11. B:  Dehydration, heat exhaustion, and heat stroke are conditions that are best avoided by encouraging clients to drink either water or sports drinks often. When individuals wait until they feel thirsty to drink, they may already have lost 1 to 2 liters of fluid. A dehydrated individual may feel less energetic and begin to develop muscle cramps. If not treated, an individual can develop heat exhaustion, which may be manifested by headaches and feelings of nausea. If heat exhaustion isn't treated, an individual may suffer from heat stroke. During heat stroke, an individual's body temperature increases, and he or she may become confused or lose consciousness. This is a medical emergency. The patient needs to have her body temperature lowered as quickly as possible.

12. D:  Labeling on food packages is helpful in determining a number of the characteristics of a food, including the ingredients, serving size, and nutrients present in the food. Food label information is based on a 2,000 calorie diet. It provides the percent daily value for the amount of fats, cholesterol, sodium, potassium, carbohydrates, and protein present in a serving size. While caffeine will be listed as an ingredient if it is present in the food, the specific amount of caffeine will not be listed.

13. D:  It is important to remember that coaching is not therapy or mental health counseling. Personal trainers should never diagnose current psychiatric problems. However, it is important to ask a person about their history—medical and otherwise—so that your sessions can be appropriate and productive. Knowing about a person's daily routine will tell you how active he or she usually is. Asking, "How would you like this work to help you?" can elicit a specific goal that the two of you can work toward.

14. A:  There are five stages of behavioral change. Listed in order of unwilling to change to readiness to change, they are precontemplation, contemplation, preparation, action, and maintenance. People in precontemplation often say, "I can't" or "I won't" about being able to change. People in the contemplation stage often say, "I just may change" or "I'm thinking about it." People in the preparation stage have actively decided to take action at some point soon. In the action stage, a person has decided to implement a consistent change, but has been implementing the new behavior for less than six months. If a person has consistently implemented a change for more than six months, he or she is in the maintenance stage.

15. B:  There are various strategies trainers can employ to effect behavior change in a client. Substitution or counterconditioning involves substituting healthy behaviors for unhealthy behaviors. Answer A is an example of social support. Answer C is an example of a reward or reinforcement system. Answer D is an example of environmental control, which is a cue that can precipitate healthy behavior.

16. C:  A relapse is when a person stops their positive behavior and, as a result, loses the positive benefits he or she had gained. Many conditions can lead to relapse; work pressures, boredom, and increased travel are only a few. Although similar, a lapse is a temporary stop in positive behavior. Had this client returned after a week or two, her exercise routine would have lapsed, but she would have likely maintained or quickly regained the positive benefits.

17. C:  A number of factors can help facilitate a beneficial working relationship between a client and a trainer. These can include being present in the moment, maintaining confidentiality, being interested in your client's life, giving helpful feedback, and treating your client in a positive way. Along those lines, it is important to accept clients at the level they are currently at, rather than comparing them to others.

18. D:  Active listening is a technique than enhances communication. It involves conveying what the client says back to the client, so that the individual feels they are being heard and understood. The client tells you how he or she feels or what he or she thinks, and you repeat or paraphrase it back to the individual. This technique provides the opportunity for clarification if the client meant something else. When actively listening, it is helpful to let the other speak without interruption and to maintain eye contact and focus on the client.

19. A:  Motivational interviewing is based on the idea that change occurs when there is an equal partnership between the client and trainer. While you are a training expert, your client is an expert is his or her life. Motivational interviewing is used in a client-centered relationship. Generative moments are powerful or negative events that have happened to a client that can spur him or her to change. Appreciative inquiry is a technique in which the trainer asks positive and powerful questions to help the client visualize potential possibilities. Change talk involves language spoken by a client about his or her desire and ability to change their behavior.

20. C:  Goals that are most helpful are those that are specific, very well defined, able to be measured, realistic, and have a time constraint on them. The actions a client needs to take should be specifically defined. For example, a goal may be that a client will walk on his treadmill at a pace of 3 mph for 30 minutes on Monday through Friday before going to work.

21. D:  Client-centered techniques include asking open-ended questions, listening actively, and frequently clarifying what the client says. These can all contribute to building rapport and a strong relationship with a client. Nonverbal communication is that which is expressed and received via nonverbal cues, such as facial expressions, gestures, and the presence or absence of eye contact. Intrinsic motivation is the motivation for change that comes from within. For example, a person may want to lose weight to feel proud or to feel like he can achieve a goal. When people are extrinsically motivated, they are motivated to achieve a goal because of an external factor. For example, someone might want to lose weight to fit into a wedding dress.

22. C:  While you should always obtain permission before posting a photo of a client on a Web site, that is not one of the critical initial pieces of information. If medical clearance is necessary, a

signature and recommendations from your client's physician should be obtained. In addition, you will need to know your client's past and present medical and health issues to create an appropriate training plan. You will also need informed consent from your client, demonstrating that he or she understands the risk and benefits of undertaking a training program.

23. A: Hypertension is defined by the Seventh Report of the Joint National Committee on Prevention, Detection, Evaluation, and Treatment of High Blood Pressure as a systolic blood pressure of ≥ 140 mm Hg and a diastolic blood pressure of ≥ 90 mm Hg on two separate occasions. In addition, current use of an antihypertensive medication is considered to be a positive risk factor for hypertension.

24. B: A client with dyspnea will have shortness of breath while resting or only with mild exertion. It is not normal, and it can be a symptom of cardiac or pulmonary disease. Orthopnea is shortness of breath that occurs when one is lying down. It is relieved by sitting upright or standing. Ischemia occurs when there is a lack of blood flow and oxygen to the heart. This causes pain in the chest or pain that has radiated to the neck or arm. Syncope is a loss of consciousness that usually occurs when the brain does not receive enough oxygen.

25. C: When an individual has intermittent claudication, he or she will develop pain in a specific area with exercise due to inadequate blood flow to that specific muscle. This pain can be reproduced from day to day. It usually does not occur when a client is sitting or standing. People with coronary artery disease or diabetes are prone to developing intermittent claudication. However, once the exercise that precipitated the pain has stopped, the pain should go away within one to two minutes.

26. D: The popliteal artery, located behind the knee, can be difficult to palpate. The carotid pulse is felt by placing one's fingers lightly in the lower neck, along the medial aspect of the sternocleidomastoid muscle. The brachial pulse can be palpated between the triceps and biceps muscles on the anterior and medial aspect of the arm, near the elbow. The radial artery can be palpated on the anterior arm, near the wrist.

27. A: Normal blood pressure is classified as a systolic pressure of less than 120 mm Hg and a diastolic pressure of less than 80 mm Hg. If either the systolic or diastolic pressures are elevated on multiple occasions, an individual's blood pressure is considered to be high.

28. B: BMI stands for body mass index, and it can be calculated by dividing an individual's weight by height squared. In this example, BMI = 80 kg / (1.75 m)$^2$. This results in a BMI of 26.1. BMI values fall into a range. The normal range is 18.5–24.9. The overweight range is 25–29.9. The obese class I range is 30–34.9. The obese class II range is 35–39.9.

29. D: The Rockport 1-mile walk test involves having a client walk as fast as he or she can for a distance of 1 mile. The individual must not run at all during this test. At the end of the test, the individual's pulse and heart rate are measured. The Queens College Step Test involves having an individual step up and down on a standardized step height continuously for 3 minutes and then measuring his or her pulse and heart rate after the 3 minutes.

30. B: A sit-and-reach test can measure the flexibility of an individual's lower back, hip, and hamstrings. A one-repetition bench press is used to assess muscular strength or muscle force. The push-up test and the curl-up test are used for measuring muscle endurance.

31. A: The hip joint, as well as the shoulder joint, can move in all directions. They are ball-and-socket joints. A hinge joint can only move in one plane, such as with knee flexion and extension. A cartilaginous joint is a strong joint that is very slightly movable, such as intervertebral joints. A pivot joint is a joint in one plane that permits rotation, such as the humeroradial joint.

32. C: The respiratory system involves the lungs and is where the exchange of oxygen for carbon dioxide occurs. The cardiovascular system, which involves the heart and blood vessels, is responsible for delivering oxygen and nutrients to all tissues in the body, regulating the body's pH level to prevent acidosis or alkalosis, and maintaining fluid volume to prevent dehydration.

33. B: In passive stretching, a client remains relaxed, allowing a trainer to stretch the client's muscles. Ballistic stretching, which involves a bouncing-like movement, can cause injury to muscles if not performed carefully. Static stretching involves movements that are deliberate and sustained. Active stretching involves stretching muscles throughout their range of motion.

34. D: Flexibility training has several benefits, including increased circulation, increased range of motion, improved muscle coordination, and decreased future chance of muscle injury.

35. B: Rhabdomyolysis, caused when an individual exercises too excessively, results in muscle damage and breakdown. These breakdown products, which can include protein and myoglobin, then enter the bloodstream and have the potential to harm the kidneys. Kidney failure, and possibly death, can result. Symptoms of rhabdomyolysis can include muscle swelling, pain, and soreness. Myoglobinuria and proteinuria describe the conditions of having myoglobin and protein in the urine. However, they do necessarily reflect a cause. Dialysis is a treatment for kidney failure.

36. A: While a linear periodized training program involves having a progressive increase in the workout intensity over the course of a week, a nonlinear periodized training program involves a variation of intensity over the course of a week. A weeklong nonlinear periodized training program can target muscle strength and power. A "power" training day involving power sets can also be implemented. This program may be more conducive to individuals with scheduling conflicts.

37. C: To calculate an individual's target heart rate, first one needs to estimate the person's maximal heart rate. This is estimated by subtracting a person's age from 220. In this example, the person's maximal heart rate is 220 − 50 = 170. Using this number, the target heart rate can be calculated. The recommended target heart rate is between 50% and 85% of the maximal heart rate. This would be 170 × 0.50 = 85, and 170 × 0.85 = 145. So, the individual's target heart rate is estimated to be between about 85 and 145 bpm.

38. A: A training program needs to balance many different variables to be effective. A trainer needs to take a client's goals, daily routines, and preferences into account to create a routine that will be followed. Each training session should include a warm-up phase, a workout or endurance phase, and then a cool-down phase.

39. C: It is important that a training session is not too intense. The "talk test" is a simple way to get a handle on the intensity of the endurance or workout phase. A client should be able to talk or answer a trainer's questions without gasping for breath. Not being able to speak easily can indicate that the workout is too intense. Cardiovascular, muscular, and orthopedic injuries are more likely to occur when a workout is too intense.

40. B: Osteoporosis is a disease that involves a loss of bone mineral density. Osteopenia is a milder form of osteoporosis. Although people with osteoporosis are more susceptible to fractures due to the thinning of their bones, they are appropriate candidates for flexibility training programs. These programs can help improve posture and maintain the alignment of the spine. However, the program should avoid repetitive exercises that involve twisting or flexing of the spine. Everyone who participates in a flexibility training program should be taught proper breathing techniques.

41. A: A person's flexibility is reflected in his or her ability to move a joint, without pain, through a range of motionVarious factors are associated with increased flexibility. Younger people are more flexible than older individuals, and women are more flexible than men. Warmer, more relaxed muscles allow more joint flexibility than colder muscles. Individuals who are physically active are often more flexible than those who are not. In addition, the joint structure and health of the joint and its surrounding tissues affect an individual's flexibility.

42. D: If their medical issues allow it, individuals over the age of 65 can and should participate in exercise training programs. Aerobic, or cardiorespiratory, exercise can decrease morbidity and mortality rates in older individuals. The recommendations are for older individuals to engage in moderate intensity aerobic activity for 30 minutes, 5 days a week (150 minutes total), or to engage in vigorous-intensity aerobic activity for 25 minutes, 3 days a week (75 minutes total). People can also do a combination.

43. B: Recent research supports a role for exercise programs during pregnancy. Goals of this program can include reducing low back pain and decreasing the risk of developing gestational diabetes. However, there do exist a number of absolute contraindications. Some of these include ruptured membranes, placenta previa after 26 weeks of gestation, premature labor, preeclampsia, and high-risk multiple gestation pregnancies. In contrast, relative contraindications include the individual being a heavy smoker, having poorly controlled diabetes or seizures, or having poorly controlled hypertension or hyperthyroid disease.

44. C: Diabetes can lead to kidney problems (nephropathy), trouble seeing (retinopathy), and decreased sensation of peripheral nerves (peripheral neuropathy). If these conditions are present, a trainer needs to adapt an exercise program accordingly. Some precautions that can be taken include keeping the blood pressure stable for retinopathy, avoiding exercise requiring high levels of coordination for peripheral neuropathy, or avoiding prolonged exercise for nephropathy.

45. A: People who are obese have a BMI greater than or equal to 30. These individuals are at a high risk of cardiac problems, certain types of cancers, and diabetes. Among other areas, training programs can focus on weight loss, promote appetite control, and lower the risk of associated medical issues. Weight loss should be gradual—not more than 1 kg per week. Aerobic training sessions five to seven times a week lasting 45–60 minutes per session may be helpful.

46. D: Obtaining informed consent at the beginning of a professional relationship can protect against potential legal action. An informed consent document will discuss the reason for the training program, the risks or discomfort that a client may experience, the responsibilities of the client, the benefits the client may reap, and it will offer the opportunity for a client to ask related questions. Fee structure and payments are not part of the informed consent.

47. A: When describing the anatomy of bone, the epiphysis is the end of the bone and the diaphysis is the shaft of the bone. The periosteum is a membrane that covers the surface of a bone, except at

the articular surfaces (joints). The endosteum is the lining of the bone marrow cavity and contains the cells necessary for new bone development.

48. D: A synovial joint is the most common joint found in the body and is made up of two articulating bones. Synovial fluid is present in the synovial cavity, which is lined by a synovial membrane. The joint is surrounded by a fibrous capsule, which can be supported by ligaments. Sometimes, a synovial joint may contain other structures, such as menisci (for example, in the knee) or fat pads. There are subtypes of synovial joints, including a hinge joint, ball-and-socket joint, and a pivot joint.

49. C: Leg raises are one exercise that works the hip flexor muscles. These muscles include the iliopsoas, rectus femoris, sartorius, and pectineus. Exercises for hip extension include squats or leg presses. Hip extensor muscles are the hamstrings and the gluteus maximus. Hip abduction exercises can be done with an exercise machine. Muscles involved with hip abduction include the tensor fascia latae, sartorius, and gluteus minimus and medius. Leg curl exercises involve knee flexion. Muscles involved with flexion of the knee are the hamstrings, gracilis, and popliteus.

50. C: The central nervous system is comprised of the brain and the spinal cord and is responsible for receiving, analyzing, interpreting, and acting on sensory information. The central nervous system is comprised of the peripheral and autonomic nervous systems. The autonomic nervous system is responsible for functions such as respiration, digestion, making hormones, and maintaining heart rate. The autonomic nervous system can be subdivided into the sympathetic nervous system, which is activated when the body is "stressed" and causes an increase in heart rate and respiratory rate and the parasympathetic nervous system, which is "in control" when the stressful stimulus is no longer present.

# Photo Credits

**Licensed Under CC BY 4.0 (creativecommons.org/licenses/by/4.0/)**

Muscles: "The Three Connective Tissue Layers" by Openstax Anatomy & Physiology Chapter 10.2 (https://cnx.org/contents/FPtK1zmh@8.25:bfiqsxdB@3/Skeletal-Muscle)
Muscle Fibers: "Muscle Fibers" by Openstax Anatomy & Physiology Chapter 10.2 (https://cnx.org/contents/FPtK1zmh@8.25:bfiqsxdB@3/Skeletal-Muscle)
Human skeleton: "Human skeleton front en" by Mariana Ruiz Villarreal (https://commons.wikimedia.org/wiki/File:Human_skeleton_front_en.svg)
Cardiovascular System: "Circulatory System en edited" by Mariana Ruiz Villarreal (https://commons.wikimedia.org/wiki/File:Circulatory_System_en_edited.svg)
Respiratory System: "Respiratory system complete en" by Mariana Ruiz Villarreal (https://commons.wikimedia.org/wiki/File:Respiratory_system_complete_en.svg)
Muscular System: "Overview of Muscular System" by Openstax Anatomy & Physiology Chapter 11.2 (https://cnx.org/contents/FPtK1zmh@8.25:FL6Dj0EF@3/Naming-Skeletal-Muscles)
Respiratory System and Heart: "Pulmonary Circuit" by Openstax Anatomy & Physiology Chapter 20.5 (https://cnx.org/contents/FPtK1zmh@8.25:GqYHW4Z4@3/Circulatory-Pathways)

**Licensed Under CC BY-SA 3.0 (creativecommons.org/licenses/by-sa/3.0/deed.en)**

Heart: "Heart diagram blood flow en" by Wikimedia user ZooFari (https://commons.wikimedia.org/wiki/File:Heart_diagram_blood_flow_en.svg)
Planes of Movement: "Human anatomy planes" by YassineMrabet (https://commons.wikimedia.org/wiki/File:Human_anatomy_planes.svg)

# Secret Key #1 - Time is Your Greatest Enemy

To succeed, you must ration your time properly. The reason that time is so critical is that every question counts the same toward your final score. If you run out of time, the questions that you do not answer will hurt your score far more than earlier questions that you spent extra time on and feel certain are correct.

## Pace Yourself

Wear a watch. At the beginning of the test, check the time (or start a chronometer on your watch to count the minutes), and check the time after each passage or every few questions to make sure you are "on schedule."

If you are forced to speed up, do it efficiently. Usually one or more answer choices can be eliminated without too much difficulty. Above all, don't panic. Don't speed up and just begin guessing at random choices. By pacing yourself, and continually monitoring your progress against your watch, you will always know exactly how far ahead or behind you are with your available time. If you find that you are one minute behind on the test, don't skip one question without spending any time on it, just to catch back up. Take 15 fewer seconds on the next four questions, and after four questions you'll have caught back up. Once you catch back up, you can continue working each problem at your normal pace.

Furthermore, don't dwell on the problems that you were rushed on. If a problem was taking up too much time and you made a hurried guess, it must be difficult. The difficult questions are the ones you are most likely to miss anyway, so it isn't a big loss. It is better to end with more time than you need than to run out of time.

Lastly, sometimes it is beneficial to slow down if you are constantly getting ahead of time. You are always more likely to catch a careless mistake by working more slowly than quickly, and among very high-scoring test takers (those who are likely to have lots of time left over), careless errors affect the score more than mastery of material.

# Secret Key #2 - Guessing is not Guesswork

You probably know that guessing is a good idea - unlike other standardized tests, there is no penalty for getting a wrong answer.  Even if you have no idea about a question, you still have a 20-25% chance of getting it right.

Most test takers do not understand the impact that proper guessing can have on their score.  Unless you score extremely high, guessing will significantly contribute to your final score.

## Monkeys Take the Test

What most test takers don't realize is that to insure that 20-25% chance, you have to guess randomly.  If you put 20 monkeys in a room to take this test, assuming they answered once per question and behaved themselves, on average they would get 20-25% of the questions correct.  Put 20 test takers in the room, and the average will be much lower among guessed questions.  Why?
1. The test writers intentionally writes deceptive answer choices that "look" right.  A test taker has no idea about a question, so picks the "best looking" answer, which is often wrong.  The monkey has no idea what looks good and what doesn't, so will consistently be lucky about 20-25% of the time.
2. Test takers will eliminate answer choices from the guessing pool based on a hunch or intuition.  Simple but correct answers often get excluded, leaving a 0% chance of being correct.  The monkey has no clue, and often gets lucky with the best choice.

This is why the process of elimination endorsed by most test courses is flawed and detrimental to your performance- test takers don't guess, they make an ignorant stab in the dark that is usually worse than random.

# $5 Challenge

Let me introduce one of the most valuable ideas of this course- the $5 challenge:

*You only mark your "best guess" if you are willing to bet $5 on it.*
*You only eliminate choices from guessing if you are willing to bet $5 on it.*

Why $5? Five dollars is an amount of money that is small yet not insignificant, and can really add up fast (20 questions could cost you $100). Likewise, each answer choice on one question of the test will have a small impact on your overall score, but it can really add up to a lot of points in the end.

The process of elimination IS valuable. The following shows your chance of guessing it right:

| Eliminate this many choices | Chance of getting it correct |
|---|---|
| 0 | 20% |
| 1 | 25% |
| 2 | 33% |
| 3 | 50% |
| 4 | 100% |

However, if you accidentally eliminate the right answer or go on a hunch for an incorrect answer, your chances drop dramatically: to 0%. By guessing among all the answer choices, you are GUARANTEED to have a shot at the right answer.

That's why the $5 test is so valuable- if you give up the advantage and safety of a pure guess, it had better be worth the risk.

What we still haven't covered is how to be sure that whatever guess you make is truly random. Here's the easiest way:

*Always pick the first answer choice among those remaining.*

Such a technique means that you have decided, **before you see a single test question**, exactly how you are going to guess- and since the order of choices tells you nothing about which one is correct, this guessing technique is perfectly random.

This section is not meant to scare you away from making educated guesses or eliminating choices- you just need to define when a choice is worth eliminating. The $5 test, along with a pre-defined random guessing strategy, is the best way to make sure you reap all of the benefits of guessing.

# Secret Key #3 - Practice Smarter, Not Harder

Many test takers delay the test preparation process because they dread the awful amounts of practice time they think necessary to succeed on the test. We have refined an effective method that will take you only a fraction of the time.

There are a number of "obstacles" in your way to succeed. Among these are answering questions, finishing in time, and mastering test-taking strategies. All must be executed on the day of the test at peak performance, or your score will suffer. The test is a mental marathon that has a large impact on your future.

Just like a marathon runner, it is important to work your way up to the full challenge. So first you just worry about questions, and then time, and finally strategy:

## Success Strategy

1. Find a good source for practice tests.
2. If you are willing to make a larger time investment, consider using more than one study guide- often the different approaches of multiple authors will help you "get" difficult concepts.
3. Take a practice test with no time constraints, with all study helps "open book." Take your time with questions and focus on applying strategies.
4. Take a practice test with time constraints, with all guides "open book."
5. Take a final practice test with no open material and time limits

If you have time to take more practice tests, just repeat step 5. By gradually exposing yourself to the full rigors of the test environment, you will condition your mind to the stress of test day and maximize your success.

# Secret Key #4 - Prepare, Don't Procrastinate

Let me state an obvious fact: if you take the test three times, you will get three different scores. This is due to the way you feel on test day, the level of preparedness you have, and, despite the test writers' claims to the contrary, some tests WILL be easier for you than others.

Since your future depends so much on your score, you should maximize your chances of success. In order to maximize the likelihood of success, you've got to prepare in advance. This means taking practice tests and spending time learning the information and test taking strategies you will need to succeed.

Since you have to pay a registration fee each time you take the test, don't take it as a "practice" test. Feel free to take sample tests on your own, but when you go to take the official test, be prepared, be focused, and do your best the first time!

# Secret Key #5 - Test Yourself

Everyone knows that time is money. There is no need to spend too much of your time or too little of your time preparing for the test. You should only spend as much of your precious time preparing as is necessary for you to pass it.

Once you have taken a practice test under real conditions of time constraints, then you will know if you are ready for the test or not.

If you have scored extremely high the first time that you take the practice test, then there is not much point in spending countless hours studying. You are already there.

Benchmark your abilities by retaking practice tests and seeing how much you have improved. Once you score high enough to guarantee success, then you are ready.

If you have scored well below where you need, then knuckle down and begin studying in earnest. Check your improvement regularly through the use of practice tests under real conditions. Above all, don't worry, panic, or give up. The key is perseverance!

Then, when you go to take the test, remain confident and remember how well you did on the practice tests. If you can score high enough on a practice test, then you can do the same on the real thing.

# General Strategies

The most important thing you can do is to ignore your fears and jump into the test immediately. Do not be overwhelmed by any strange-sounding terms. You have to jump into the test like jumping into a pool—all at once is the easiest way.

## Make Predictions

As you read and understand the question, try to guess what the answer will be. Remember that several of the answer choices are wrong, and once you begin reading them, your mind will immediately become cluttered with answer choices designed to throw you off. Your mind is typically the most focused immediately after you have read the question and digested its contents. If you can, try to predict what the correct answer will be. You may be surprised at what you can predict.

Quickly scan the choices and see if your prediction is in the listed answer choices. If it is, then you can be quite confident that you have the right answer. It still won't hurt to check the other answer choices, but most of the time, you've got it!

## Answer the Question

It may seem obvious to only pick answer choices that answer the question, but the test writers can create some excellent answer choices that are wrong. Don't pick an answer just because it sounds right, or you believe it to be true. It MUST answer the question. Once you've made your selection, always go back and check it against the question and make sure that you didn't misread the question and that the answer choice does answer the question posed.

## Benchmark

After you read the first answer choice, decide if you think it sounds correct or not. If it doesn't, move on to the next answer choice. If it does, mentally mark that answer choice. This doesn't mean that you've definitely selected it as your answer choice, it just means that it's the best you've seen thus far. Go ahead and read the next choice. If the next choice is worse than the one you've already selected, keep going to the next answer choice. If the next choice is better than the choice you've already selected, mentally mark the new answer choice as your best guess.

The first answer choice that you select becomes your standard. Every other answer choice must be benchmarked against that standard. That choice is correct until proven otherwise by another answer choice beating it out. Once you've decided that no other answer choice seems as good, do one final check to ensure that your answer choice answers the question posed.

## Valid Information

Don't discount any of the information provided in the question. Every piece of information may be necessary to determine the correct answer. None of the information in the question is there to throw you off (while the answer choices will certainly have information to throw you off). If two seemingly unrelated topics are discussed, don't ignore either. You can be confident there is a relationship, or it wouldn't be included in the question, and you are probably going to have to determine what is that relationship to find the answer.

## Avoid "Fact Traps"

Don't get distracted by a choice that is factually true. Your search is for the answer that answers the question. Stay focused and don't fall for an answer that is true but irrelevant. Always go back to the question and make sure you're choosing an answer that actually answers the question and is not just a true statement. An answer can be factually correct, but it MUST answer the question asked. Additionally, two answers can both be seemingly correct, so be sure to read all of the answer choices, and make sure that you get the one that BEST answers the question.

## Milk the Question

Some of the questions may throw you completely off. They might deal with a subject you have not been exposed to, or one that you haven't reviewed in years. While your lack of knowledge about the subject will be a hindrance, the question itself can give you many clues that will help you find the correct answer. Read the question carefully and look for clues. Watch particularly for adjectives and nouns describing difficult terms or words that you don't recognize. Regardless of whether you completely understand a word or not, replacing it with a synonym, either provided or one you more familiar with, may help you to understand what the questions are asking. Rather than wracking your mind about specific detailed information concerning a difficult term or word, try to use mental substitutes that are easier to understand.

## The Trap of Familiarity

Don't just choose a word because you recognize it. On difficult questions, you may not recognize a number of words in the answer choices. The test writers don't put "make-believe" words on the test, so don't think that just because you only recognize all the words in one answer choice that that answer choice must be correct. If you only recognize words in one answer choice, then focus on that one. Is it correct? Try your best to determine if it is correct. If it is, that's great. If not, eliminate it. Each word and answer choice you eliminate increases your chances of getting the question correct, even if you then have to guess among the unfamiliar choices.

## Eliminate Answers

Eliminate choices as soon as you realize they are wrong. But be careful! Make sure you consider all of the possible answer choices. Just because one appears right, doesn't mean that the next one won't be even better! The test writers will usually put more than one good answer choice for every question, so read all of them. Don't worry if you are stuck between two that seem right. By getting down to just two remaining possible choices, your odds are now 50/50. Rather than wasting too much time, play the odds. You are guessing, but guessing wisely because you've been able to knock out some of the answer choices that you know are wrong. If you are eliminating choices and realize that the last answer choice you are left with is also obviously wrong, don't panic. Start over and consider each choice again. There may easily be something that you missed the first time and will realize on the second pass.

## Tough Questions

If you are stumped on a problem or it appears too hard or too difficult, don't waste time. Move on! Remember though, if you can quickly check for obviously incorrect answer choices, your chances of guessing correctly are greatly improved. Before you completely give up, at least try to knock out a couple of possible answers. Eliminate what you can and then guess at the remaining answer choices before moving on.

## Brainstorm

If you get stuck on a difficult question, spend a few seconds quickly brainstorming. Run through the complete list of possible answer choices. Look at each choice and ask yourself, "Could this answer the question satisfactorily?" Go through each answer choice and consider it independently of the others.  By systematically going through all possibilities, you may find something that you would otherwise overlook.  Remember though that when you get stuck, it's important to try to keep moving.

## Read Carefully

Understand the problem.  Read the question and answer choices carefully.  Don't miss the question because you misread the terms.  You have plenty of time to read each question thoroughly and make sure you understand what is being asked.  Yet a happy medium must be attained, so don't waste too much time.  You must read carefully, but efficiently.

## Face Value

When in doubt, use common sense.  Always accept the situation in the problem at face value.  Don't read too much into it.  These problems will not require you to make huge leaps of logic.  The test writers aren't trying to throw you off with a cheap trick.  If you have to go beyond creativity and make a leap of logic in order to have an answer choice answer the question, then you should look at the other answer choices.  Don't overcomplicate the problem by creating theoretical relationships or explanations that will warp time or space.  These are normal problems rooted in reality.  It's just that the applicable relationship or explanation may not be readily apparent and you have to figure things out. Use your common sense to interpret anything that isn't clear.

## Prefixes

If you're having trouble with a word in the question or answer choices, try dissecting it.  Take advantage of every clue that the word might include.  Prefixes and suffixes can be a huge help.  Usually they allow you to determine a basic meaning.  Pre- means before, post- means after, pro - is positive, de- is negative.  From these prefixes and suffixes, you can get an idea of the general meaning of the word and try to put it into context.  Beware though of any traps.  Just because con- is the opposite of pro-, doesn't necessarily mean congress is the opposite of progress!

## Hedge Phrases

Watch out for critical hedge phrases, led off with words such as "likely," "may," "can," "sometimes," "often," "almost," "mostly," "usually," "generally," "rarely," and "sometimes."  Question writers insert these hedge phrases to cover every possibility.  Often an answer choice will be wrong simply because it leaves no room for exception.  Unless the situation calls for them, avoid answer choices that have definitive words like "exactly," and "always."

## Switchback Words

Stay alert for "switchbacks."  These are the words and phrases frequently used to alert you to shifts in thought.  The most common switchback word is "but."  Others include "although," "however," "nevertheless," "on the other hand," "even though," "while," "in spite of," "despite," and "regardless of."

## New Information

Correct answer choices will rarely have completely new information included.  Answer choices typically are straightforward reflections of the material asked about and will directly relate to the question.  If a new piece of information is included in an answer choice that doesn't even seem to relate to the topic being asked about, then that answer choice is likely incorrect.   All of the information needed to answer the question is usually provided for you in the question.  You should not have to make guesses that are unsupported or choose answer choices that require unknown information that cannot be reasoned from what is given.

## Time Management

On technical questions, don't get lost on the technical terms. Don't spend too much time on any one question. If you don't know what a term means, then odds are you aren't going to get much further since you don't have a dictionary. You should be able to immediately recognize whether or not you know a term. If you don't, work with the other clues that you have—the other answer choices and terms provided—but don't waste too much time trying to figure out a difficult term that you don't know.

## Contextual Clues

Look for contextual clues. An answer can be right but not the correct answer. The contextual clues will help you find the answer that is most right and is correct. Understand the context in which a phrase or statement is made. This will help you make important distinctions.

## Don't Panic

Panicking will not answer any questions for you; therefore, it isn't helpful. When you first see the question, if your mind goes blank, take a deep breath. Force yourself to mechanically go through the steps of solving the problem using the strategies you've learned.

## Pace Yourself

Don't get clock fever. It's easy to be overwhelmed when you're looking at a page full of questions, your mind is full of random thoughts and feeling confused, and the clock is ticking down faster than you would like. Calm down and maintain the pace that you have set for yourself. As long as you are on track by monitoring your pace, you are guaranteed to have enough time for yourself. When you get to the last few minutes of the test, it may seem like you won't have enough time left, but if you only have as many questions as you should have left at that point, then you're right on track!

## Answer Selection

The best way to pick an answer choice is to eliminate all of those that are wrong, until only one is left and confirm that is the correct answer. Sometimes though, an answer choice may immediately look right. Be careful! Take a second to make sure that the other choices are not equally obvious. Don't make a hasty mistake. There are only two times that you should stop before checking other answers. First is when you are positive that the answer choice you have selected is correct. Second is when time is almost out and you have to make a quick guess!

## Check Your Work

Since you will probably not know every term listed and the answer to every question, it is important that you get credit for the ones that you do know. Don't miss any questions through careless mistakes. If at all possible, try to take a second to look back over your answer selection and make sure you've selected the correct answer choice and haven't made a costly careless mistake (such as marking an answer choice that you didn't mean to mark). The time it takes for this quick double check should more than pay for itself in caught mistakes.

## Beware of Directly Quoted Answers

Sometimes an answer choice will repeat word for word a portion of the question or reference section. However, beware of such exact duplication. It may be a trap! More than likely, the correct choice will paraphrase or summarize a point, rather than being exactly the same wording.

## Slang

Scientific sounding answers are better than slang ones. An answer choice that begins "To compare the outcomes…" is much more likely to be correct than one that begins "Because some people insisted…"

## Extreme Statements

Avoid wild answers that throw out highly controversial ideas that are proclaimed as established fact. An answer choice that states the "process should used in certain situations, if…" is much more likely to be correct than one that states the "process should be discontinued completely." The first is a calm rational statement and doesn't even make a definitive, uncompromising stance, using a hedge word "if" to provide wiggle room, whereas the second choice is a radical idea and far more extreme.

## Answer Choice Families

When you have two or more answer choices that are direct opposites or parallels, one of them is usually the correct answer. For instance, if one answer choice states "x increases" and another answer choice states "x decreases" or "y increases," then those two or three answer choices are very similar in construction and fall into the same family of answer choices. A family of answer choices consists of two or three answer choices, very similar in construction, but often with directly opposite meanings. Usually the correct answer choice will be in that family of answer choices. The "odd man out" or answer choice that doesn't seem to fit the parallel construction of the other answer choices is more likely to be incorrect.

# Additional Bonus Material

Due to our efforts to try to keep this book to a manageable length, we've created a link that will give you access to all of your additional bonus material.

Please visit http://www.mometrix.com/bonus948/nasm to access the information.